Circling Dixie

CIRCLING DIXIE

Contemporary Southern Culture
through a Transatlantic Lens

HELEN TAYLOR

RUTGERS UNIVERSITY PRESS
New Brunswick, New Jersey, and London

Library of Congress Cataloging-in-Publication Data

Taylor, Helen, 1947–
    Circling Dixie: contemporary southern culture through a transatlantic lens / Helen Taylor.
        p.   cm.
    Includes bibliographical references (p.   ) and index.
    ISBN 0–8135–2861–5 (cloth : acid-free paper) — ISBN 0–8135–2862–3 (pbk. : acid-free
paper)
        1. Southern States—Civilization—20th century. 2. Southern States—Civilization—
20th century—Foreign public opinion, British. 3. Public opinion—Great Britain.
4. Popular culture—Southern States. 5. Popular culture—Southern States—Foreign
public opinion, British. 6. Great Britain—Civilization—American influences.
7. Southern States—Relations—Great Britain. 8. Great Britain—Relations—Southern
States. I. Title.
F216.2.T39 2000
975'.043—dc21   00–028079

British Cataloging-in-Publication data for this book is available from the British Library

Manufactured in the United States of America

For Ida M. Taylor and Derrick Price

Contents

Acknowledgments

This is a book about journeys, reciprocal exchanges, and influences. In the years since I began to write it, I have taken many real and metaphorical journeys (not to mention false starts, wrong turns, and doses of travel sickness) and drawn on countless resources. I could never have completed the long road to publication without the help of my universities, colleagues, family, and friends (not to mention the kindness of strangers).

I am grateful to the universities of Warwick and Exeter, which granted me study leave and research funding in order to complete this book. The British Academy has supported travel and conference funding.

I am indebted to my family and many colleagues and friends who have put up with, read, listened to, and made suggestions for parts of this book. Ida M. Taylor and Geoffrey Howard Taylor have always loyally and lovingly supported and believed in me. Anthea Callen, Gill Frith, Judith Glushanok, and Anne Janowitz have been absolutely wonderful friends in need, and their spirits and courage revived and renewed my own on countless occasions. Richard Dyer has shown continuing enthusiasm for my project and offered suggestions for reading, theater, and film; he has always boosted my flagging confidence, even through dark times of his own. The late Joseph Logsdon was a wonderful cosponsor of my 1998 conference entitled "New

Orleans in Europe," and he kindly endorsed the New Orleans chapter; his loss in 1999 was a major blow for southern scholars. Diane Roberts read several chapters in draft and sent encouraging and helpful advice, as well as assisting me with material on the League of the South. Ed Gallafent found the most esoteric books for me in his haunting of secondhand bookshops, and his wise counsel at Warwick made all the difference. I owe much to former and present colleagues at the universities of Warwick and Exeter, especially Bridget Bennett, Regenia Gagnier, Jeremy Treglown, and Ginette Vincendeau. Cora Kaplan, Richard Gray, and Richard King have been strong intellectual mentors and good friends over the years.

Rosan and Frank de Caro were fine companions on my travels around the South in 1995 and 1996, and their hospitality and scholarly local knowledge were much appreciated. My oldest southern friend, Marie Blanchard, and her husband, Neal, were also cheering company.

I am grateful to the following individuals who have generously given me advice, allowed me to interview them, sent me research materials, or helped in other ways: Maya Angelou, Connie Atkinson, Ian Bell, Patricia Brady, Lord Melvyn Bragg, Zane Branson, Lyons Brown III, Andrew Didlick, Peter Dunderdale, Sir Richard Eyre, Andy Fagg, Alice Hall Farley, Lady Antonia Fraser, Maureen Freely, Simon Frith, Beverly Gianna, Lennie Goodings, Robert A. Gross, Sir Peter Hall, Simon Hawtrey-Woore, Nicholas Herbert-Jones, Kit Hesketh-Harvey, James Kent, John Long and the Ken Colyer Trust, Colin McArthur, Alison Menzies, Muriel Mitcheson Brown, Alan Munton, Philip Nobile, Jeff Nuttall, Mark Ottaway, Victor Perkins, Jim Porteous, Elly M. Taylor, Emma Tennant, Jill Terry, Allen Toussaint (with special thanks for the ride in the gold Rolls Royce), Thomas M. Verich, Rosella Mamoli Zorzi, and everyone involved in the Tennessee Williams/New Orleans Literary Festival and the London South Bank Festival of the South. I thank Clare Bainbridge for her Web searches on Maya Angelou.

Kate Fullbrook, a longtime friend, offered scrupulous and shrewd comments on each chapter that forced me to think again and thus to improve the book considerably. Jane Gaines's comments on early drafts, and Linda Wagner-Martin's on the whole manuscript, were incisive; I valued their constructive criticism. Leslie Mitchner has been the best kind of editor, urging me to write, supporting me at every stage, and offering pertinent comments and prompt and helpful advice along the way. Grace Buonocore copyedited with great care.

As I said at the outset, this is a book about a convoluted series of journeys. My favorite traveling companion, Derrick Price, has gone along all the way, carrying my (various kinds of) baggage, guiding me through cyberspace, making me laugh, and sharing the pleasures of the trip. He is the main reason I got there in the end.

Circling Dixie

PROLOGUE

I began to write this book by posing myself a series of what I thought would be simple questions. Why was the culture of the American South so appealing to me, and why did the South suddenly seem to be everywhere I looked? Why did I look back on the years I lived there with such extraordinarily mixed emotions of yearning and abhorrence? Why was *Driving Miss Daisy* such a comforting film to my middlebrow relatives, and why were my students and friends so envious of my regular trips to New Orleans? Was there a reason for so many British theaters to be producing Tennessee Williams plays, for the British press to be printing long articles about rumored sequels to *Gone With the Wind*, and for an adoring crowd of Cornish people to have queued round the block to see Maya Angelou read poetry in a seaside ballroom?

These questions proved far from simple, however, and threw up more problematic issues about the ways we understand cultures and engage with a nation's, region's, or city's cultural artifacts. In order to address them, however imperfectly, I undertook a series of real and virtual journeys, and this book is an attempt to record the results of one Briton circling the Dixie of her onetime home and long-term imaginative desire.

Of course, the story of the South has been told in terms of journeys other than my own. There are real journeys of settlement and migration, colonial struggles and exploitation, slave markets and movements, the Underground Railroad, the March to Atlanta, the Great Migration, and the Freedom Rides. Besides these, there are cultural, often metaphorical journeys. These range from slave narratives smuggled out to the North, spirituals and blues songs carried by singers and players north to Chicago or New York, crossover plays and films that draw on southern local color but involve international companies and audiences, and musical and literary artists clustering together into supportive communities. Many of these have involved other trajectories across continents, notably Europe and Africa. Transatlantic exchanges and mutual influences have been a significant part of the development of southern culture in all its manifestations—from architecture and literature to music and cuisine.

For Europeans looking imaginatively across the Atlantic, American culture is not only a site of desire, fascination, and envy but also a space of interaction and reciprocity. Europeans do not situate themselves as passive consumers of that rich culture; as with their own, they respond to its many dimensions with consciousness of their own histories, cultural forms, and individual and social identities. America feels curiously familiar to Europeans because they have close connections with a U.S. culture that has been to a great extent formed and transformed by European genres, styles, and artists. And because of their close colonial and postcolonial relations with African nations, Europeans are intrigued by the correlations between the oldest continent and the New World and the links and tensions between all three continents throughout what can be seen as both a black and white Atlantic. The narrative of European-southern connections is only just beginning to take shape.

The transatlantic lens through which I view the flow of southern culture within Britain is intended to cast light on the ways in which key examples of this culture are produced and reproduced as a result of these crossings. The book's title is intentionally ambiguous. *Circling Dixie* suggests the international circulations of southern cultural forms themselves and also those appropriations and critical responses that circle around, and back to, the American South. The focus is on the contemporary, specifically after World War II, when the South (for positive as well as negative reasons) has moved further than ever before into the center of American social and cultural life. As a result, its history has been revised, it has engaged anew with national and international concerns, and it enjoys a more cosmopolitan cultural life.

This is where I came in. As a child growing up in England during the fifties and sixties, I was both fascinated and appalled by a South that I first knew only through Hank Williams, Paul Robeson, and the Dixie Cups songs, as well as from television footage of assassinations and ugly white faces screaming at black kids walking to newly integrated schools. When I first went to live in Baton Rouge, Louisiana, in 1969, I became fascinated by the way those images of the South had been constructed for me and how British culture had made sense (albeit very partial and fragmented) of this mythified and demonized place.

Tracking the relationships between nations, regions, peoples, and cultures leads one into byzantine mazes. The subject is huge, and there are many narratives to be told about the global influence of southern culture. Several of them, such as Elvis Presley's life after death or the media success of evangelical preachers, are already well documented, while journalists increasingly relish gothic and bizarre tales of a region that still contains many anachronistic and eccentric elements within a homogenizing nation. My exploration is structured around a series of significant, representative cultural case studies that have been particularly informed by a transatlantic (Europe–North America) and circum-Atlantic (Africa–Europe–North America) axis. Thus my focus is on examples of the region's culture that are internationally celebrated but whose transnational formations have been critically neglected.

First, I discuss the twentieth century's two most commercially successful and resonant American novels-made-films focused on the South, Margaret Mitchell's *Gone With the Wind* and Alex Haley's *Roots*, which treat the plantation myth and the slave South in very different ways. Margaret Mitchell's book (1936) and David O. Selznick's film (1939) were praised from their first appearance and have continued to enjoy popular acclaim, despite their reactionary racial politics and nostalgia for an Old South most Americans now recognize as discredited. The American Bicentennial publication of Alex Haley's symbolically titled "autobiography" about slavery and its aftermath, *Roots* (1976), was intended to shame international opinion into revising the plantation myth at the heart of the 1930s Mitchell classic. Chapter 2 focuses, however, on the commercial pressures and ploys operating to breathe new life into *Gone With the Wind* for the post-war era, especially through sequels, a TV miniseries, and other fictional revisions. Chapter 3 then discusses the flawed ambition of Alex Haley, including the complex set of journeys (some of dubious authenticity) taken by the author in his attempt to write the definitive epic story of the African American race. Both chapters account for the uneasy tension between different versions of the South's troubled history and the ways in which these versions have drawn on, been validated in or challenged by, and circulated around three continents.

The South of popular representations returns repeatedly to the plantation, the rural, and the small town. Southern cities lack the cultural weight and glamour of America's major West and East Coast cities, and a mere handful have become cultural centers. Chapter 4 focuses on one exceptional city that has long held a reputation as a weighty and glamorous mecca for literary and musical artists and cultural production of many kinds: New Orleans. Known as "America's European Masterpiece," it is the southern city with the closest ties to its European colonial history and to European artistic practices and modes of cultural production. The chapter examines changing postwar representations of this city, both from New Orleanians themselves and also from Europeans drawn to the city's charms. The chapter also discusses some of the contradictions and constraints faced by southern cities when promoting cultural tourism in a region still regarded as racially and socially divided and troubled.

A Streetcar Named Desire provided the first huge fillip to New Orleans's postwar tourist industry. Tennessee Williams's play (1947) and the Elia Kazan film (1951) put the city on the map and made the playwright's name. Williams went on to acquire a great international reputation and to have his plays produced and read in many countries. He had a great affection for and close relationship with Britain, and chapter 5 examines the ways in which this one European country increasingly took him to its heart and reinterpreted his work with a European flavor. It examines the 1990s British theatrical bandwagon of Williams productions. Transatlantic tensions operating over his lasting reputation are aired, especially relating to the writer's friendship with Maria St. Just and the engagement of Britain's top directors and actors with the more problematic and obscure plays.

The book ends by focusing on an African American southern autobiographer who has made her reputation out of a circum-Atlantic career in writing and public performance. Maya Angelou has become one of the United States' most acclaimed international figures, and she has done more than most artists to attempt symbolically to bring together the three continents of the black and white Atlantic route, from Africa through Europe to the American South. Angelou combines a long career in the arts of performance—music, dance, and oratory—and a commitment to a very southern pedagogical and messianic ambition. A Europhile who has lived in exile in Africa and (unusually for an African American writer) finally settled in the Deep South, she embodies, and expresses some of the incoherences and problems of, those very cultural flows with which this book is concerned.

1

LOOKING
TRANSATLANTICALLY

Look one way, the South is the heart of darkness in *Missis-sippi Burning*. Look the other, it's the embarrassingly stereo-typical but oddly redeemed drama of family values, roots, racial peace, and national healing of *Forrest Gump*.

"It's America's will-o'-the-wisp Eden."
—Peter Applebome, *Dixie Rising* (1996)

Anyone who attempts to define the South is doomed to frustration. A region of extraordinary contrasts, inspiring both delight and repug-nance, it defies simple exegesis. The South inspires the most lavish praise as well as the most vindictive criticism. It seduces with luxuri-ant foliage, hot and sultry nights, luscious food and drink, and its famed hospitality and southern belles; but it is also a place whose racial history and attitudes to violence and unorthodox sexuality will turn one's stomach. In numerous accounts, documentary or fictional, those apparently opposed but in fact closely allied Souths, the gothic and romantic, the tragic and homely, the violent and the healing, *Mississippi Burning* and *Forrest Gump*, explode or uneasily coexist.

European and American visitors alike are lured into listening to southern song and storytelling and marvel at the sense of family con-tinuity, place, and history that still holds sway. Southerners assure themselves, with William Faulkner's Quentin Compson, that they "don't hate" the South, which has given many people good reason to hate it. Commentators in recent years have debated whether there is still such a place as "the South" and have argued about whether America itself has been Southernized, or the South Americanized. And for those who grew up after World War II, the South has not only spawned much of the popular music and some of the best literature and film of the era; it has also produced some of the period's most haunting images: white troops beating up and shooting blacks and whites fighting for civil rights; the assassinations of John F. Kennedy and Martin Luther King; a white state governor calling for "segregation now, segregation tomorrow, segregation forever."

The three most universally recognized names in English are said to be Jesus, Coca Cola, and Elvis Presley. Two of those three come from the American South, even if their global reputations have obliterated their origins in (respectively) Atlanta, Georgia, and Tupelo, Mississippi. The South in general, and New Orleans in particular, are known for giving birth to America's only original art form, jazz. John Shelton Reed reminds us that the South has given us those commercial institutions most signifying Americanness, Holiday Inns and Kentucky Fried Chicken (and of course Coke).[1] Atlanta is the home of Ted Turner and CNN, as well as Margaret Mitchell and *Gone With the Wind*; the Olympic Games—the first ever in a southern city—were held there in 1996. The last two Democratic presidents have been southerners: the first person from the Deep South to win the post for more than a century, Jimmy Carter of Georgia, and Bill Clinton, once governor of Arkansas, the first Democrat in living memory to be elected to a second term. Through most of the 1990s, the most powerful Washington politicians, both Democratic and Republican, were southerners.

The post–World War II decline of northern "Rust Belt" cities and the rise of "Sunbelt" hi-tech, agribusiness, and service industries attracted investment and federal (especially military) expenditure to the South. As a result, between 1970 and 1990, the South's population grew by 40 percent (twice the national rate) and at the millennium accounted for one-third of the national population, as it did in 1860, the height of its success just before the Civil War. In 1993, more than one-half of America's new jobs were created in the South, and states such as Florida, Texas, and Georgia experienced population explosions. A relatively buoyant southern economy, employment opportunities, mild weather, and low property prices drew people of all races and ages to work or retire there; both white Americans and (more surprisingly) African Americans reversed the long-term pattern of migration northward and headed South in significant numbers. The South has ensured its international position in the twenty-first century by building highways, airports, sports stadia, hotels, and gambling riverboats; air-conditioning in public buildings makes summertime bearable. This economic success also led to a creeping national adoption of conservative political, religious, and moral values traditionally associated with southerners. So, as the South has fully entered the American mainstream—politically, culturally, and socially—it has influenced the terms of political and cultural debates. Although the South is still remembered for the "burden" of its history of slavery, secession, war, racist conservatism, and violence, its more liberal racial attitudes (and, to some extent, practices) have convinced the wider nation that it has "risen again" to assert a new national and international importance.

Cultural phenomena once associated with an insular, nostalgic South—such as evangelical religion and country music radio—have caught the imagination of the entire nation and moved beyond its shores. From a reputation as the unhealthy, backward-looking "Other" of a progressive democratic country, the South seems to be sloughing off many of its negative as well as more decadent associations. Its much touted characteristics of sectional parochialism and traditionalism are said to be disappearing. The postwar tourist boom has opened up dramatic new opportunities in cities such as Miami, Charleston, and New Orleans; in national parks such as the Smokies; and in music theme-parks such as Dollywood, Graceland, and Nashville's Grand Ole Opry. "America's gone South," wrote British journalist Jonathan Freedland, quoting a historian as saying, "'The South didn't win the war, but it's winning the peace.'"[2]

A DIFFERENT PLACE?

That said, "the South" (wherever you believe that region to lie—and scholars are notoriously vague or disputatious about this) is still internationally regarded as a discrete, distinctive place, very different from any other region of the United States or anywhere else, for that matter. Nonsoutherners are in no doubt about the significance of crossing the mythic Mason-Dixon line; many northerners perceive the South negatively and see it as barely integrated into the Union.[3] It is startling to meet northerners who—even at the turn of the century—have no intention of traveling to the South yet harbor the most exaggerated, sweeping prejudices about the whole region. It is, of course, true that, in terms of advances in civil rights, education, gender and race equality, religious reforms, and so on, the South (to put it politely) has dragged its feet behind much of the rest of the nation. For the whole of the twentieth century, it had the highest national levels of poverty, unemployment, child mortality, and illiteracy. De facto segregation continues to operate fairly rigidly in churches, subdivisions, schools, and restaurants, and the memories of slavery and civil rights struggles for identity politics have ensured a lingering suspicion and distance between the races. The powerful evangelical churches and televangelism are associated with profoundly conservative racial and sexual agendas. Mixed dating and friendships are rare, and white flight to the suburbs has raised ever higher barriers between races and classes.

It is now commonly accepted, however, that these generalizations no longer apply only to the South; divisions along race and class lines, conservative social and racial agendas, segregated schooling, unions in retreat, and an enthusiasm for country music are all national phenomena that reflect the power and influence of the South on national culture. In 1974, John Egerton published an influential book whose title, *The Americanization of Dixie: The Southernization of America*, summarized well the reciprocal relationship of the postwar shift. Egerton, uneasy about new developments, bemoaned the fact that the South and the rest of the country were "not exchanging strengths as much as they [were] exchanging sins," while in a 1996 response to this thesis, Peter Applebome argued the South had offered the nation "a calm in [its] storm . . . a sense of history, roots, place, and community . . . the purest kernel of conservative values and politics in a conservative era it [had] largely created."[4]

EUROPE AND THE SOUTH

In light of the South's recent national and international importance, it is hardly surprising that Europe has begun to pay special attention. For a long time, there have been strong personal and cultural relationships between Europe and the region—from musicians living and playing in European countries to a future president (Clinton) studying as a Rhodes scholar at Oxford University. Especially since the 1950s, Europeans have constituted an enthusiastic following for southern cultural forms, especially music, and kept those forms alive through devoted recording and buying of music, patronage of musicians and concerts, and informal support and friendship networks.

And, to European eyes, the whole region has a special character. In 1994, the London South Bank Centre hosted a major cultural festival, "The American South." Its artistic director, Nancy Covey, wrote in the festival brochure that she had asked people where and what they thought "the South" actually was. Everyone, she said, had a different idea, but all agreed on one thing: "a common feeling of southern heat. Images of hot, humid summers . . . searing Bar-B-Q's and spicy crawfish boil; but also the heated passions of the Civil War, the Peace Marches, Sunday revival meetings and the continuing sense of struggle combining to create a view of family and history quite different from the rest of the country."

"Heat" may seem a strange organizing principle for a festival, but it is an apt synecdoche for the South, and one that gets right to the heart of a region that has so fascinated the world, for the "Hot South"—as opposed to, say, the "Wild West"—is a region of increasing international fascination. Long associated with hot passions and tempers—of the blues, the Ku Klux Klan, voodoo, and rock and roll—the South is a region associated deliciously with forbidden and guilty desire, racial and sexual violence, and excess of all kinds. Such associations have lingered since the mid-nineteenth century, when Harriet Beecher Stowe's international best-seller *Uncle Tom's Cabin* (1852) first defined it to the world as a gothic, demonic region and abolitionist writers invented it as "an 'eastern,' erotically-charged, pagan, authoritarian, chaotic Other *within* the occidental, quotidian, Christian, chaste, orderly democracy of the United States."[5] To most of those who wrote about and excoriated the South (from Garrison to Longfellow, and including Stowe herself), it was a place of the gothic and darkly romantic imagination, since few of them actually ventured to the South.

Yet, from the earliest writers who visited the region—figures such as northerners William Cullen Bryant, Walt Whitman, and Edward King and British writers Frances Trollope and William Thackeray—to modern commentators such as V. S. Naipaul, Jonathan Raban, and John Berendt, there is always a strongly felt sense that the South is unutterably *different* (whether for better or worse) and that it involves different kinds of perception and judgment than those in the rest of the United States. In the antebellum South, the wild and difficult terrain and the horrors and peculiarities of slavery and its legacy tended to make writers perceive it in tragic or gothic terms (for instance, as some vision from Dante's *Inferno* or as Paradise Lost).[6] Twentieth-century visitors have expected to find scenes straight from Edgar Allan Poe but instead have reveled in the sensual delights of the region's exotic foods, varied landscape, and strangenesses. And increasingly, for advertisers, the South is becoming associated with what the American West once signaled, namely, independence, individualism, escapism, and freedom.

In contemporary accounts of the region, there is considerable reliance on a mythical South that is familiar from literature, film, and song: a world slightly out of control, saturated in lust and criminality, haunted and obsessed by its "moonlight and magnolias" past, incestuous, and sick at heart. The taken-for-granted decadence for which the South is so renowned—from Tennessee Williams's plays to southern evangelists' notorious adulteries—seems profoundly at odds with America's dreams and aspirations. Thus it is celebrated or vilified as that Other Place, an exotic site that is more deviant, dangerous, and depraved than anywhere else on the North American continent. The contemporary South is the America everyone knows and loves or loathes—but it is also *not* America. For Europeans, it seems to share a troubled and profound burden of history; a confused but lasting caste and class system; ethnic and racial conflicts that have lasted centuries; the experience of having a war fought (and lost) on its own land; a resistance to Yankee (indeed, twentieth-century) progressivism, progress, and efficiency; and a most un-Puritan delight in sensual pleasures such as good food, music, and porch-sitting rather than deferred gratification, hard work, and fast food. That the South is now not the nation's number one economic problem but its "main engine of economic growth" is still obscured by the dominant image of a laid-back South that so appeals to the outsider.[7]

THE SOUTHERN CULTURAL INDUSTRIES

In cultural terms, the South has long had a distinguished international reputation—all the more remarkable because those cultural industries have sprung predominantly from the region's poorest and most disempowered peoples. It goes without saying that southern music, from blues and jazz through bluegrass and rockabilly to rock and roll and new country, has been celebrated globally, especially since World War II, when bands began to travel widely and radio and records disseminated every kind of music to vast audiences. Household names, from Leadbelly, Bessie Smith, and Louis Armstrong to Dizzy Gillespie, Hank Williams, and Patsy Cline, have made the music of the South a world music that is reproduced often without reference to, or knowledge of, its southern origins or qualities. Over several decades, there has been a large appetite for southern evangelical religion, encompassing gospel music and singers such as Mahalia Jackson as well as high-profile preachers from Billy Graham to the founder of Moral Majority, Jerry Falwell. Though painting is not one of the South's greatest exports, the canvasses of John James Audubon, Aaron Douglas, and Jasper Johns have attracted attention. Southern writers have found international acclaim, through both publication and distinguished film and television adaptation (often scripted by the writers themselves). While global television carried live footage of struggles over bussing, the burning of black churches, the Ku Klux Klan, and Christian fundamentalist hysteria and hypocrisy, in recent decades the South has been re-presented and repositioned to signify very differently. The cultural industries, including tourism, have worked hard to market a South rich in heritage and cultural diversity, treading carefully to avoid the inevitable historical memories of uglier times and the ever present reality of minority group unemployment, poverty, and racial oppression in a region still caricaturable through God, guns, and the Confederate flag.

In the 1990s, cities such as Atlanta, Memphis, and New Orleans, all with large black populations and black mayors and city councils, promoted themselves vigorously, walking a careful line between the nostalgia market for the Old South of plantation homes and Civil War battle sites ("the Confederate Trail") and the New South market for younger visitors, with live music, multimedia museums and exhibits, and multicultural events. While this promotion often focused on music rather than other cultural forms, in order to cast tourist nets wide and remind tourists of the wide-ranging heritage on offer, southern cities began to develop differentiated self-definitions.

A 1995 British newspaper advertisement for Nashville ("Music City, USA") records the many kinds of music for which the city is famous, and against a large photograph of a riverboat it assures the potential tourist: "For every Nashville sound there's a Nashville sight. . . . To country add a hotel with 4 acres of atrium. To reggae add a full-scale replica of the Parthenon (yup, that Parthenon). . . . To rap add plantation houses that didn't go with the wind. To gospel add four 100-plus shop malls. . . . To cajun add 611 restaurants, 11 museums, 3 art galleries, 12 golf courses and one almighty 1,500-seat dance hall." Music is seen as pivotal to a cultural experience of a southern city both proud of its sustained past and yet magnificently geared up for the postmodern experience demanded by the 1990s tourist. This bricolage of old and new, European and American (yup, that Parthenon), southern traditional and up-to-the-minute tourist orthodox (golf, malls, museums), follows international trends in ensuring that the unique, exceptional qualities of the South will coexist with middle-class, predominantly white tourists' expectations. Carefully excluded are reminders to those tourists of the harsher social and political realities of the region, especially its volatile and violent racial heritage. Visitors of any race do not take well to overt warnings about avoiding poor (usually black), crime-ridden areas of town. Southern cities are busily and heavily policing tourist areas in an attempt to draw in revenue from visitors by pretending racial strife and problems are gone with the wind.

THE BURDEN OF HISTORY

Southerners have to perform a difficult balancing act. The United States is associated in world consciousness with the present and future, rather than the past. Its cultural contribution to the twenty-first century is defined overwhelmingly in terms of "the New"—modernity, modernism, postmodernism. To Europeans especially, the United States is the innovative, young nation that lacks the solid sense of history and heritage that characterizes the Old World. It is credited with producing mainly vernacular forms linked to a democratic rather than elitist culture but—in postmodern discourse—characterized by superficiality, eclecticism, and a lack of cohesion or profundity and associated with callow youth rather than the wisdom of age. Most of all, U.S. culture is accused of lacking a sense of history. However unfair and ahistorical these associations, they are remarkably persistent. In terms of the American South and southern culture, however, such generalizations are particularly problematic. One of the main reasons the South orients itself frequently toward, and tends to such sentimentality about, Europe is that it has a deep sense of a shared history and the burden and authority of the past, and more than any other region it is reluctant to leave its complex history behind.

Of course, there are many ethnic and racial groups of Americans within other regions who have a profound historical sense. But the pervasiveness of this sense is found mainly below the Mason-Dixon line. One need only point to southern obsessions with the Confederate flag, Civil War battle sites, genealogy, and the conservation and restoration of old (well, nineteenth-century) buildings; the dominance of southern gothic, in literature and film; the enormous respect paid to the region's musical traditions and oldest musicians; and the focus of southern tourism on heritage and history rather than the futuristic or pastiche. Two of Faulkner's most quoted lines summarize it to perfection: "The past is never dead. It's not even past."[8] Whatever their racial or ethnic origins, southern artists of all kinds are steeped in, haunted by, and ironically engaged with their own history and self-conscious about the violent, tragic history of slavery; defeat in what many euphemistically call the "War between the States" or defensively the "War of Northern Aggression"; and a heritage of racial conflict and resulting sociopolitical upheavals. Slavery and the Civil War stand at the heart of the South's sense of history, but the predominantly English, African American, and Celtic concern with roots, family, and generational and social continuities all guarantee that, however Americanized and homogenized it becomes, the South will shed at its peril that consciousness of past in present that so enriches its various cultures and daily life. John Berendt, a New York journalist who wrote a celebrated study of contemporary Savannah, summarized the difference between the American North and South thus: "In New York, you might say, or write, 'Before going out, Mrs. Jones put on her coat.' In Savannah, you would say, 'Before going out, Mrs. Jones put on the coat her third husband gave her before he committed suicide.'"[9] Although this is an amusing caricature of a singularly inward-looking, heritage-obsessed southern town, it reflects a widely held view of southerners as always conscious of past in present, always eager to ask strangers where they come from and to which church they belong. A genuine passion for and reluctance to let go of its history help explain the concern with place, home, and family that gives a rich texture to southern life.

Images of the South have become a familiar part of the cultural scene, in many films, TV series, and advertisements. Although all things American are—in advertising terms—"aspirational," the Deep South in particular has become a favorite reference point for publicity images of many kinds. Ironically, it is for the very qualities that have been seen to hold the South back, economically, socially, and racially, that the South is being celebrated: a refusal to change or modernize, a reluctance either to stop the party in order to get the work done or to welcome progressive reforms in regional, racial, and gender affairs. The postwar New South of "Sunbelt" industries, African American state and city politicians, and front porches abandoned for TVs and PCs does not feature large in advertising campaigns. Just as the West is still represented predominantly as "Marlboro Country," so the South seems to stand as the nation's *id*: a site of carnival, play, desire, abundant and deviant sexuality, and lawless violence.[10] Despite that, it is also a place where people value roots and where class, gender, and race demarcation lines are clear (albeit often uncomfortable or dangerous). It is the region in which the past is always calling, where there is a suspicion of the new or new-fangled.

The unchanging, conservative South is epitomized in the long-running, highly successful Jack Daniel's poster and newspaper advertising campaign. Since 1955 (a very long time in advertising history) the same individual, Ted Simmons of Simmons Durham, has produced copy and photographs in identical format, giving vignettes of life in the Jack Daniel's company town. Every week, in the quality British press, grainy black-and-white photographs accompanied by a paragraph of text illustrate the process of production and way of life in a tiny town called (deliciously) Lynchburg, Tennessee. There, old white men continue the process of their ancestors—dating from 1866—of smoothing the liquor through hard maple charcoal and laying it down for a long time in an "aging house" until absolutely ready. These same ageless men, with whom we feel we are familiar from *The Waltons* and *The Beverly Hillbillies,* live in the company town, also known mythically as "The Hollow," and drink the whiskey, ensuring a peaceful continuity within a time-honored region. Jack Daniel's sour mash, marketed as a man's drink and iconized by rocker-bikers ("Easy Riders") and movies such as *A Few Good Men* and *Scent of a Woman* (both 1992), has captured an essence of southernness that has had huge international appeal. This is a South where (white) men are real men, drinking is serious, the small town offers a high-quality, low-stress life, and the past is respected at all levels of production and consumption. As a 1997 London Underground billboard advertisement for the whiskey proclaimed, "Jack Daniel's Country is old country where change occurs, but tradition governs." Or, a year later, and more succinctly, "Trendy since 1866."

THE SOUTH AND BRITAIN

In the final decades of the twentieth century, saturation advertising and film with a southern theme reinforced British fascination with the American South. There is a strong affection between the South and Britain, in terms of both sociohistorical roots and ties and cultural and mythic connections. In terms of demographic influence, however, it is not a specifically *English* connection, of the kind that exists in New England and other northern states that saw a great deal of English immigration. The earliest census in 1790 (albeit disputed by some historians) established that the majority of Europeans in the southern states were *Celtic* rather than English—Scottish, Irish, Scotch-Irish, Welsh, and Cornish—and by the time of the Civil War the South's white population was more than three-quarters Celtic. From the late seventeenth century to the American Revolution, the southern backcountry was flooded with one of those groups, the Scotch-Irish, and it is said that their heritage and style are the characteristics most associated with southerners over the past two centuries: herding rather than tilling, leisurely, musical, tall-tale telling, violent, clannish, family-centered, fiercely Protestant, with a strong sense of honor.[11] Indeed, the term most used, usually pejoratively, to describe poor white southern frontiersmen from the mid-1700s is the Scottish term for a noisy, boasting fellow, a "cracker."

The white cracker has acquired a new spin in recent years. The neo-Confederate, white supremacist League of the South was set up to defend the notion of the true South as Celtic, thus by definition white; other Souths (notably African American) thus become illegitimate and inferior.[12] The league's central text, written by board member Grady McWhiney, is *Cracker Culture*, which argues, as Diane Roberts puts it, "Celtic culture rolls down uninterrupted through two millennia from Queen Boudicca in her chariot to Cale Yarborough in his stock car."[13] Arguing euphemistically for "heritage not hate," among other things the league has declared a wish to return to British spelling, seeing the American Webster's dictionary as an example of "cultural ethnic cleansing" (15). The Celtic card is being played belligerently against what is perceived as a politically correct celebration of multicultural southern diversity. Leftist Celtic organizations such as the Scottish Nationalist Party and Plaid Cymru are embraced for their nationalist separatism, which is (mis)interpreted as conservative supremacism. In the case of Scots nationalism the movies *Rob Roy* and *Braveheart* are highly recommended; the league Web site recommended that all "Southrons" (Walter Scott's pejorative term) should go to see *Braveheart*, a film also endorsed strongly by the Ku Klux Klan and John Birch Society.[14] And The League of the South is not the only white supremacist group to have resorted to Celtic mythology. The twentieth-century rededication of the Klan was inspired by D. W. Griffith's *The Birth of a Nation* (1915), the film version of Thomas Dixon's novel *The Clansman* (1905). In Dixon's novel, cross burning is used by the Klan after the old practice in the Scottish highlands for calling clans together. In 1915, on Stone Mountain, Atlanta, the second wave of the Klan revived the Scottish practice and burned a cross during Thanksgiving weekend; thus the pernicious practice always associated with Klan intimidation was born. The Celtic cross has become a potent symbol of a rash of "patriot movement" groups in the States, such as Christian Identity, the North American Liberation Association, and Neo-Nazis.[15]

THE WALTER SCOTT FACTOR

Of all Celtic influences on the American South (apart from a general recognition of the supreme importance of Scottish and Irish music), one name, that of Walter Scott, is the most cited. Plantation houses and humble street names alike testify to the enthusiasm Victorian southerners had for reading his work; his novels still sit proudly on southern bookshelves. Scott's historical novels inspired a tradition of cavalier romances by writers such as William Alexander Carruthers, in tomes called *The Cavaliers of Virginia* (1834) and *The Knights of the Golden Horseshoe* (1841). The renowned slave Frederick Douglass, when choosing his own name rather than a slave master's, settled on Douglass after a character in Scott's *The Lady of the Lake,* ironically because a northern abolitionist suggested it. It is common to blame Scott for much of the romanticism and feudal aspirations established firmly within the nineteenth-century South and still continuing into the present century. Mark Twain famously attacked "Sir Walter Scott with his enchantments" for checking progress in the South and for the South's embrace of "dreams and phantoms . . . decayed and swinish forms of religion . . . sillinesses and emptinesses, sham grandeurs, sham gauds, and sham chivalries of a brainless and worthless long-vanished society." To him, Scott's "jejune romanticism of an absurd past that is dead" was largely responsible for the Civil War itself.[16]

The Cavalier myth, in which the Old South was created by an aristocracy of English Cavaliers fleeing Cromwell, is blamed for many of the South's most persistent and damaging myths about itself. W. J. Cash, in the most famous deconstruction of this myth, saw Scott as central to the ideology of the medieval southern gentleman, living in a world "wholly dominated by ideals of honor and chivalry and *noblesse*." He argued that Scott "was bodily taken over by the South and incorporated into the Southern people's vision of themselves" and that his books inspired southerners to see themselves as "the chivalry."[17] Even in twentieth-century southern historiography, Scott's influence is recognized. The South is described as the region most enthusiastically supportive of the American Military-Industrial Complex, especially since World War II. Militancy and martial behavior have long been dominant in the South (partly because of engagement with Native American uprisings and slaves): "Many southerners, weaned on the novels of Sir Walter Scott, were obsessed with a sense of honor."[18] And, alert to the resonances of this Cavalier myth, Brown-Forman Beverages Worldwide, which owns Jack Daniel's, has a "Tennessee Squire Program" that makes loyal Jack Daniel's drinkers "squires" who co-own plots of land in Lynchburg. The company will cheerfully acknowledge the playful spuriousness of this "program" (they boast that the late Frank Sinatra was a squire, who circled his helicopter over his designated plot—though there is no legal entitlement), but it illustrates how saturated the contemporary South still is in its feudal mythology.

DIALOGUES WITH BRITAIN

Many British cultural influences on, and dialogues with, the South have partly made it what it is. British speech patterns, dialects, and pronunciations have endured there, with southerners retaining many words and pronunciations common in seventeenth- to nineteenth-century Britain. Critic Cleanth Brooks argued for more than fifty years that southerners speak an older, purer form of "King's English" than most English-speakers and that there are clear links between southern English and the English of southwest Britain; other sociolinguists have published lists of southern words that demonstrate the persistence of terms from Chaucer and Shakespeare.[19] Despite Jefferson's Anglophobia, there has been less effort in the South than North to break the colonial connection. The Yankee tradition in the Jacksonian era to Americanize the language and literature, along with tariffs and economic rivalry, have no counterpart in the South. Northern cities, with strong immigrant voices in the urban culture, have no counterpart in the South. Fawning over the British monarchy has persisted longer in southern states.[20] English influence, widely recognized in New England and the earliest English colonies, endures in the South through the names of English former plantations and colonies, now states, as well as cities and towns: Virginia (for Elizabeth I), Carolina (Charles I), Georgia (George II), the James River (James I), Birmingham, Norfolk, Richmond, Raleigh, and so on. British folk music is acknowledged as a major source for the "country" element in country and western music. Although it is well known that European Gothic inspired both prominent state capitols and major plantation houses, it is less frequently recorded that southern Episcopalian ecclesiastical architecture was often modeled on English parish churches. British literature, too, was very important to the planter and politician in antebellum culture: Victorian figures such as Arnold, Carlyle, Mill, Tennyson, Browning, and Darwin were read avidly; Carlyle reciprocated this admiration with his enthusiastic espousal of the Confederate cause, while Browning's robustly optimistic Christian work inspired the establishment of hundreds of Browning Societies throughout the South. In New Orleans, as Anglo-southerners tried to capture and control the Creole-French tradition, the nineteenth-century Mardi Gras "krewes" (itself a term invented to sound like archaic English) invoked Milton's *Comus* and *Paradise Lost* and Spenser's *Faerie Queene* in order to accumulate cultural capital.[21] English Victorian attitudes to sexuality echoed southerners' own patriarchally repressed views: the white Madonna southern belle on her pedestal owes much to the Angel in the House of Coventry Patmore and Tennyson's *Idylls of the King.*

And many parallels exist between colonial attitudes to the colonized, as described and defended in Victorian discourses, and the
South's defense of the "peculiar institution of slavery." Of course,
conservative and progressive politicians alike pointed fingers at Britain to make points for and against chattel and wage slavery, and the
institution of slavery bound together British and southern trade and
other relationships throughout the eighteenth and nineteenth centuries. The abolition debate on both sides of the Atlantic shared ideas,
champions, and documents; proslavery southern writers such as James
Henry Hammond felt obliged, after the abolition of slavery in Britain, to defend themselves against their own compatriots and those
English abolitionists who began to stir up northern opposition to the
"peculiar institution." In the years and months leading up to secession, there was strong support at all levels of British society for the
Confederate cause. And, in 1845, years before the Civil War began,
freed slaves Frederick Douglass and Harriet Jacobs traveled to England
(and Douglass first to Ireland). While there, Douglass promoted his
Narrative of the Life of Frederick Douglass, an American Slave, while
Jacobs worked as nursemaid to a child whose mother had just died;
he found ready support for his abolition cause, and she (whose *Inci-
dents in the Life of a Slave Girl* was to appear more than a dozen years
later) would later work in the antislavery reading room above the
North Star offices in Rochester and try unsuccessfully to find a British publisher for her own slave narrative.

Indeed, a literary relationship has been one of the most enduring links and exchanges between Europe and the South. Apart from
the towering Celtic figure of Scott, there are many mutual literary
influences and admirers. In autobiographies by southern writers, from
Richard Wright to Maya Angelou, frequent reference is made to the
young writer's introduction to European, especially English, literature
and of its hold over the southerner's imagination. In an exhibition
of Mississippi fiction printed in England, mounted in 1992 at the
University of Mississippi, Americans were referred to as "literary step-
children of 'the Brits,' and no greater source of inspiration exists for
American authors than the 500-year-long tradition of English English
literature."[22] The catalog reflects on the fact that southern writers still
see theirs as a lesser literature, while English letters are the real McCoy.
Ellen Gilchrist, writing of her love for the English Faber and Faber
editions of her fiction, notes wryly, "I was raised to think I was an

Englishwoman who only happened to be living in the Mississippi delta because my family were colonists"(22); indeed, on the dust jacket of her first British collection, the 1982 Faber *In the Land of Dreamy Dreams*, she describes herself as "an Englishwoman and a Scot" (23). Richard Ford offers a telling anecdote about English cultural imperialism; renting a converted barn from an Englishman, he found himself avoiding meeting his landlord on rent-collection days: "Probably, he imagined, I was ducking my rent. But I was only ducking him—his choice of words—my own hold on literature being, then as now, somewhat fragile" (27).

THE BRITISH TAKE ON SOUTHERN CULTURE

The affection felt by southerners for Europeans, especially the British, is well reciprocated. The closeness of ties is manifest in genealogical, cultural, and political terms, not to mention a shared heritage and guilt about the slave trade and slavery itself. The South appears in British culture through a number of stereotypes: there is the simple South of comical accents and mountain people or small-town folk asleep on front porches; the romantic antebellum South of courtly beaux and beauteous belles; and, most familiar in recent years, the violent or gothic South of evil stirrings behind the magnolia in moonlight, usually some terrible racial or sexual sin or secret. Since in recent decades the South has acquired a less conservative and separatist reputation within the United States, international attention has focused less on its violent past and more on its cultural production and tourism possibilities. This does not mean that, whenever another death row prisoner's case is highlighted or an abortion clinic is firebombed, the South's murky history and characteristics are forgotten; it does mean that these no longer obscure its heterogeneous cultural forms and achievements.

You do not have to look far to see how British culture is infused with reminders and traces of those many cultures. For a start, there is the omnipresence of southern music, on disc, radio, and TV, in film and in church services, and over supermarket loudspeakers. My files bulge with documents on British events relating to American Civil War weekends, the Southern Skirmish Association reenacting battles, a Minstrel Spectacular (reviving in the 1990s the much discredited "Black and White Minstrel Show" of the 1950s and early

1960s), and *Gone With the Wind*–themed weddings. There are restaurants and bars called The Big Easy, Old Orleans, and The Jefferson Experience; a music-oriented pub at the end of my street was renamed The Louisiana. New Orleans jazz groups, Cajun and zydeco bands, gospel and country singers abound, as do informal publications linking them. On BBC as well as independent TV and radio, popular series focus on country, jazz, and soul.[23] Most of all, there is no decline in enthusiastic homage paid to "the King," Elvis. The 1990s growth in saturation television and newspaper coverage of his birthday (especially in 1997, the twentieth anniversary of his death) reflects the passionate national involvement in the singer: Elvis fan clubs, memorabilia collections, "Elvis Rooms," tribute concerts, and themed holidays ("Have an Elv of a Time for Just £49"), Elvis impersonators (Hull's Bobby Memphis, Swansea's Elvis Patel), travel clubs ("Memphis is Mecca"), and two exclusively Elvis-themed shops in London, Elvisly Yours and The Elvis Shop. The year 2000 saw a West End opening of a new comedy by Lee Hall, *Cooking with Elvis*.[24]

In the last years of the century, a fascination with all things southern grew and grew. Supermarkets sold Cajun dishes; bourbons with reassuring names like Old Forester, Old Times, and Southern Comfort; and "dairy cocktails" in such flavors as "Louisiana Peach," "Mississippi Mud," and "Wild Jack Chaser." Secondhand bookshops and libraries boasted novels by prolific writers Frank Yerby and Frances Parkinson Keyes, as well as crime and gothic best-sellers by John Grisham and James Lee Burke. The romance section of large stores is crammed with titles such as *Riverboat Seduction*, *Moon over Black Bayou*, and *Southern Passions*, while there is a new taste for movie adaptations of southern writings, from *Steel Magnolias* (1989) to *Midnight in the Garden of Good and Evil* (1998).

SOUTHERNNESS, HYBRIDITY, AND CULTURAL FLOWS

I have suggested that the definition of "southernness," and the qualities distinguishing southern cultures from those of the rest of the United States, have eluded and fascinated readers and writers alike. In the 1990s, there was no diminution in the number of colloquia, journals, books, and informal debates about the nature, future, and mind of the South. In postwar years, a key moment that focused global attention on the South and all things southern was the election of President Jimmy Carter in 1976. In this description, historians William J. Cooper Jr. and Thomas E. Terrill spell out the different, apparently opposing Souths embodied within the president himself:

> Carter was perceived both as a modern man and as a rural rustic. He symbolized the modern South—desegregated, upwardly mobile, more cosmopolitan in its politics, a champion of agribusiness, well educated, adroit in public imagery. But he was also perceived as a simple peanut farmer and small-town Southern Baptist from a rural fantasyland where few people wore shoes, neighbors were neighborly, and traditional values and ways persisted—except for Jim Crow, which had wondrously vanished one warm summer morning.[25]

These two very contradictory Souths might lead one to abandon the quest for a clear and simple definition of "southern." Rather than seek an authentic "southernness," we should recognize that southern culture is itself hybrid, the product of black and white Atlantic or transatlantic intercultural influences and movements—a living process of "call and response." Postcolonial discussions of culture have rejected the search for origins and roots, concentrating instead on notions of hybridity and crossover.[26] Paul Gilroy and Edward Said have written of the ways in which, paradoxically, imperialism has brought the world closer together, Gilroy using as metaphor for cultural exchange the ship's voyage, routes rather than roots, Said emphasizing the fact that empire meant the interrelationship of cultures.[27] Said talks of "the interdependence of cultural terrains in which colonizer and colonized co-existed and battled each other through projections as well as rival geographies, narratives, and histories." This emphasis on the battle for meaning opens the way to see all cultures as heterogeneous, differentiated, and nonmonolithic. Gilroy focuses on "diaspora cultures," with identity defined as "a process of movement and mediation."[28] Both men, refusing the notion of origins, follow post-1960s trends among poststructuralists, radical geographers, and multiculturalists in recognizing the importance of rethinking modernity in terms of cultural exchange, fusion, and flow. Emphasizing his hostility to the narrow Afrocentrism he discerns within the black community, Gilroy cites Nelson Mandela as a powerful advocate for his argument. On first visiting the States, President Mandela told his audience he had found solace listening to Marvin Gaye's "What's Going On?": "When we were in prison, we appreciated and obviously listened to the sound of Detroit"(96).

Now, not all black culture is southern, and Motown is a mid-western phenomenon. But, with this anecdote, Paul Gilroy reminds us of the many journeys—some into exile—made by African Americans across the Atlantic, with all the subsequent rich cultural dialogues and mixtures. A good example of this is a form of music closely associated with blacks. Jazz was always hybrid, played from the outset by mixed-race and white musicians, using European forms and often relying on extended visits to Europe.[29] For many critics, the idea of appropriating jazz or black fiction for Afrocentrism is to distort and diminish it, since it is "inextricably linked to European practice." Jazz in particular is today an "international 'language,'" and if one thinks of the growing worldwide reputation of black writers, fiction is fast catching up.[30]

In recent years, scholars have become fascinated by the idea of circulating and dynamic, rather than fixed, cultures. "Authenticity" and "origins" are seen as political inventions, thus politically loaded. A search for roots has been transformed into a tracing of routes, and cultures are now seen as intersections of meanings. American culture has become a "superculture," detached from roots, being adapted, absorbed, and mediated through the processes of globalization and transnational communities (especially via the airwaves, the Internet, and tourism). Cultural imperialism is being replaced by postimperial notions of a global, mass-mediated culture that takes particular local forms, adopted, assimilated, appropriated in various ways.[31] Nelson Mandela listened to Motown in jail; a Serbo-Croat family sang "Deep River" to tourist Maya Angelou when she entered their store; Elvis Presley loved to watch British Monty Python tapes on TV; at the 1996 summit meeting between Presidents Yeltsin of Russia and Clinton of the United States, a Finnish professor sang Presley songs translated into Latin.

This is not to suggest, in some Pollyanna-ish way, that such appropriations bring the world together in loving harmony. What it does highlight is the tendency of critics, at this millennial and postcolonial moment, to foreground links rather than barriers between peoples and cultures. Eschewing the pure, fixed, essential, timeless and universal, they favor the hybrid, dynamic, local, in process and in performance. Going along with all these images of cultural flows and dialogues is a notion much associated with the Caribbean and—within the United States—Louisiana, "creolization." Paul Gilroy has defined the "Black Atlantic" world of routes between Africa, Europe, and the United States, while Joseph Roach coined the term "a circum-Atlantic world," which, in his words, "insists on the centrality of the diasporic and genocidal histories of Africa and the Americas, North and South, in the creation of the culture of modernity."[32] In terms of the South, historian Charles Joyner adopts the view, expressed first in 1938 by Bronislaw Malinowski, that the black and white races "exist upon elements taken from Europe as well as from Africa." Thus all southerners enjoy a shared heritage and identity: "Whether expressed with the virtuosic frenzy of a Dizzy Gillespie or an Elvis Presley, or with the laid-back quietude of a Lester Young or a Willie Nelson . . . every black Southerner has a European heritage as well as an African one, and every white Southerner has an African heritage as well as a European one."[33]

German critic Berndt Ostendorf follows Joyner's line by challenging what he sees as the orthodox American Manichean opposition between "Eurocentrism" and "Afrocentrism." He favors "a genuine Creolization . . . a hybridization and *metissage* of what used to be rigid categories of belonging" and argues for a "circumatlantic Creole mindset."[34] He is, however, alert to the dangers of too vague a definition of creolization erasing a sense of history and cultural memory (so crucial in the South), in such a way that the chamber of commerce and tourist trade can oversimplify or mythify complex groups of people and cities within the Americas. For example, he quotes writer Barry Ancelot describing tourists' simplistic expectations of southwestern Louisiana Cajuns: "The French who seek vestiges of former colonials find instead French-speaking cowboys (and Indians) in pick-up trucks. They are surprised that the Cajuns and Creoles love fried chicken and iced tea, forgetting this is the South; that they love hamburgers and coke, forgetting this is the United States. . . . American visitors . . . too, [look] in vain for traces of Longfellow's Evangeline."[35]

So how can Europeans and Americans alike consider the paradox of a region that is steeped in a singular social and especially racial history, developed from its own particular cultural roots, and that is also a hybrid, performative mixture of European, African, and Protestant American routes? Is there a single southern culture, or, as Richard Gray suggests, "a rich, pluralistic, sometimes warring and at other times embracing series of influences and energies: not so much southern culture, really, as southern *cultures*"?[36] Are there not also multiple responses to, and interpretations of, that culture(s) in a wide variety of readerships, audiences, spectators, and tourists? These questions have intrigued many southern commentators, and thus one of the most exciting challenges we face is the documentation of the ways southern culture has circulated through different continents, cultures, and countries. Being a sickly traveler myself, I know that too much flow and flux produces a yearning for home, roots, and settled relations. While it is important to acknowledge the global march of Americanization, it is also necessary to examine the details of where and how American cultures affect and interact with specific locations and times. So this book addresses these issues through a close focus on particular British dialogues in southern culture, informed and mediated as those are by transatlantic and circum-Atlantic forces. Just as the South cannot be seen in sociopolitical isolation, Britain's postcolonial late-twentieth-century relationships with America and Africa will come into frame as a transatlantic lens is trained on its engagement with the postwar South.

In the late 1930s, BBC employee Ursula Branston followed in the footsteps of a few eccentric Englishwomen of the mid-nineteenth century: she resigned her London-based job, took a ship to Baltimore, and then published an account of her extensive travels in the South.[37] In her preface, she reveals that apparently arbitrary mixture of cultural products and references that first led to a fascination with the region: "I went to America to see the South. Why the South? . . . Because of Henderson's *Jackson*, Marian Anderson's voice, Bill Robinson's taps; because of the word 'sharecropper' and a review in a London paper of *The River*; because I heard, in the distance, of WPA and TVA and CCC; because Battleship won the Grand National, and people said that mint julep was the most subtle drink on earth" (5).

Half a century later, the black British journalist Gary Younge was inspired by the television series documenting the civil rights era, *Eyes on the Prize*, to take a Greyhound bus trip from Washington to New Orleans, tracing the route of the 1960s antisegregation Freedom Riders. He, too, had been long fascinated by the South. Why? "It could have been with the televising of Alex Haley's *Roots*, which I was forced to stay up and watch. My brothers and I could recite the lineage all the way from Kunta Kinte down to Haley himself. . . . It could have begun when I was studying *To Kill a Mockingbird* for English O level, or watching Alice Walker's *The Color Purple*. . . . Or maybe it was B. B. King's blues and Billie Holiday's 'Strange Fruit.'"[38]

But however different the elements of Branston's and Younge's desire, the same serendipitous mixture of cultural forms, a cocktail of (mostly popular) music, film, literature, with a dash of vibrant politics, has long constituted British fascination for the region. At present, few British tourists venture much farther into the South than Florida, for Disney World and Epcot, so it remains largely a "virtual" site of myth and imagination. And yet it is becoming one of North America's most familiar regions to us, as familiar in popular representations as "the West" and the major urban centers of Los Angeles and New York. Its dramatic rise in national economic, political, and cultural status is paralleled by its rising international reputation. Europeans, too, look to the "will-o'-the-wisp Eden" for inspiration, nostalgia, and utopian visions. This book aims to examine some of the complex ways in which the British have engaged creatively with the cultural movements and products of the South and, via many different transatlantic and black and white Atlantic routes, have helped reinterpret and revivify its images and history.

2

"GONE WITH THE WIND" INTO THE MILLENNIUM
Sequels, Borrowings, and Revisions

If one were to look back over the twentieth century and ask which single work of art proved to be its most popular and enduring, reaching the largest global audiences and achieving most purchase within world culture, there is probably only one choice: *Gone With the Wind*. Reputed to have sold more copies than any other book (except the Bible), this novel-made-film, in all its manifestations—book, film, video, soundtrack, memorabilia, sequel, plagiarized novel, fictional reworking, biographical and critical study, not to mention countless advertisements, spoof posters, songs, heritage plates, pop-up books, themed restaurants, and colloquial expressions—has reached a vast worldwide market.[1] Margaret Mitchell's novel, *Gone With the Wind* (1936), a long and loving backward glance at the traumatic American Civil War and the devastation of the South, sealed in celluloid immortality through its highly successful 1939 David O. Selznick film version, is instantly recognized, much cited and quoted, and has come to be associated in the international mind with American southernness, indeed with nineteenth- and twentieth-century America itself.

The novel belongs to a long tradition of southern plantation fiction and white apologist historiography. It focuses on the South's most dramatic historic period, secession, followed by the 1861–1865 "War between the States" (Civil War), the bloody demise of plantation culture and the slave economy, and the violent chaos of Recon-

struction. Although this period had been fictionalized by other southern writers, Mitchell was unique in focusing on such a complex sweep
of history from the perspective, and through the experiences, of a
young white woman who begins by expressing boredom at the
thought of war, then lives through extreme reversals of fortune and
wealth, loses parents, husbands, a child, and many friends, and yet
survives to rebuild her plantation home, way of life, and self-esteem.

The story revolves around Scarlett O'Hara, daughter of Irish landowner Gerald, who has made the plantation Tara into one of
Georgia's finest. She is unrequitedly in love with Ashley Wilkes, who
marries his cousin Melanie. As war begins, Scarlett has to protect her
family and the pregnant Melanie. Staying in Atlanta with relatives,
she faces Sherman's army and (with the help of a frightened, inex-
perienced slave, Prissy) delivers Melanie's baby as the city goes up in
flames. During Reconstruction, she pragmatically does business with
the Yankees and so prospers and restores the fortunes of Tara, while
simultaneously protecting her close circle's involvement with the Ku
Klux Klan. During the course of the narrative, she marries three
times—first, for spite at Ashley; second, to pay off Tara's postwar taxes;
third, for fun. This third husband, Rhett Butler, shares his wife's prag-
matism, blockade-running during the early part of the war and only
later joining the Confederate army. He engages in lucrative deals with
the federal army from the start of the conflict and right through Reconstruction. Enraged at his wife's love for Ashley and selfish disen-
gagement from him and their daughter, Bonnie Blue, who dies in a
riding accident, he leaves her. The book ends with Scarlett realizing
how much she loves him and resolving to get him back—by returning to her beloved Tara to plan her strategy.

Gone With the Wind (known familiarly as *GWTW*) has sealed in
popular imagination a fascinated nostalgia for the glamorous southern plantation house and an ordered hierarchical society in which
slaves are "family" and there is a mystical bond between landowner
and the rich soil those slaves work for him. It has spoken eloquently,
albeit from an elite perspective, of the grand themes (war, love, death,
conflicts of race, class, gender, and generation) that have crossed continents and cultures. For women reader-viewers, Scarlett O'Hara has
provided a rich source of imaginative play and has stood for a quality of female strength, power, and bloody-mindedness that is rare in
twentieth-century fiction and film. Characters (Scarlett, Mammy,

Rhett), iconic sayings ("Tomorrow is another day"), and dramatic moments (Atlanta burning and "birthin' babies"), in film as well as novel, acquired international significance for *GWTW* enthusiasts and inspired a tradition of writing and filmmaking that keeps the work alive, in both its imitations and detractions. Even when, in recent years, African American writing and film, from *The Color Purple* to *Beloved*, have embarrassed *GWTW* fans into a recognition of its historical distortions and the southern belle and her beau are now the subject of TV soap opera and satire, the original retains its popular mystique.

From its first publication and the film that followed the novel faithfully, there are many—not least black and white southerners anxious for their region to be represented as modern and progressive—who have wished this work would fade away and occupy a minor role in the representational history of the American South, to be overtaken by versions of the American Civil War of greater verisimilitude and relevance for a multicultural American society. During the decades since the civil rights movement, and especially in a racially sensitive postcolonial world climate, this glorification of a lost world of slavery and socioeconomic exploitation has seemed anachronistic and racially provocative. However, the publicity machine for *Gone With the Wind* ignores such political sensitivities, invoking its character as a work that is "timeless," "legendary," and "immortal." And although there is some truth in the claim that *Gone With the Wind* appeals enormously to very different nations and cultures, it is important to remember that the legend and longevity of this work have been carefully nurtured by the many groups and individuals—publishers, literary estate, film and television companies, porcelain figurine makers and so on—who have profited handsomely from the work's "universal" success.

EUROPE'S "GONE WITH THE WIND"

My interest in this chapter is not to rehearse the debates about the original novel and film but rather to discuss the ways in which European audiences and financial interests have shared in this bonanza and allowed *GWTW* to "endure." Published in the pre–World War II depression 1930s, this epic work addressed issues close to European hearts: economic and social upheavals, the inevitability of an imminent catastrophic war. As the world recovered from war and the Holocaust in the forties and fifties, it was a costume drama and heroic story for drab, utilitarian days. In the final three decades of the century, it became a feminist, or "me-generation" text, as well as a fin-de-siècle wallow in nostalgia for days of certainty, continuity, and order. There are still fascinating histories to relate about the popular significance of and relationships with this work in, say, Finland, Germany, or the Netherlands. For example, after many years of local people's failed attempts to create a Margaret Mitchell Museum in Atlanta, the project succeeded only with enthusiastic injection of capital support from the German company Daimler-Benz AG. It would be impossible to do justice to the complex subject of European popular and critical reception within different countries and cultures. The focus of this chapter is the legacy of *GWTW* in Britain and Ireland.

Margaret Mitchell was unusual among 1930s southern novelists in gesturing strongly to Catholic European cultures. Scarlett O'Hara is the daughter of an Irish father, Gerald, and French mother, Ellen Robillard. Mitchell was very conscious of her own Irish maternal ancestry and throughout the novel drew on a romantic Celtic mythology to explain the O'Haras' passionate love for family ties and the land itself. The very name of the plantation, Tara, has that mythic weight that both Gerald and Scarlett draw on to justify the white South's defense of its property—houses as well as slaves. Meanwhile, Ellen's Frenchness is that element of refinement and elegance that made rough farmer Gerald marry her. It also signifies the deep passion that she suppresses (for lost love, her French cousin Philippe) but that emerges in her willful daughter, Scarlett. Scarlett O'Hara, the hybrid product of these two characters and cultures, bridles against the orthodox manners and mores of conventional American southern society, invoking and expressing her Irishness and Frenchness in various ways, from working on the land she loves to keep Tara within the family to appreciating the fancy bonnet Rhett brings her from Paris.

Mitchell's reference to these European cultures within her own work undoubtedly appealed to European readers and audiences. When other writers turned their attention to the ur-text, as either inspiration or model, they recognized that the ethnic mix within *GWTW* was one of its most appealing features and so followed suit. During the 1980s, two sequels to the original novel were commissioned; one was published and made into a television series. A French writer was taken to court on a *GWTW*-plagiarism charge, while a distinguished American southerner who had lived most of his life in France published a trilogy, closely following Margaret Mitchell's subject matter. None of these works broke the mold of the original. All played their part in keeping it alive. The Celtic theme was used to a more politically reactionary effect than in Mitchell's and Selznick's work, and the French perspectives cast little new transatlantic light on the old story. The real effect of European engagement with *GWTW* was that European (mainly British) writers and actors, and Europe-based companies (publishing, film, TV, and publicity) financed and profited from new versions of the work to ensure the longevity of the *Gone With the Wind* story well into the twenty-first century.

THE SEQUEL TO "GONE WITH THE WIND"

The Mitchell Literary Estate's commissioning of a sequel to Margaret Mitchell's novel in the 1980s played the most significant part in ensuring new life for the work. This was an obvious commercial move for a literary estate hungry for greater profits, and—hot on its heels—a TV industry eager for a blockbuster miniseries. I say an obvious move, because the genre of the sequel has become an important contemporary Western cultural phenomenon. Although it is by no means a new form, in the last two decades of the twentieth century, mainstream Hollywood and book publishers have found the sequel to be a money-spinner—easy to market on the back of the original and guaranteed enthusiastic ready-made audiences and readers. The proliferation of sequels to such successful films as *Jaws*, *Lethal Weapon*, or *Terminator* is paralleled by fictional sequels to, and rewritings of, titles by Jane Austen, Charlotte Brontë, and Daphne du Maurier.[2] In the case of film, the sequel has become such a cinematic cliché that it tends to cheapen the status of the original; in the case of fiction, it tends to enhance the original work's classic status and indeed—in the case of *popular* fiction (Daphne du Maurier's *Rebecca* being one of the best examples)—to add gravitas.

There is a distinction to be made here between the sequel and the reworked, or intertextual "literary echo," novel. The "echo" begins with the original and then plays games with readers' knowledge and expectations of the characters and narrative development; it invites them into a knowing literary conceit, teases and pleases them with surprises and shocks. As in Jean Rhys's *Wide Sargasso Sea*, a version of the *Jane Eyre* story that forces readers to rethink their understanding of the original, or Graham Swift's *Last Orders* (1996), which recalls and offers a contemporary commentary on William Faulkner's *As I Lay Dying* (1930), the "ghostly presence" of the first writer informs but does not determine the subsequent work.[3] The sequel, however, is restricted by the terms of the original. However much a writer wishes to create original material, she or he will be judged in terms of the faithfulness to the ur-novel, thus preventing too radical a departure from its terms, characters, and narrative thrust. Sequels must probably always disappoint, since readers' imaginary scenarios and fantasies about what happens in the aftermath of beloved novels will require of the second work extremely high levels of insight into the enigmas and unresolved questions within the first. The sequel, or "classical progression," must offer a narrative of continuity and must be seen to be a labor of love and respect, not subversion or parody.[4] It is thus an impossible task to produce a sequel that challenges the terms and tone of the original without drastically damaging reader expectations. This was one of the problems facing any new version of *GWTW*.

The epic nature of southern history has invited sequels: Margaret Walker has long planned a sequel to her *Jubilee* (1966); Alex Haley produced a sequel to *Roots* (1976); Kyle Onstott's "Falconhurst" and John Jakes's "North and South" series were followed by a southern trilogy from Julian Green. Margaret Mitchell herself joked about a second *GWTW*, *Back with the Breeze*, "a highly moral tract in which everyone, including Belle Watling, underwent a change of heart and character and reeked with sanctimonious dullness."[5] Despite desperate pleas from publishers and readers, Mitchell always refused to write a sequel and enjoined her executors to refuse to allow such a publication by any other writer. Anne Edwards, Mitchell's first biographer, wrote a sequel entitled *Tara*, but it was refused permission for publication by the estate and is now sealed in a vault, never to see the light of day. However, after the death of the writer's brother, Stephens (who abided by his sister's wishes until his final days), his sons and heirs decided to capitalize on the lucrative possibilities of such a commission and ignored Mitchell's injunction. After long deliberation and rumored bids from writers as disparate as lesbian American novelist Rita Mae Brown and British romance queen Barbara Cartland, they hired as near a clone of Margaret Mitchell as could be found: Alexandra Ripley, southern author of such historical sagas as *On Leaving Charleston* (1981) and *New Orleans Legacy* (1987). The sequel was promised in 1989 or 1990, to coincide with the film's fiftieth anniversary, around which much media publicity was anticipated. The eventual publication, in 1991, was said to be late because Ripley's first draft was refused by the estate; she claims difficulties with an editor. It hardly mattered, since the suspense only aroused further interest in the book.

Scarlett: The Sequel to Margaret Mitchell's "Gone With the Wind" ends by reuniting Scarlett and Rhett, but only after a long series of picaresque adventures involving trips to Charleston, Savannah, Atlanta, and finally—for much of the book—Ireland. Scarlett hands over the management of Tara to sister Suellen and with her considerable wealth goes off to get Rhett back, as we knew she must. Rhett, who (as Mitchell made him promise) returned to Charleston, is living with his mother and working as an upmarket camellia grower and fertilizer salesman. After some skirmishing and a passionate roll on the beach after a near drowning (an encounter that fortuitously impregnates our heroine), Rhett rejects her and marries a dull schoolteacher, who later conveniently dies in childbirth. Scarlett secures the major shareholding in Tara, then turns her back on the South, and, inspired by Irish relatives she met in Savannah, sails to her father's birthplace, county Meath, influenced by Gerald O'Hara's memories and love of the Irish soil. Her destination is Adamstown, home of her one-hundred-year-old grandmother Katie Scarlett, and nearby Tara, that mythic place that gave its name to Scarlett's family plantation. Buying a huge, decaying estate called Ballyhara, Scarlett becomes known as "the O'Hara," the most significant landowner and citizen. Taking on a series of curiously feudal roles and responsibilities, she exercises power with benevolent tyranny.

The members of her extended family are all active in the Fenian Brotherhood, and for a while—until she begins to hunt and socialize with the Anglos—she finances their activities. An Irish witch delivers her of a daughter, Cat, by cesarean section on Halloween night. The members of the O'Hara clan are idealistic and eminently superstitious, and their revolutionary fervor is finally condemned as pathological and murderous—especially when they try to turn on the newly reunited Scarlett and Rhett, in the final chapter huddled together with their daughter fearing for their lives. As one would expect, this implausible saga has a neat, conservative happy ending, the nuclear family reconstituted with Cat, substitute for the dead daughter Bonnie Blue.

Scarlett appeared in September 1991 in eighteen languages, including Japanese and Chinese, and forty countries simultaneously. It became the fastest-selling book in publishing history, with 5.5 million copies sold worldwide in its first two months. By 1993 it had sold more than twenty million copies worldwide. On 4 October 1991, the *New York Times* ran a full-page advertisement from Warner Books boasting of its success as the "record-breaker for biggest first day sales" and "the overnight national bestseller," quoting booksellers across the land on the lines of people waiting to buy, the "epidemic of Scarlett fever," the mobbing of one store from opening bell to closing time, and so on. The William Morris Agency director of foreign rights described it bombastically as the most successful publication of all time.

The British press dutifully reported the phenomenal sales success of the book, while enjoying the irony of the almost universally dreadful critical reviews it received in its first weeks. As one journalist observed, "Rarely can a novel which has received so many dreadful reviews have achieved such remarkable sales figures." Marilyn Warnick, attending the Frankfurt Book Fair for the *Daily Telegraph*, commented that it was easy to identify the publishers of *Scarlett* walking the aisles. "They were the ones gloating that they didn't give a damn about the most appalling worldwide reviews in history since there are already 1.6 million copies of the book in print in the US, 250,000 in the UK and Commonwealth and 600,000 in Germany."

These sales figures seem considerably at odds with the millions the publishers claim were sold in the first months, but then the whole marketing information is notoriously unreliable. There are few, including the publishers, who deny that this sequel was about money. Journalists salivated over Alexandra Ripley's large advance, though it is impossible to establish what it was.[6] The press had a field day mocking the whole enterprise. The London-based magazine *Girl about Town*, noting that *GWTW* had sold more than any other book except the Bible, remarked: "Ms Ripley will no doubt shortly be able to buy herself all the ante-bellum mansions she desires. Watch out for the film, the who'll-play-Scarlett hype, the sequel of the sequel, the overkill, and the overkill of the overkill."[7]

Overkill it may all have been, but it certainly worked. The book was carefully, lavishly, and glossily marketed and hyped. The mass-circulation American *Life* magazine and British *Daily Express* newspaper published tempting extracts. Enormous secrecy surrounded the whole project, with stories of Ripley's daughters typing the manuscript to prevent secretaries blabbing about the plot and armed escorts delivering the text to its British printers. All bookshops and reviewers were denied copies of the book until publication day, "in case they broke wind." No one was to reveal whether or how Scarlett got Rhett back, and publication day was dubbed "Scarlett Day" in order to focus media attention. That day, 25 September 1991, Alexandra Ripley gave a worldwide press conference in New York, while at midnight, in London, in the absence of a real author, Scarlett and Rhett look-alikes drove up to the Covent Garden bookshop Books Etc. and signed copies for (a handful of) purchasers. A Scarlett ball was held at Osberton Hall, Nottinghamshire.

All these measures, matched by even more lavish and extravagant hype in the States, ensured the kind of publicity that produces early sales and keeps the book at the front of the shop. *Scarlett* sold well all over the world; Britain was no exception. And press coverage, including early reviews, emphasized the whole packaged deal and its tenuous relationship to literary matters or merits. Journalist Peter Guttridge of the *Independent* saw it as a merely cynical marketing exercise: "Ripley's novel is a sequel to the film in the age of the miniseries. It is written with space for adverts." Novelist Sally Beauman expressed a common view, "God preserve the novelist from the literary estate."[8]

"CUSTODIAN OF A GREAT AMERICAN MYTH": ALEXANDRA RIPLEY

Beauman's comment was shrewd, suggesting as it did the many constraints under which such a writer must operate. The sequel writer of any novel that is still in copyright is vulnerable to the self-interest and manipulations of heirs and estates. Furthermore, as is the case with sequels in general, any writer accepting such a lucrative contract must face up to the inevitable comparison with the original. "Custodian of a great American myth" and "monster undertaking" are how journalists summed up Ripley's task, one she herself called "impossible."[9] Her novel would never be read as a discrete work on its own terms; it would have to be judged against a much loved and acclaimed original with classic status. The marketing took the "more of the same" line; the book jacket of *Scarlett* directly emulated that of the reissued original novel, using identical size and similar colors and poses of Scarlett against indeterminate landscape of land and sky, with cameo inset on the side. The choice of Ripley, and the subsequent publicity for her book, needed to walk a fine line between reverence for the original and excitement about its sequel.

Ripley's greatest asset, from the estate's perspective, was her southernness: "I got it because I'm a real Southerner," she said to interviewers, emphasizing that the South is "a way of life," "a way of thinking," not just an issue of geography.[10] This is, of course, a considerable simplification; other southerners undoubtedly offered themselves, but Ripley won. And—despite the establishment of an I Won't Read the Sequel Club in Atlanta—the choice of a southerner was undoubtedly shrewd. It enabled the estate to argue a spurious kind of continuity with the original (despite Mitchell's fierce opposition to a sequel) and to sell writer and book as products of a peculiarly southern sensibility—a factor that was to prove a sticking point with the *next* sequel. In the publicity pack, Ripley herself talked of the "awesome burden" with which she was entrusted and said she had been "terrified some Yankee was going to do it." At the publicity interviews, she celebrated her own southern femininity, claiming she had been raised as a "real lady of the South" who admired Melanie and Ashley Wilkes, a "perfect woman" and "a gentleman," and found it hard to identify with the selfish, unscrupulous Scarlett.[11]

More to the point was Ripley's practice in writing southern historical novels comparable in scope and theme with Mitchell's original. She had already positioned herself in the mainstream of southern romance; every previous novel she had written had been compared with *Gone With the Wind*, so the challenge of picking up Mitchell's pen was one for which she was well primed. In one interview, she said she "couldn't resist the challenge to meet Miss Mitchell head on, in single combat"—though this metaphor is hard to reconcile with her preparation for the writing: copying out in longhand more than two hundred pages of the original novel to emulate Mitchell's style and faithfully preserving most of Mitchell's characters unchanged.[12] She claimed to have studied Mitchell's style so minutely that she became "a vivisectionist, a lab technician," terms suggesting more the humble assistant and follower than original, creative interpreter.[13]

"Combat" is hardly the metaphor, either, for Ripley's omissions and evasions. Her contract, almost certainly influenced by Mitchell's devout Catholic heirs, proscribed any interracial sex scenes, steamy sex, and homosexuality; Ripley was glad to comply. Indeed, she went further; assuming a mildly politically correct persona, she agreed that racial issues might have been a prickly issue. "I couldn't lie about what things were like in the Nineteenth Century . . . so I just tiptoed around it," she told her *Newsday* interviewer.[14] "Things" were, of course, the contest over freed Negroes' rights in the Reconstruction South, followed by the "redemption" of white power. Her white characters would have brutally ensured the restoration of land and wealth, denying freed blacks access to land, property, the vote, and education through physical intimidation and political chicanery. Ripley acknowledged to her interviewer: "I'm sure there was also a lot of long-suppressed anger [among former slaves], but I didn't bother with that. It's not my story. . . . I'm not a sociologist. I'm a novelist." Her narrative decisions, then, included killing off Mammy early on, removing Prissy to another place, and giving the extremely docile former slaves minor, insignificant roles. Slave dialect is almost completely absent, as is any discussion of racial issues. The only two black characters given any profile are Scarlett's maid in the South, Pansy (a little in-joke, given the name Mitchell originally chose for Scarlett herself), and a caricature of "Queen of Sheba," rich Charleston whorehouse madam and indispensable ladies' sempstress. Most significant of all, halfway through the action she removes Scarlett to Ireland, where she retraces her roots and reestablishes her plantation home in the Anglo-Irish estate, Ballyhara. The political struggle on which she focuses is that between the Anglo-Irish and Irish nationalists in the shape of the Fenian Brotherhood. "Mercifully," she said, "everybody is white, so I don't run into that minefield." The defiant tone of the writer's comments can leave readers in little doubt as to her political commitment and racial allegiance.

The book jacket of Ripley's novel, pledged to follow Mitchell's trajectory, claims to "seamlessly pick up the narrative, bringing us back to Tara and the people we remember so well." *Scarlett* takes its eponymous heroine through a series of picaresque adventures during which she gains control of Tara, establishes her own Tara in the land of origins, and regains the loving arms of Rhett Butler. In terms of the focus on the importance of dynasty and land to Irish southerners, and of love as well as independence in women's lives, she continues Mitchell's 1930s preoccupations, the products of Mitchell's family, race and class. Both novels construct a mythic southern dynasty derived from an idealized version of Irishness—one steeped in hedonism, cunning, family loyalty, and passion, contrasted with the pallid refinement and genteel style of the Anglo-Saxon and French South. Ripley enacts Mitchell's revenge or retribution fantasy, continuing Scarlett's career as shrewd capitalist ("I am the O'Hara of Ballyhara," she cries) but also making her symbolically restore the rights, dignity, and honor of the defeated and broken-hearted South.[15] In case this smacked too uncomfortably of the white South's "redemption" of its powers after Reconstruction, it all takes place many thousands of miles away.

CRACKER CULTURE

Ripley's novel, however, has an interesting contemporary spin. It appeared in 1991, three years after the first publication of a key historical study of Celtic southernness written by a respected, if controversial, southern scholar. Grady McWhiney's *Cracker Culture*, which, as I discussed in chapter 1, has become the bible of the extreme rightwing League of the South, could well have provided some of the historical inspiration and backbone for the novel.[16] Ripley claimed to have read widely in scholarly materials; given the critical attention McWhiney received at the time *Scarlett* was being written and the similarity of their interests, it is unlikely she was ignorant of the book or its central argument. McWhiney focuses on Celtic (Irish, Scottish, Welsh, and Cornish) immigration and cultural assimilation into the South from the seventeenth century to the Civil War. In a polemical prologue, Forrest McDonald argues that, over the centuries, conditions in the English Uplands, Wales, Scotland, and Ireland became unsympathetic to Celtic "traditional ways" and that by migrating to the American South such ways could be preserved and flourish: "In a manner of speaking, their entire history had prepared them to be Southerners" (liii).

McWhiney himself claims that the English/Celtic cultural conflict within the British Isles shaped the entire history of the United States, notably exporting there a sectionalism that "exploded into the War for Southern Independence" (7). English northerners and Celtic southerners are predictable types: Yankees are commercial, disciplined, hardworking, and WASPishly uptight, while southerners (like their

Celtic ancestors) are fond of idleness, sensual, good at conversation and leisure pursuits—in short, a lot more fun than the English and Anglo-Yankees. This thesis sees the "leisurely Celtic lifestyle" as central to "Cracker culture" (144), a lifestyle shared by poor and wealthy southerners alike. Shared at least by male whites: McWhiney notes without irony that they "much preferred to enjoy life while their animals, their women, or their slaves made a living for them" (41). He documents the way northerners and Europeans described southerners in the terms often ascribed to premodern British Celts (and, indeed, as McWhiney astonishingly does not acknowledge, to blacks): superstitious, degenerate, licentious, uncontrolled, violent, savage, and barbaric. The antebellum South, in this account, was created and developed by white Celts and then suffered from the cultural imperialism of a North dominated by English peoples and values that were forced onto the South and its Celtic people. The Civil War was the rerun of a former struggle between the English and Celtic cultures, and white crackers (like their Celtic ancestors) "would fight, even if beforehand they knew that their cause was lost" (217).

McWhiney's book has been seen as part of a backlash against postmodern historians and cultural critics who argue that one can no longer speak of a separate "North" and "South" and that "the South" is a largely politically motivated construct of right-wing ideologues who are still fighting a virtual Civil War. It is also seen as a defensive response to liberal academics' championing of African American sociopolitical history and their arguments about the "Africanization" and multicultural nature of southern culture itself. McWhiney's subtext is pretty clear: the South's Celtic settlement, rather than any other, was the central determining factor in its separate development and unique culture. The "cracker," rather than being a buffoon loafer in the region's history, should be seen as its most authentic character type; the Celtic heritage of the American South therefore becomes its myth of origin. The Civil War is the last standoff between Celtic man and his long-standing English oppressor.[17]

A CELTIC SCARLETT

Whether or not she had read this reactionary book that has been challenged by most other southern historians and cultural critics, Ripley adhered to its ideological line fairly closely and produced a romantically charged fictional version of the thesis. In many ways, the novel attempts to legitimize those Celtic southern myths of origin and centrality (a very white version that excludes other ethnic groups, especially African Americans) and also to confirm white southerners' sense of themselves as semiaristocratic descendants of Irish kings. Indeed, the first half of the novel may be read as setting up the competing national cultures within the South in order to establish a kind of authenticity within Ireland itself, near the historic site of Tara, where Scarlett settles and establishes a new dynastic line with daughter Katie (Cat). After burying Melanie and Mammy, Scarlett socializes with Rhett's (very English) Charleston-based mother, Eleanor Butler, and tries unsuccessfully to fit into demure Anglo ways, later moving on to Savannah and her maternal grandfather, the French Pierre Robillard, who demonstrates the rigid *froideur* of the French, from which she flees. Finally, triumphantly, Scarlett discovers her paternal heritage by going to meet a bunch of Irish cousins living in genteel poverty in Savannah, providing an occasional base for another cousin, the priest and Fenian gunrunner Colum, who persuades her to return to her father's native land.

Irishness, in Savannah and later in County Meath, constitutes the "bit of rough" Scarlett has always craved: physical ease and sensuality, simple pleasures such as music and dance, and a chaotic and friendly intergenerational family life. For the white southerner who wishes to validate an authentic vernacular southern style that has no associations with the region's slave history, a celebration of folk culture to the tune of "Peg in a Low-Back'd Car" or "The Wearing of the Green" must have seemed a shrewd alternative. And Gerald O'Hara's choice of the name "Tara" for the plantation he won at poker invites a mythic reworking of Celticness, returning Scarlett to her father's homeland that is essentially a female space ("to anyone with a drop of Irish blood in them the land they live on is like their mother," as Gerald reminds her).[18] It is there that she is converted to the Fenian cause, persuaded of the parallels between her own desire to restore Tara to "rightful" hands after the imperialist ravages of the Union army and the desire of Irish nationalists to throw off the tyranny of English home rule and get back Ireland for its "own" people. Colum tells his wide-eyed cousin:

> Remember your South, with the boots of the conqueror upon her, and think of Ireland, her beauty and her life's blood in the murdering

hands of the enemy. . . . Do you but think of it now, Scarlett, when your Tara was being taken from you. You battled for it. . . . With all your will, all your heart, all your wit, all your might. Were lies needed, you could lie, deceptions, you could deceive, murder, you could kill. So it is with us who battle for Ireland. (565)

Thus Ripley draws on the two very disparate histories to link together the two main parts of Scarlett's story and to elevate her heroine's individual quest into an epic one. By taking Scarlett back to the real Tara, and the real rather than yearned-for birthplace of her father, Gerald, Ripley animates a whole mythic space that gives the land and the plantation Tara their suggestive resonance in the original work and ensures a receptive readership from the many Irish Americans, especially perhaps in the South. Furthermore, this schematic parallelism allows Ripley to tap into a mass international readership that is assumed to be able to absorb facile historical lessons and accept a simple colonialist model of power relations.

During the 1990s, the "Troubles" in Northern Ireland were at their height and were the subject of serious peace talks only in the latter part of the decade; no Irish or British citizen could be in any doubt of the complexity of the situation within the province, and only the most naive or blinkered ever saw the conflicts in terms of a one-dimensional imperialist model of Englishness oppressing Irishness. To an American, and especially Catholic Irish American, reader, this simplistic model has often been invoked—especially for Noraid fund-raising for Sinn Féin during a period of violent and often random attacks on both the military and civilians within Northern Ireland and the British mainland. *Scarlett* follows a well-worn trail in drawing deeply from the well of sentimentality and passion both Celtic and non-Celtic Americans feel for that country. Despite the long history of fierce anti-Catholicism within American mainstream politics, it has been virtually obligatory for modern U.S. presidential contenders, beginning with John F. Kennedy, through Ronald Reagan, to Bill Clinton and Newt Gingrich, to establish their leadership credentials by tracing some Irish family roots. For these politicians, as for the vast majority of readers, Ireland is so steeped in mythic properties, such a site of desire and longing, where the unpleasant realities of social and racial conflicts, not to mention the political fray, may disappear in a cloud of Celtic twilight and leprechaun-leaping superstition. It is also arguable that Ripley's implied international reader had even hazier notions about nineteenth-century Irish nationalist struggles than about the Reconstruction and redemption South.

The critical response to the novel, on both sides of the Atlantic, was generally damning, with the exception of some protective southern journalists. Reviewers condemned Ripley for avoiding complex racial and ethnic issues, as well as misrepresenting the complexity of Irish people and politics. American critic Patricia Storace accused Ripley of "whistling Dixie" and bowing to a "literary Nuremberg law" by accepting the contractual clause forbidding the representation of miscegenation, while M. G. Lord deplored the removal of Scarlett from a South of "poll taxes, grandfather clauses or other obstacles to black suffrage" to a "Disney World" Ireland. British writer Kate Saunders described the Irish characters as "hundreds of grinning, bare-footed leprechauns who speak like fund-raising pamphlets for Noraid." The *Irish Independent*'s Justine McCarthy believed that, with Tom Cruise's return from Eire to Hollywood, the Irish movie industry should be grateful to Ripley "for creating a gap in the County Meath market for film locations."[19] None made the connection between lines of attack on the book by pointing out that the novel she had written was as polemical as the original. Its audacity, and strongly antiliberal line, lay in its epic and romantic celebration of Celtic white southernness that simply rendered southern African Americans irrelevant and aspired to take cracker history and culture to new mythic heights. Mammy's killing off in chapter 1 was symbolically apt. As African American critic Alvin Poussaint predicted (arguing that the sequel failed to "take corrective action" over *GWTW*'s political agenda), "the white thing will be re-awakened, without much critical outlook."[20] The reawakened "white thing" was to pop up with the serialization of the novel, not on film but on worldwide television.

THE CELLULOID SEQUEL: "SCARLETT" THE TV MINISERIES

During December 1994, British satellite TV viewers were treated to eight hours of the much hyped sequel to *Gone With the Wind*, the miniseries *Scarlett*. It came from an American-European co-production consortium comprising RHI Entertainment Inc., CBS, Beta-Films (Kirch Group), and Silvio Berlusconi Communications. John Erman, responsible for other southern epics such as *Roots, Roots II, Queen,* and the TV version of *A Streetcar Named Desire*, directed; three of the key actors in *Scarlett*—Ann-Margret, George Grizzard, and Paul Wingfield—had appeared in his earlier epics. Apart from these three, the series boasted an array of major American and British stars such as Sir John Gielgud, Dorothy Tutin, and Sean Bean. The leading roles of Rhett and Scarlett were given to experienced British film and TV actors, Timothy Dalton (well known especially for his James Bond) and Joanne Whalley-Kilmer, known for distinguished parts in British and U.S. theater and for leading roles in *Scandal*, *Shattered*, and *The Singing Detective*.

The series boasted a $40 million production budget including a six-month shoot that incorporated 200 speaking roles, 2,000 extras, 120 Scarlett costume changes, and 53 locations in England, Ireland, and Charleston. It was to be broadcast simultaneously around the world, same date, time, and commercials. Although this did not happen, it enjoyed international screenings in the last months of 1994. Robert Halmi Sr., chairman of RHI, who had assembled this international partnership, paid $9 million for its rights, the highest price ever paid for such a property.[21] Like David O. Selznick before him, Halmi was an experienced, successful producer, described as one of the world's most ambitious and influential.

It was a story to warm all British hearts at the tail end of the early 1990s recession. The "legendary," "much coveted" role of Scarlett O'Hara, after a two-year search involving twenty thousand applicants, £200,000 of the producer's money, and seven phone number changes to avoid harassment, was offered to Joanne Whalley-Kilmer. British headlines crowed: "Briton to star in Scarlett role"; "GONE WITH THE BRITS"; "Southern Belle Role Goes to Northern Star"; "Jealousy as Joanne is the new Scarlett."[22] The selection of an up-and-coming rather than established star was eccentric in the 1930s, but in the 1990s (with such huge investment at stake and the high risks involved with expensive projects and unbankable stars) it seemed perverse. Hollywood's megastars—Demi Moore, Meryl Streep, or Kim Basinger—were seen as having a divine right of first refusal.

Of course, Robert Halmi Sr. was modeling his own "search for Scarlett" on David O. Selznick's, asserting with his predecessor that he wanted the *right* actor, not simply the expected face, in this important role. He followed Selznick's brilliant technique of making an international publicity stunt out of the search for his leading actress. Surveys were commissioned and encouraged; open casting sessions were held in Atlanta, London, and elsewhere; names were bandied about, and the press teased with clues. In the United States, the *National Enquirer*'s poll of one hundred people from five major cities yielded a preference for Julia Roberts, with Kevin Costner or Alec Baldwin as Rhett. *Paris-Match* invited its French readers to pronounce. They plumped for Isabelle Adjani as Scarlett, because she had "l'allure de celle qui enchaîna le coeur de Rhett Butler." Adjani's Rhett was to be Alain Delon.

More than twenty thousand unknowns, however, turned up at Halmi's home, called him incessantly, and dressed up for the open casting sessions. *People* magazine reported the excitement in Atlanta: "In a year when 18 women are running for the U.S. Senate, 410 tossed their bonnets into another ring, vying for the role of Scarlett O'Hara. . . . Students and sexagarians [sic], nurses and bank tellers, crowded into Atlanta's Civic Center on July 17 to take turns reading a scene that resounded with those most heart-felt words: 'Fiddle-dee-dee!'"[23]

Halmi gleefully called the whole circus a "feeding frenzy" but—like Selznick—chose an actress whose work he saw on celluloid and recognized as perfect for his cast. He announced the decision at a very English location, breakfast at Claridge's Hotel, London.

The problem for any starlet cast as Scarlett (and Halmi had wanted a "virtual unknown") was the inevitable comparison with Vivien Leigh. Whalley-Kilmer shared with her predecessor both extensive acting experience and minor celebrity, acquired through some roles and also marriage to a rising star—heartthrob Val Kilmer was her Laurence Olivier. She was also "discovered" by her producer when he watched her on screen (in her case, as Christine Keeler in *Scandal*). Since the whole point of the series was that it offered *Gone With the Wind* fans a second helping of their favorite dish, the actors playing Scarlett and Rhett had both strongly to recall the originals and also to stamp their own personalities on a 1990s version. As one journalist wrote: "To get inside the part of Scarlett O'Hara, she will have to summon the ghost of Vivien Leigh and recall how her inner torment inspired a performance that has lasted, unblemished, for more than half a century. A hard act to follow."[24]

The "ghost" of Vivien Leigh proved hard to exorcise. Whalley-Kilmer had to pay respectful homage, claiming greatly to admire her predecessor—"one of my idols." At the press launch, defiantly dressed in casual grunge, she responded defensively when asked whether her performance would match the "legendary" original: "It's like telling an actor you can't play Macbeth. . . . One should be allowed to re-create a role." Speaking for both of them, and playfully alluding to many a southerner's likely reaction, Timothy Dalton was more forth-right: "It's better than having any damned Yankees playing the parts."

TRANSATLANTIC TENSIONS

However, the question of emulating or matching up to the original, Oscar-winning Vivien Leigh surfaced in all discussions of the series. The U.S. *TV Guide* asked, "Will British actress Joanne Whalley-Kilmer's Scarlett O'Hara fiddle-dee-dee as well as Vivien Leigh?," while British newspapers reminded readers that this was the second time "the cream of American actresses" had been rejected in favor of a British "up-and-coming star." The "highly coveted" nature of the role was mentioned smugly by British journalists: the xenophobic *Daily Express* (9 November 1993) quoted a Hollywood source complaining: "Joanne whipped it from the bigger stars just like Vivien Leigh did more than 50 years ago. There's a strong smell of jealousy in the air."

This transatlantic tension was exacerbated when filming of the series was under way: the press gleefully reported a "clash of cultures" between the Hollywood producers and the British film crew, treated "like peasants."[25]

Robert Halmi tried to present Whalley-Kilmer as a very modern Scarlett, both successor to and contemporary reinterpreter of the great role. Scarlett, he claimed, "is idolized by millions of women who have been exposed to her extraordinary character. She was the first feminist, an independent lady who not only was strong of will but completely feminine."[26]

Whalley-Kilmer echoed this. In public interviews, she said she saw her Scarlett as a woman who, since last time, had learned a few lessons, grown and matured a great deal. Veering into psychobabble, she proclaimed: "My Scarlett O'Hara will be a very different woman. She has grown up a great deal since the end of *Gone With the Wind* and has learnt from the past. Nevertheless, when she wants something, she really goes for it. . . . But all the traits we love about her are still there; only now she'll apologise for this, realise where they're coming from and understand that it's not necessarily the best way."[27]

After the press launch, journalist Jane Thynne described the flavor of the epic as "rather more California than Georgia. Scarlett has, according to Joanne Whalley-Kilmer, been on a 'learning process,' although she remains 'very manipulative.'"[28]

Dalton's casting, though exciting considerable speculation, was more straightforward. Press reports bandied about names such as Warren Beatty, Tom Selleck, and Burt Reynolds (who had been hotly tipped to play Rhett in Anne Edwards's earlier, never-filmed *Tara: Gone With the Wind 2*). But Dalton, already an experienced theatrical actor and international star (James Bond, no less), was seen as the obvious choice, largely because of his physical similarity to Clark Gable. He had to contend with challenges to his ability to match up to the original Rhett. In interviews, he admitted he had at first regarded the idea as "like putting yourself on a cross and waiting for people to shoot arrows at you," but he decided to rise to "the challenge" and jettison any idea of emulating Gable. Cheekily commenting on Gable's hopeless southern accent and an energy Dalton did not find in the original books, he decided to forget about Gable (even if he couldn't "escape" him) and "play the part my way."

Hollywood's jealousy of Dalton's success in this "coveted" role was as intense as that of Whalley-Kilmer. The morning after the announcement, stars were reported to be furious at a British actor succeeding the legendary Gable. Robert Halmi defended his British casting: "I've had a lot of flak about having too many English people in *Scarlett*, which is an all-American drama. But the South in those days was much closer to England than the Yankees. It's natural that there's a crossover. And besides, English people can do a Southern accent better than a Yankee can."[29]

This defense of the casting on the grounds of cultural hybridity is an interesting one but almost certainly spurious. Commercial considerations were paramount. When the auction for film/TV rights was held by the William Morris Agency, no single company could afford to bid successfully. As Halmi himself said, "Everyone was scrambling for European partners."[30] The strong British element in casting undoubtedly owes something to the exigencies of his U.S.-Euro consortium. So, as with the original film, the inclusion of British stars—especially the cameo performances of distinguished figures such as Sir John Gielgud and Dorothy Tutin—was used to signify to international audiences an aura of class and classical authority.

Halmi had a grandiose vision of his *Scarlett*: "This is not a remake of *Gone With the Wind*. This is a conclusion of two very important lives in American history."[31] He ventured to suggest that this series was "probably the most important thing" he would ever do in his life—a surprising claim from a man who had a film made about his real-life involvement with Hungarian freedom fighters in World War II, who was a top stills photographer for *Life* magazine, and who had plans to do a ten-part jazz history series with Wynton Marsalis. His cast dutifully echoed this sense of being part of significant film history: Colm Meaney (Scarlett's cousin, Father Colum O'Hara) talked of his role as "like a meeting with history . . . dealing with the stuff of legend," and Annabeth Gish (Rhett's second wife, Anne Hampton) described hers as "like being a part of cinematic-television history." Costume designer Marit Allen talked of living under the "shadow" of *Gone With the Wind* but also "carrying on some wonderful legacy." Britain's greatest living classical actor, Sir John Gielgud, nudged into a similar statement, expressed a guilty feeling that he should have read all the *Scarlett* scripts, not simply the few scenes in which he appeared: apparently unable to share others' sense of destiny, he said, "I suppose I ought also to have seen *Gone With the Wind*, which I remember vaguely."[32]

Halmi's grandiose vision for the series extended beyond the casting. As befitted an international co-production, every aspect of design—setting, costume, makeup, music—was lovingly and expensively addressed. The press publicity pack (itself a work of art) boasted of the attention to detail that increasingly, pioneered by much-celebrated BBC costume drama, became a feature of the quality miniseries: "From costumes to the specially-printed notepaper on Henry Hamilton's desk; from locations and set decoration to an ocean-going, four-mast ship[,] authenticity has been the hallmark of SCARLETT, from start to finish. Indeed, it is no exaggeration to say that few productions can ever have been subject to such meticulous planning and research on the part of its Art, Design and Location departments."[33]

As further proof of its painstaking pursuit of classic status, the pack details the many locations in the United Kingdom, Ireland, and Charleston where the series was shot: Luton Hoo, Bedfordshire, with its Capability Brown–landscaped parkland and "remarkable private collection of Gothic and Renaissance works of art"; "the picture post-card village of Castlecombe [*sic*] in Wiltshire"; the State Apartments at Dublin Castle; "Catfish Row," Charleston, location of that classic film *Porgy and Bess*, illustrating "the power of Southern life to create great drama" (53-56). The snobbery invoked about all things historical, associated with privilege and heritage, carries into the series itself, with its lavish mise-en-scène: excessive space given to fancy balls, big houses, and elite activities such as hunting to hounds.

With similarly conservative effect, the series shifts the mood and emphasis of the novel. Rather than the feminine, or postfeminist, epic celebration of Celtic southernness, it offers global audiences a lavish costume romance. Probably to avoid political criticism from many sides, the Fenian struggle, and Scarlett's unwholesome role within it, is decidedly marginalized in favor of a love story amid glorious settings, together with gratuitous additions to the narrative, designed for prime-time TV. There is a fair amount of rape, whoring, scandal, raunchy sex, and murder that is not part of the novel. Scarlett's cousin, priest and freedom fighter Colum, declares love for her. The earl of Fenton, after raping Scarlett, is murdered. Scarlett is sensationally tried for the murder in the historic London Old Bailey court; she is released only after the machinations of (yes, you've guessed it) Rhett Butler. In a final break with the novel, the series ends at the mythic Irish site of Tara, with Rhett, Scarlett, and daughter Cat reunited and a sardonic exchange that undercuts any mythic pretensions. Rhett becomes uncharacteristically sentimental, telling Scarlett, "As long as we're together, the world will belong to us," to which she replies, "That's a lot of property." Each of the four episodes concludes, not with the stirring epic notes of a Max Steiner musical score, but with an intimate, schmaltzy rendition of the song "Love Hurts," placing the whole miniseries firmly within the genre of romantic melodrama.

So what did the British critics say about *Scarlett*? Perhaps because of the hefty weight of prepublicity, the sequel billed as the "TV event of the decade" and so on, critics responded with satirical or scornful dismissal. Much reference was made to their not giving a damn about the whole thing. Running headlines tell the story: "Gone . . . and Best Forgotten"; "Frankly, my dear, it's become rather tacky"; "Lost with the Sequel." It was "Southern Fried Corn", a sequel that "Returned with Flatulence." One critic gestured to the political subtext of the whole, though his tone indicated how little this really mattered: Sean Bean was "smarm on toast to Scarlett but beastly to Irish peasants (hardly helping the peace talks, but still . . .)."[34]

Ominously, all those grand European locations, classical British actors, and "authentic" period details failed to cover up a repetitive story and an unsuccessful attempt to give punters a rich second helping of their favorite dish. Thus the critical responses to the celluloid sequel were as damning as those to the novel. Hardly anyone could be found to argue that this miniseries, or the novel, was any match for the epic heroism, romantic splendor, and visual opulence of the originals.

"CUSTODIAN OF DEITIES"? A BRITISH SEQUEL

The (considerably enriched) Mitchell Estate was reputedly embarrassed by the commercial success but critical failure of both novel and miniseries. Its response was to commission a further sequel in time for the sixtieth anniversary of the original publication, perhaps to ensure a more dignified revival of the original story than *Scarlett*. Alexandra Ripley had been given a clause in her contract allowing her first refusal of a second sequel, but she declined: "I had got enough of Miss O'Hara, plus I got wonderfully, stinking rich off the first book." This time, probably with a view to finding a reliable classic sequelizer, the Mitchell Estate and its lawyers looked for their writer across the Atlantic.

The estate first approached that doyenne of the English literary establishment Lady Antonia Fraser. Fraser was best known for her popular historical biographies of figures such as Mary, Queen of Scots, and Cromwell, but she had also ventured into genre fiction, writing popular romance and detective novels. Some years earlier, she had published an ingenious sequel short story to Daphne du Maurier's *Rebecca*.[35] However, in terms of class and nationality, Fraser was an even more significant choice. From an extremely well connected English Catholic family herself, she was first married to a Scottish baron's son, Sir Hugh Fraser, of Beaufort Castle, Inverness-shire, then to the playwright Harold Pinter. Such impeccable credentials, combining Scots aristocracy and literary chic, were irresistible to an estate eager for a touch of class. Fraser declined the invitation but suggested a friend of hers, novelist Emma Tennant, author of a large number of experimental, avant-garde, and serious novels and founder-editor of a radical literary journal, *Bananas*. Tennant had a strong track record in sequel writing, having published "classical progressions" to

Thomas Hardy's *Tess of the D'Urbervilles, Tess* (1994), and Jane Austen's *Pride and Prejudice, Pemberley: The Sequel to Pride and Prejudice* (1993) and *An Unequal Marriage: Pride and Prejudice Continued* (1994); she would go on to continue Austen's *Sense and Sensibility* as *Elinor and Marianne* (1996) and *Emma* as *Emma in Love* (1996). The estate's lawyer had just read and admired *Pemberley*, so Tennant seemed a good choice to produce another "classic" sequel.

Like Fraser, a Scot who had never visited the South, Tennant's lack of southern credentials seemed at that time no obstacle to her imaginative capacity to take on the task. Indeed, her Celtic origins, coming as she did from the wealthy, elite Scots Tennant clan, were undoubtedly seen as a strong point in her favor. The American St. Martin's Press duly paid the Mitchell Estate $4.5 million for the rights to publish the book; Tennant was offered a substantial advance and promised 20 percent of the earnings, as well as shares of European book deals and the inevitable miniseries. She indicated her awareness of the enormity of the commission by referring sardonically to herself as "custodian of deities," but again the deal was all about money. The writer, not known for blockbusters, needed to pay off bills and wanted a best-seller; the estate and publisher wanted a repeat of *Scarlett*'s success, but this time for a product with a reputable literary quality. Perhaps they believed that (despite the critical flop of the British actor–heavy TV series) a serious British novelist would, like Vivien Leigh and Joanne Whalley-Kilmer, add the touch of class that only Britishness could bring.

In various interviews and informal conversations during 1995 and 1996, Emma Tennant expressed her delight in writing the *GWTW* sequel. The money would be good, of course, but since she had developed a knack for writing well-received and commercially successful sequels, this was the culmination of a whole new direction for her writing. She welcomed the return from experimental writing to a more conventional style: "I'm fascinated by the return to pure narrative. . . . It's a skill that many writers have lost, particularly those of the post-modern generation, after 'The Wasteland.'"[36] She claimed to agree with writer Andrew Davies that the gap between classic drama and soap opera had considerably narrowed. With the end of communism and socialism, furthermore, intellectual snobbery toward the genre of romance had declined, and romantic love remained the one utopian ideal. From having been very snobbish about writing romance, she had discovered its appeal and found it an important, riveting subject and genre. The whole *GWTW* sequel idea seemed such fun, and she believed she could breathe more life into its characters than Ripley. Furthermore, she was already planning a further sequel, "Scarlett's Daughter."[37] She did not appear to be concerned about the conditions written into her contract, as they had been into Ripley's. These stipulated that she had to observe strict secrecy concerning plot details (to be told to no one but the "husband and secretary" she was, erroneously, assumed to have) and adhere to Mitchell's tone, viewpoint, and characters, as well as begin her novel at the date *Scarlett* left off, 1878. Finally, while allowing for "modern sensibilities" regarding race and sex since 1936, she was to exclude "all acts of or references to miscegenation, incest and sex with another member of the same sex."[38] Not for her Sally Beauman's cry, "God preserve the novelist from the literary estate."

THE FLOP OF "TARA"

In November 1995, Tennant delivered her 575-page manuscript four months in advance of her deadline. Then the trouble began. Her St. Martin's Press editors deeply disliked the work, criticizing everything about it—characterization, story line, setting, style—in an 89-page vitriolic memo. This was described by a British literary agent as "certainly the roughest editorial reaction to a commissioned manuscript [he'd] ever seen."[39] Although a major revision might have been undertaken in response to the wholesale attack "Tara" received, Emma Tennant was so devastated, and the two sides so far apart, that after considerable legal wrangles she was dismissed by the Mitchell Estate. Hoping in vain to follow "stinking rich" Ripley's example, Tennant was paid £150,000 before tax for two years' work; itself a tidy sum, it was a fraction of the expected royalties. Along with the other unpublished sequel, Anne Edwards's *Tara*, her manuscript was to be sealed in a vault.

As I argued earlier, an undertaking involving such high reader expectations must offer a narrative of continuity rather than surprise and is restricted by the terms of the original. The constraints on any sequel writer are therefore fairly strangling; any serious novelist must strain at the bit. If one considers the draconian censorship embodied in the estate's contract, it is not difficult to see why a second

GWTW sequel must be doomed. For legal reasons, Emma Tennant is forbidden to show the manuscript to anyone or even to discuss its contents. Before the legal row, however, and in her *Telegraph* article about the whole business, she divulged certain plot details that indicate that the book would certainly be following the general trajectory of both the original and its first sequel. There was to be a dramatic fire at Tara; Scarlett and Rhett had an ecstatic honeymoon and then left Ireland for Paris, where they had a spectacular fight; they returned to the South, where the couple became involved with Boss Tweed and the Reconstruction-era President Rutherford B. Hayes; there was a passionate, for the first time sexual, reunion between Scarlett and Ashley; and it ended with the reconciliation of the central protagonists (since "an audience raised by Vivien Leigh–obsessed mothers and grandmothers are likely to have inherited the Gable fixation at the breast").[40] Tennant was concerned by Ripley's casual dismissal of Ashley Wilkes and Scarlett's first two children, Wade and Ella; she reintroduced and used them to create new tensions in the central love relationship. It is, of course, difficult to comment on a manuscript one is not allowed to see. It might be worth suggesting, however, that Emma Tennant is respected for an ironic, knowing, postmodern cleverness; her published sequels tend to have a lightness of touch and considerable use of humor. If the style of "Tara" followed suit, it would almost certainly go down badly with the conservative, fairly unironic factions involved in the ongoing *GWTW* project.

At the heart of the editors' attacks on Tennant's manuscript, there seemed to lie considerable hostility toward the British approach to an American, and southern, treasure; the touch of class the commission seemed to require was clearly too esoteric or eccentric for this quintessentially American task. Tom McCormack, the St. Martin's chairman, was specific in finding an "unAmerican sensibility" about the manuscript, indicating it needed "different visions, almost a different sensibility."[41] In Emma Tennant's own account of her sacking from the project, it is clear that his ideal British writers were the middlebrow best-selling writers James Herriott (of veterinary tales *All Creatures Great and Small* fame) and M. M. Kaye, author of *The Far Pavilions*.[42] He reacted angrily to the enthusiasm of the British managing director of Little, Brown, United Kingdom, Philippa Harrison (who had offered a large sum for the book), since in his view European responses to "Tara" were irrelevant in the United States. "Philippa can do what the hell she wants for England, but her ability to judge books for America is in my opinion not to be counted on." A senior editor at St. Martin's, Hope Dellon, was even more explicit: "Basically, it wasn't Southern enough." Tennant herself concluded, after meeting McCormack, that there was an irreconcilable gulf betweeen the estate's desire for a "quality novel" and St. Martin's preference for a middlebrow blockbuster. In an interesting comment on the "Tara" controversy, Laurence J. Kirshbaum, president of *Scarlett*'s publisher, Warner Books, observed how perilous the whole business of a second sequel was likely to be: "You're dealing with so many expectations. . . . Time only makes the process more difficult because *Gone With the Wind* looms larger and larger in our collective memory as the years go by."[43]

The publishers have undoubtedly developed impossible expectations of any sequel writer, aware that the scrutiny given to the next version will be even harsher and more merciless than it was for the first. Big bucks are at stake; a failure of nerve may well have prompted their withdrawal from "Tara." However, the secret of Tennant's brusque treatment may lie in a proprietorial belief that this mythic work, which seems to have captured some central spirit of twentieth-century American life that has also proved exportable and translatable across the world, cannot be allowed imaginative play by outsiders. Starring roles on celluloid are one thing (and even those arouse the jealous ferocity of Hollywood and American fans and critics), but the creative fictional treatment of Mitchell's epic work by a nonsoutherner may be seen as the last straw—especially by a writer so sophisticatedly playful as Emma Tennant, who may well have lacked the gravitas (or lumpen seriousness) expected of such an endeavor.

TWO FRENCH "GONE WITH THE WINDS," A PLAGIARISM CASE, AND A FIFTY-YEAR-OLD MANUSCRIPT

It is easy to become romantic about transatlantic relations, but the Tennant case is a salutary reminder of the limitations of entente cordiale. A further example of the ferocious protectiveness of the *GWTW* myth by the Mitchell Estate was graphically illustrated in a legal case that occurred some time before the Tennant episode. It was surely no coincidence that, in the very week Ripley's sequel was launched, a French best-selling novel, published nine years earlier and following closely the narrative line of *GWTW*, was banned on a plagiarism charge.[44] Régine Deforges's *La bicyclette bleue* (1982) had been followed by two sequels. Opening on the eve of mobilization, 1939, it follows the fortunes of Léa Delmas, a seventeen-year-old beauty living on a Montillac estate, who lives through World War II and undergoes a series of amorous adventures. Unrequitedly in love with Ashley Wilkes–style Laurent, who marries his Melanie, cousin Camille, she has a passionate and volatile relationship with a Rhett-type called François, who joins the French Resistance. The many plot and character parallels were acted on as late as 1991, when the Mitchell Estate (represented by the Trust Company Bank of Atlanta, Georgia) slapped a writ on the author and the publisher, Editions Ramsay, and took the case to the Paris court. The court was impressed by the prosecutor's evidence of literary borrowings, despite the defense's claim that Deforges, who acknowledged the "involuntary assistance of the late Margaret Mitchell," was merely "borrowing its essence." Mitchell's heirs were awarded damages of £214,000.

It is significant that one of the major planks of the defense's case rested on the degree of explicit sexuality in the two books and the extent to which the two heroines—Scarlett and Léa—indulged in the pleasures of the flesh. The Paris *avocat* told the court that Scarlett had only one pleasurable carnal experience with Rhett, in a violent scene, and that Rhett was little more than a *canaille* (rotter) and *fripouille* (rascal), Scarlett a mere *coquette*. Léa, by contrast, was a sensual woman who offered herself to the men she loved "without reserve, without prejudice, in all simplicity." This 1990s reinterpretation was not, however, accepted as justification of an intertextual revision of the earlier work, and the court decided it was a case of plagiarism (though Deforges's two sequels are so far unaffected by this decision). This case is a further example of the sharp-eyed, hungry determination of the Mitchell Estate to preserve the unique position of *GWTW* in the marketplace on its terms and to protect it from commercial exploitation by anyone other than itself. Given its puritanical and repressive restrictions on the two sequel writers, it may also indicate another example of the estate's skills at censuring any writer or work that offered a contemporary gloss on female sexuality and sexual pleasure.

Sequels and borrowings of the original work have multiplied since

1936, and France, like other European countries, has remained fascinated with the text. But there is one French novel that owes to Margaret Mitchell the delay of its completion and publication for fifty years. One of France's most distinguished men of letters, Julian Green (1900-1998), born of American parents in Paris the same year as Mitchell and the first foreigner to be elected to the Académie Française, dropped the novel he was writing after the publication of its famous predecessor; he felt his own had been preempted. He continued to write about the South, and in 1958 his play *South*, set on the eve of the American Civil War, was premiered to great praise in London.[45] Around fifty years after beginning the manuscript, in 1987 he published his saga of the American South, significantly in French, *Les pays lointains*, translated for the British and American market as *The Distant Lands*, followed by two sequels, *The Stars of the South* and *Dixie*.[46] Their first appearance in the French language (and *Dixie*, as I write, is still untranslated) testifies to the popularity of the subject matter in the hands of a trusted literary figure. Audiences on both sides of the Atlantic have been fascinated by this Francophone southerner; the novels have sold more than a million copies.

"THE DISTANT LANDS"

For the purposes of this discussion, the first volume is of most interest, since it is the one Green himself originally abandoned as being too close to Margaret Mitchell's novel. *The Distant Lands* was written by a man whose entire life and career were spent in France but who felt that his heritage was southern, that he himself was at heart a southerner. As its title suggests, it reads like a nostalgic tribute to a region and historical moment that are now distant in time and memory. In many ways, the tortured heroine, Elizabeth, an English girl who is brought in penury to live in the Deep South in her teens and who learns to love it (refusing to leave after the death of husband and lover), speaks for Green's own imaginative yearnings for a region he never knew but that resonated mythically through his parents' (especially his mother's) memories and fantasies.

The novel covers a short but significant span of southern history, 1850 to 1855. Secession and war are still some way off, but they are constantly the subject of dinner table and whispered (usually male) conversation. Elizabeth Escridge and her mother, Laura, arrive at

Dimwood Plantation, Georgia, home of Laura's cousin William Hargrove, where they have been given charitable shelter since Laura's widowhood and loss of family home. Laura establishes her daughter's security and desirability and then leaves—with various endowments from male American relatives—for England. Elizabeth is left, dreaming of the Devonshire countryside, to face the mysteries, hauntings, delights, and seductions of a classical southern plantation, lowered shutters, oak alley, heady magnolia, deadly wood, and all. The book covers a restless and uncertain period of national turbulence, including the debate over California as slave or free state and the Fugitive Slave Act. Inevitably, the publication of *Uncle Tom's Cabin* presages a new urgency in the crisis of North-South relations. These national upheavals operate, however, as little more than colorful contexts for the central drama surrounding the beautiful and desirable Elizabeth, who proves both susceptible to every handsome male visage that happens along and irredeemably romantic and idealistic in relation to her "Romeo," Jonathan Armstrong, who serenades her through the magnolia but then leaves to marry another. After many travels between big houses in Savannah and Virginia, she settles for marrying her guardian's son, Ned, after a night of passion that compromises them both. Back at Dimwood, Jonathan addresses her intimately at a ball and gets champagne in his face from jealous Ned; a duel ensues, in which both men die. Ned's son is thereafter publicly named after his father but privately after Elizabeth's lover.

Along the way, the novel takes in many of the usual southern elements familiar to readers of the plantation novel: magnificent balls, secret assignations, and duels; superstitious and vaguely sinister slaves; family histories of tragedy, broken hearts, and suicide; large houses that conceal sexual and racial secrets. True to the form of the post-1960s liberal novel of this genre, *The Distant Lands* contains a certain amount of discussion of abolitionism and the arguments around slavery, while making clear the ways in which the myopic and greedy white South brought the war inexorably upon itself. Furthermore, the novel features a family that has fled from the West Indies, one of whose members (the significantly Catholic Aunt Laura) has borne a mixed-race daughter. This woman, the inevitable dusky beauty, has driven men, and specifically one man, crazy with desire. In this respect, Green has broken the unspoken taboo of the white southern epic, respected by Mitchell herself and, in their sequels, by Ripley and

Tennant: the specter of miscegenation and the white South's fascination with and desire for the black body. The tone of the novel,
with its emphasis on a somewhat decadent, inward-looking, tragi-
gothic society, reminds the reader more often of Poe, even Faulkner,
than of the more feisty and polemical Mitchell.

One wonders why Green decided to finish the novel fifty years
after its conception and why it has attracted so many readers' imagination. Had *Gone With the Wind* never existed, it might have been
necessary to commission this novel, which examines, rather super-
ficially, the nature of a wealthy and stagnant society doomed to
disappear within a decade. Green's lovingly detailed accounts of
sumptuous houses, furnishings, and meals (there are mouthwatering
accounts of dinners and even a recipe for mint juleps), as well as his
scrupulous accounts of the historical minutiae of the South's political history in the early 1850s, all offer a certain narrative pleasure.
Yet the first novel does not reach the Civil War, so it lacks those dramatic events that challenged and changed that class of southerner
from its complacency and self-assurance and that forced its women
to abandon obsessive concerns with courtship, marriage, and ward-
robe. The novel returns to the nineteenth-century plantation novel,
spicing up its tale of beaux and belles with a postbellum awareness
of some racial politics, the war and devastation to come—but it is by
no means clear to what ideological end. As Elizabeth's husband, Ned,
dies in her arms after his duel, he urges her not to return to England
with mother Laura: "You'll suffer over there because you belong to
us. Our South will be the dream that will stay with you until you
die, the dream of distant lands where you experienced love, and you
will cry."[47] Given the novel's dedication, "To the memory of my
mother, daughter of the South," it is tempting to see Green's work
(completed in his late eighties) as a deeply nostalgic tribute to a lost
motherland, a culture that is still—for Green as for many others—
absurdly idealized and politically deeply suspect.

However, the novelist's European roots and preoccupations give
this work a rather original twist on the southern myth. Unusually,
its heroine is first-generation English, cast into a set of interconnected
families of English and Scots heritage. A devout Catholic, Green gave
decidedly lukewarm portrayals of Protestants of any race. Considerable emphasis is laid on English snobbery, obsession with tradition,
repression, and dullness; Welshness, in the form of the plantation

master's repulsive confidante, Miss Llewellyn, is sinister and devious; and Scottish Presbyterianism is positively humorless and dour, sexually frigid, and thus liable to hysteria. Julian Green mocks English class aspirations, even to the extent of giving Elizabeth's mother a second husband named Lord Fidgety.

What strikes a British reader most is the curious way in which this novel is not simply a reworking of the *Gone With the Wind* story, spiced up by reasonably human slaves and copious references to *Uncle Tom's Cabin*, but is also a southern *Jane Eyre*. Elizabeth is notable for her innocence (though without Jane's plainness) and sexual ignorance; for much of the early part of the story she is, like Jane Eyre, a rather bored and homesick bystander in a large house in which she is tolerated as a charity case. Though the master of the house suppresses his desire for her, others arouse her sensuality, and, like Jane, she falls in love in a scented garden. Most significantly, her true love's mistress, then wife, is the nymphomaniac Annabel Darnley, whose "exotic blood" makes her a "vampire," a "female monster" who forges a "diabolical link" with her husband (755-757). Elizabeth is positioned symbolically between this sexually crazed union and her guardianship by Charlie Jones and his Presyterian wife, who reads *Pilgrim's Progress*, then her repressed St. John Rivers–like husband, Ned, who gives way to lustful excesses in the first days of their courtship and marriage but is soon alarmed by and refuses her powerful sexual demands. In Brontë's more subtle novel, female desire is problematized and explored through the insanity—related closely to overt sexual expressiveness—of Bertha Mason, mirrored in Jane Eyre's own suppressed sexuality and confused Christian morality. In Green's more rambling and muddled novel, the anti-Catholic prejudices of the English lead to a cheerless, repressive deceitfulness and moral and sexual torpor. By the end of its more than nine hundred pages, the reader might feel that Elizabeth discovers how much fun sex can be largely in response to the sheer tedium of living through a very dull narrative. Unlike his more famous female predecessors, Green can never convince us that his protagonist's dilemmas and problems carry a weightier symbolic or metaphoric meaning. Elizabeth cannot satisfactorily represent either the repressed force of female desire or the spirit of a New South waiting to be born. Even the transatlantic take on the southern story, with its original ethnic and religious elements, cannot endow this novel with the epic weight for which it strives.

The novelist was right to abandon his story when Mitchell published hers; he helped keep the plantation novel tradition alive but took it no further than Mitchell herself, nor indeed than William Faulkner, Ellen Glasgow, or John Jakes. What is most significant about *The Distant Lands* and its sequels is the fact that Green and his publishers felt that the late 1980s were the appropriate time to go into print and that, as sales figures testify, the market responded enthusiastically. From the successes of Julian Green's trilogy, not to mention Alexandra Ripley's sequel and countless romantic, gothic, and "bodice-ripper" novels that offer watered-down versions of the ur-text, the plantation theme and Civil War novel are as popular as ever. *GWTW* is still with us and lives to another day.

"GONE WITH THE WIND" AT THE MILLENNIUM

In May 1996, the urbane magazine *Vanity Fair* ran a long photo feature entitled "Scarlett 'n the Hood," offering a designer-led travesty of plantation legend and urban black chic.[48] It opened with a mockup of the archetypal still of Rhett bearing Scarlett upstairs in his arms, an image so well known it has become one of the most quoted of our time. In place of Clark Gable and Vivien Leigh (or, indeed, Ronald Reagan and Margaret Thatcher, a much celebrated 1980s pastiche) it featured black models Charlton Cannon and Naomi Campbell, resplendent in creations oozing silk, lace, and marabou from the couture collections of Dior, Charvet, and Vivienne Westwood. In this version, white male designers played Mammy (a bearded Gianfranco Ferre of Dior), Prissy (Charles Andrews), and a nameless "house servant" (John Galliano). There were 1990s homoerotic innuendos, as Prissy and Mammy attended intimately to the body of Scarlett, dubbed "the first supermodel." Playfully transgressive, this pastiche served as a reminder of how many details of this one literary and film text—characters, images, settings, significant scenes, key phrases—have acquired general cultural familiarity and thus how easy it is to parody. In such ways does *Gone With the Wind* become constantly updated and reinvigorated as a myth of today.

This has not been entirely plain sailing, however. Toward the end of the century, publishers, filmmakers and writers have strained to titillate new markets. Although the first sequel was a commercial success, in a politically sensitive decade it was a dire critical failure; the

Mitchell Estate's commission of a British writer with considerable literary credentials testified to a certain unease or embarrassment. The hostility of Warner Books toward Emma Tennant's second sequel, especially belittling her European interpretation of the story, suggested an oppressive appropriation of the original that augurs badly for any further interpretations. The estate found that the "classic" sequel eludes it, but—to its shame—endorsed and benefited from a progressed story that foregrounds and argues forcefully a distastefully reactionary, indeed racist version of the southern story. The restrictions placed on the sequel writers, forbidding a challenging and historically (especially racially) more honest reading of that murky period of southern history, have doomed writers to self- or publisher-censored blandness and inconsequentiality. And even a major writer such as Julian Green seems to have been constrained by the original story in such a way that he could bring no new insights to bear on the subject.

In the last months of 1998, the final chapter of the sequel saga was announced.[49] Mitchell's trustees commissioned best-selling author Pat Conroy to write a first-person novel, *The Rules of Pride: The Autobiography of Capt. Rhett Butler*. Conroy wrote the preface to the sixtieth-anniversary edition of *GWTW*, describing its importance thus: "To Southerners like my mother, *Gone With the Wind* was not just a book, it was an answer, a clenched fist raised to the North, an anthem of defiance." Rather than sequel, he preferred to call his version a "companion" to the original, but one that differed markedly from the others. First, he planned to kill off Scarlett O'Hara, in a scene he boasted would be "the most memorable literary death since Anna Karenina threw herself under a train." Second, he refused to accept the censorship of subject matter imposed on, and accepted by, both Ripley and Tennant. Conroy claimed that the trustees' demand for no homosexuality or miscegenation led him to suggest that his novel would begin with the sentence "After they made love, Rhett turned to Ashley Wilkes and said, 'Ashley, have I ever told you that my grandmother was black?'" It will be interesting to see whether Conroy's "companion" piece provides a fresh way into the original's subject matter and tone or whether it will emerge as fairly empty parody. And, in terms of that death scene, it seems unthinkable that any *woman* writer would have dared to draw such a final line under one of the most celebrated female protagonists of literature and film.

To kill off Scarlett is a clear denial of the pleasure women reader-viewers have always enjoyed in the ambiguous ending of novel and film, and also to close off future possibilities for a millennial heroine. It remains to be seen whether Conroy's book inspires an outpouring of alternative sequels, copies, pastiches, or even "literary echoes" that will give the text vibrant new life. Maybe his intervention will ensure that there will be an indifferent silence.

I suspect, even before *The Rules of Pride* appears, that *Gone With the Wind* has done its ideological work. Indeed, its power must not be underestimated. *GWTW* was able to hold its own as a world cultural icon throughout two-thirds of the twentieth century. At the 1996 Olympics, international visitors poured out of Atlanta Airport asking to see Tara; a year later a German-sponsored Margaret Mitchell Museum opened to satisfy tourist demand; memorabilia collectors and anniversary watchers are well served by an efficient, lucrative *GWTW* industry; a respected Scottish novelist had a go at writing a second sequel to the novel; an English journalist complained that the thirty-six-tape "audio books" version of the novel occupied an entire seat of her car; across the world TV comedies, chat shows, and arts programs reference the work constantly. Its manifold global circulations and reinterpretations have coincided with and imaginatively play into a rise in reactionary movements such as the League of the South and the new academic challenge to multiculturalism, "white studies," together with neofascist groups in many European countries. Maya Angelou warns, "You are gone but not forgotten / Hail, Scarlett. Requiescat in pace."[50]

Gone With the Wind still speaks, sometimes through echoes, and it still urgently needs to be answered back. One dramatic response came in the 1990s, when the house in which Margaret Mitchell wrote the novel was repeatedly attacked by arsonists, a demonstration of one attempt to overthrow the myth. In the next chapter, I discuss the most successful fictional, African American attempt to do so: Alex Haley's *Roots*.

3

EVERYBODY'S SEARCH
FOR ROOTS
Alex Haley and the Black and
White Atlantic

Gone With the Wind created, and perpetuated, a white myth of the South for international readers and audiences throughout the century. In the bicentennial year, 1976, however, a work appeared that looked set to sweep Scarlett, Rhett, and their faithful Mammy into historical oblivion. Alex Haley's autobiography, Roots, was quickly dubbed "the black Gone With the Wind," its author hailed as a new national hero.[1] The book, filmed immediately for television, brought to audiences on both sides of the Atlantic a new awareness of black heritage, genealogy, and pride. Over the next thirty years, however, the halo slipped, Haley was discredited in certain quarters, and serious questions were raised about the mythic qualities of the book and the heroic status of its author. This chapter follows the progress of Roots over those decades and recounts both a transatlantic and circum-Atlantic tale.

Roots begins in the year 1750 and records the story of the original ancestor of former Coast Guard journalist Alex Haley. Kunta Kinte, a Gambian Mandinka warrior, is captured into slavery and taken to the American South, where he becomes the first of a long line culminating in Alex, his brothers, and his sister. The book records the horrors of the Middle Passage, the cruelties and deprivations of slavery, the separation of families, economic and sexual exploitation, the rise of abolitionist fervor, secession, the Civil War, the emancipation of slaves, and gradually a new prosperity for what became the Haley family. The main story ends with Alex's grandfather hanging up his sign, in 1893, "W. E. Palmer Lumber Company," and his wife giving birth two years later to Alex's grandmother Bertha. The final chapter records, in abbreviated form, the successful professional careers of Alex and his siblings, as well as an account of his journey to Africa to hear about his "roots" from the Gambian griot.

Roots was an instant success. Its advance print run of 200,000 sold out at once; 1.5 million hardback copies were sold in the first eighteen months, and millions have sold since. The novel was translated into at least thirty-three languages and distributed in twenty-eight countries. Among many major awards, it won the prestigious Pulitzer Prize. By the mid-1980s, 276 colleges and universities had adopted the book for black history curricula; it was popularly recognized as a sort of black family Bible.

In January 1977, the twelve-hour television miniseries was broadcast over eight consecutive evenings on ABC-TV to record American audiences. ABC research estimated that 130 million viewers saw some part of the series; virtually three-quarters of the TV audience watched the eighth (final) part. (The previous record was set by the first broadcast of *Gone With the Wind* in November 1976, which attracted 65 percent of the audience.) The huge success of the TV series (in Britain as well as in the United States) was both astonishing to all concerned and seen by some as a major cultural event. "Haley's Comet," *Time* magazine called it; black readers claimed it was the most important civil rights event since the 1965 Selma, Alabama, march. In Britain, reporting on the impact of the first U.S. broadcasts, the *Daily Express* (3 February 1977) referred to the way "30 million Americans fought blizzards, ice and fellow commuters to be home in time for *Roots*," and the *Daily Mail* reported the cancellation of night school courses, a huge drop in restaurant business, and the emptying of bars and hospital wards. In the *Sunday Telegraph* (30 January 1977) the series was described as "the most traumatic event in the nation's broadcasting since Orson Welles's 'War of the Worlds' produced panic in the 1930s." Audience figures were all the more amazing because 90 percent of the TV audience was white. Indeed, *Roots* became the film trade's dream "crossover": a feature that appealed to the urban black mass market as well as the majority white audiences. The TV series won 145 different awards, including 9 Emmys.[2]

Roots enjoyed huge commercial and popular spin-offs. Fifty cities declared "Roots Weeks"; the governor of Tennessee (Haley's home state) proclaimed 19-21 May 1977 "Alex Haley Days"; and the Gambian government pronounced Kunta Kinte's home in Juffure a national shrine and began to market "Roots trips." T-shirts, plaques, and "Roots music" recordings appeared; "Root-tracing kits" with imitation parchment genealogical charts became the rage (among whites as well as blacks). Schools were sent supplementary materials to use with the book and show, and colleges gave students credit for simply watching the miniseries. New black babies were named Kunta Kinte and Kizzy, after the show's main protagonists. In Eddie Murphy's successful comedy *Coming to America* (1988), HRH Akeem (Murphy) entered a barber's shop and was proclaimed by the barber "a Kunta Kinte"—an authentic African.

Haley himself became a folk hero. Letters arrived from all over the world addressed to "Alex Haley, 'Roots,' America." He was said to be the third most admired black man among black American youth (after Muhammad Ali and Stevie Wonder). In the prestigious "Black One Hundred," a list of the most influential blacks, Haley is listed above major writers James Baldwin and Toni Morrison. He was invited to meet presidents and crowned heads, to front TV commercials, and to speak on talk shows, at prestigious lecture venues, and at autograph parties. There were keys given by many U.S. cities, special citations from the U.S. Senate and House of Representatives, and profiles galore in magazines and newspapers. Two black colleges, Fisk and Lane, placed him on their boards, and dozens of publishers and hundreds of individuals sent him manuscripts for endorsement and patronage. At the 1996 Atlanta Olympic Games, to commemorate *Roots'* twentieth birthday, a vast statue of the writer was unveiled.

The (mainly white) critics who have enthused most about *Roots* have made large, often extravagant claims for it. Despite a damning indictment of its literary style, writing in 1979, Leslie Fiedler recognized the cultural significance of the book and TV series. Noting that Kunta Kinte had become a household name, he said, "With *Roots*, a Black American succeeded for the first time in modifying the mythology of Black-White relations *for the majority audience*" (a majority that was, of course, white), and he goes on to argue how unlikely it might have seemed that this book, "like Mrs. Stowe's, [would] be 'read equally in the parlor, the kitchen and the nursery,' but be condensed in the Reader's Digest and assigned in every classroom in the land."[3] Almost a decade later, Harold Courlander (who had by then won a plagiarism suit against Haley) noted: "*Roots* continues to be read and quoted, is found everywhere on library shelves, is a cornerstone of various Black studies programs. . . . In short, the book has an established place in contemporary American literature and will be spoken of, no doubt, for some time to come."[4] Historian Willie Lee Rose described *Roots* simply as "the most astounding cultural event of the American Bicentennial."[5]

Roots must be the only nonreligious text to have achieved such universal success and endorsement. *Gone With the Wind* has outsold it but rarely found itself on a school or college syllabus, praised by political leaders or judges. This smash hit made its author a multimillionaire, national black hero, and international roving ambassador. For African Americans, deprived for centuries of their ancestral homes and families, enslaved and exploited, denied basic human and civil rights, including the right to literacy, this book offered a fresh perspective on their history, genealogy, and community.

ROOTS, NOT ROUTES

The word *roots* recurs in many a discussion of the South and its meanings. A word traditionally associated with southerners' tendency to stay in the same place, to focus on and value a family and home, during the twentieth century it has become a term of nostalgia and desire. Critic John Egerton believes the South shares with the rest of the nation, since World War II, a lost sense of rootedness that has produced "a steady erosion of the sense of place, of community, of belonging."[6] For others, that very sense of roots and connections (however eroded they may be within a new postindustrial region) is precisely what the nation looks to the South to represent and uphold.

On the other hand, within postcolonial discourse, the word has developed reactionary connotations. As I discussed in chapter 1, "routes" rather than "roots" have been identified as the most meaningful way of configuring the contemporary world. Defining "the Black Atlantic," Paul Gilroy focuses on cultural exchange and flow rather than origins and fixed, pure identities. For him, the ship's voyage is the perfect metaphor for hybrid black Atlantic identities and relationships. A voyaging ship was a productive and imaginative way

out of a rather narrow Afrocentrism, a way of seeing crisscross movements of black people—through physical journeys as well as cultural
and political exchanges—as a means of looking afresh at questions
of nationality, identity, and historical memory. Slaves who traveled
from Africa to America via the Middle Passage, black slaves in British
ports, Harlem Renaissance writers, intellectuals and jazz musicians
who traveled to London and Paris (often to settle)—all were shaped
by and helped shape a black Atlantic consciousness and memory. Origins were impure and mixed; the interesting questions were those of
process rather than point of departure, diasporic circulation rather
than starting points and roots. "Roots" were associated with reactionary and nostalgic forces.

This all makes sense, until one focuses on Haley's *Roots*, the postwar, postcolonial text that most successfully foregrounded the historical struggles and present dilemmas of African Americans and—by
analogy—displaced and rootless blacks everywhere. *Roots* took the
ship's voyage as one of its central themes and metaphors, not of hybrid exchanges but of diasporic peoples' loss of, and need for, origins. This work, about the routes of one family and indeed one man,
Haley himself, argues passionately for the need to discover roots, to
locate and celebrate origins, to find the single identifying moment
for black identity. It is an unashamedly Afrocentric vision, leading
American blacks back to a Rousseauesque vision of original purity and
innocence, to the Paradise Lost of one of their earliest societies. Luck-
ily for Haley, its somewhat lukewarm working title, *Before This Anger*, was changed by shrewd editors to the more resonant and mythic
final name.

In the 1870s, the writer Albion W. Tourgée had reflected on the
black freedman: "The white man traces his ancestry back for generations, knows whence they came, where they lived, and guesses what
they did. To the American Negro the past is only darkness replete
with unimaginable horrors. Ancestors he has none."[7] More than a
century later, Toni Morrison remarked that in America the past
is always either absent or romanticized. Slavery, so much of the
world's past, has been erased from memory; that institution that had
"broke[n] the world in half" had made blacks the first truly modern
people. Her own much acclaimed novel *Beloved* (1987) was intended
to return slavery to the heart of Afro-America's political and literary
culture. "Slavery wasn't in the literature at all," she said. "We have

to re-inhabit those people."[8] *Beloved* is certainly the most harrowing, profound, and brilliant study of slavery, but it is unfair to claim that this subject did not exist in the literature. It is true that the most famous, notorious novel about slavery, *Uncle Tom's Cabin* (1852), had been written by a northern white woman, Harriet Beecher Stowe. Morrison may have been suggesting that there was no adequate literary treatment, especially by an African American. However, in many different kinds of discourse through the twentieth century, notably through autobiographies by writers such as Richard Wright and Zora Neale Hurston, novels such as Ernest J. Gaines's *The Autobiography of Miss Jane Pittman* (1971) and Sherley Anne Williams's *Dessa Rose* (1986), and essays by Ralph Ellison, James Baldwin, and Alice Walker, there were concerted attempts to begin to trace, and root, ancestors and to rescue the past from those nameless horrors. In a few notable works—Margaret Walker's *Jubilee* (1966) and Alice Walker's *The Color Purple* (1982)—the terrible, inadequately recorded and much mythified story of slavery and its aftermath were reexplored imaginatively and reexamined from a strongly feminist perspective.

However, the only work to achieve huge popular sales, appeal to a vast global multiracial market, and command large peak-time audiences on television was *Roots*. Published in a year when the whole nation was trying to heal wounds and emerge whole and unified, and even elected President Carter from the Deep South to confirm that process, *Roots* became a myth in its own right. The ripples were felt as far as India and Australia. Justice V. R. Krishna Iyer, judge of the Supreme Court of India, said: "The dignity of a race is restored when its roots are known . . . and that explains how Gandhi in India could resist the imperial rulers with knowledge of our strength and sustenance from our roots. *The Discovery of India* by Nehru was prompted by the same urge to trace one's roots which induced Alex Haley to research the Black Americans' roots."[9] In an article about the opening of an Australian museum dedicated to the British convicts from which many Australians are descended, the *Observer* (16 July 1995) described a *"Roots*-style voyage of genealogical discovery." After Haley's death, the Reverend Jesse Jackson said simply, "He lit up the long night of slavery. He gave our grandparents personhood. He gave *Roots* to the rootless."[10]

BRITAIN AND AFRICAN AMERICAN CULTURE

The impact of this single work reverberated across the Atlantic. Until relatively recently, African American culture was recognized in Britain almost entirely through black music and sports, with the occasional film star such as Sidney Poitier thrown in for good measure. Of course, black and white intellectuals had long had links, from the Harlem Renaissance onward, with black thinkers and artists; but they were in a small minority. In the late 1970s, however, a new popular enthusiasm began to develop for African American literary culture. Until then, the occasional British intellectual (black or white) might have read imported copies of Richard Wright's *Native Son* (1940) or Ralph Ellison's *Invisible Man* (1952). But during the eighties and nineties, general readers and school and college students alike took with enthusiasm to writers such as Alice Walker, Toni Morrison, Maya Angelou—even, perhaps, Langston Hughes and James Baldwin (though living contemporary male writers have been relatively neglected). Steven Spielberg's film of *The Color Purple* (1985) was as huge a hit in Britain as in the States, and his controversial *Amistad* (1997) is a major example of a 1990s vogue for film treatments of slavery. African American experience and cultural forms have come to signify a certain kind of exotic and exciting marginality, one that has added a new dimension to the British love affair with the States. And since most of those cultural producers come from the South, or at least write about the South, southern history, and southern people, a significantly different perspective is added to British cultural associations with that mythic site.

Many reasons may be adduced for this. Teachers in British schools who now have power over curriculum choices came to maturity in the 1960s, when civil rights and black consciousness produced charismatic leaders—from Martin Luther King Jr. and Malcolm X to Coretta Scott King and Angela Davis—whose words and actions resounded through that decade. Editors of new, small, feminist, Third World, and left-wing publishing houses shared that formation and quickly realized how popular and lucrative reprints of African American texts could be. Indeed, in their seventies and eighties heyday, the two main British feminist presses were kept afloat largely by their two biggest-selling authors—Maya Angelou for Virago, Alice Walker for the Women's Press. The Pulitzer Prize for *The Color Purple*;

Spielberg's hit film version; the Nobel Prize for literature for Toni Morrison; the much acclaimed television series shown in Britain in the late 1980s, *Eyes on the Prize: America's Civil Rights Years, 1954–1965*; the new evidence of a conspiracy to murder Martin Luther King; the films of Spike Lee and the controversies over rap music; the 1990s media spectacle of the Clarence Thomas sexual harassment hearing, the O. J. Simpson trial, the rise, fall, and rise of Mayor Marion Barry: these and more created a climate of intense interest in all things African American.

And at the beginning of this new wave was Alex Haley's *Roots*. Published at a moment when the eyes of the world were focused on the United States' celebrations of its two-hundred-year-old democracy, it was the first African American book to be a British best-seller, to be serialized in the conservative newspaper the *Daily Express*, and to attract mass audiences for its 1977 weekly television screenings. This was probably the first time an African American cultural product other than music, boxing, or athletics was discussed in the British home, classroom, and hair salon. This single work, conventional in form, uneven in literary quality, aimed at a middlebrow *Reader's Digest* market, precipitated a transnational interest in and awareness of the history of slavery that has paved the way for greater works and more challenging versions of that history.

"THE GRIOT FROM TENNESSEE"

Alex Haley played his legendary role well to an admiring international audience.

> I acknowledge immense debt to the griots of Africa—where today it is rightly said that when a griot dies, it is as if a library has burned to the ground. The griots symbolize how all human ancestry goes back to some place, and some time, where there was no writing. Then, the memories and the mouths of ancient elders was [*sic*] the only way that early histories of mankind got passed along . . . for all of us today to know who we are.

With these words, he concluded his acknowledgments page. The tribute to the African griots he paid here, and in the final chapters of the book—not to mention at countless lectures and interviews after publication—was paid back to him by selected African American critics. For instance, his biographer, Mary Siebert McCauley, entitled her study "Alex Haley, a Southern Griot."[11] In an issue of the *Black Scholar* published only months after the first transmission of the television miniseries, black columnist Chuck Stone praised Haley for producing, as he had intended, "the symbol [sic] saga of all of us of African ancestry." Calling him "the griot from Tennessee," he praised Haley for "painstakingly unraveling the umbilical cord that had stretched a tortured distance from Africa to America."[12] For many critics and millions of readers and TV viewers, Haley unraveled that umbilical cord by using his own family's story, and his griotlike powers, to link the preliterate African past to his own literary, professional present via the terrible saga of slavery. The griots passed stories on orally, "for all of us today to know who we are." Haley, as befitted a contemporary figure who was the culmination of centuries of oppression and resistance, slavery and freedom, gave his story massive prepublicity circulation on campus lecture tours and in popular journals.

Already a race hero for his ghost authorship of *The Autobiography of Malcolm X* (1965), Haley welcomed claims made for the vast symbolic importance of *Roots* for his race and nation. Although usually regarded as a novel, it was published originally as nonfiction, supporting Haley's apparently thoroughly researched claims that the book told the true story of his ancestors, traced back to the Mandinka tribe of Juffure, the Gambia. This was no tale found in books; it was a culmination of an epic quest. Haley had heard fragments of it first at his grandmother's knee in Henning, Tennessee, and had subsequently traveled the world, interviewing people, seeking sources, and eventually being led to an old African griot who revealed the name of his original ancestor Kunta Kinte.

The problem with this romantic account is that it has been disputed by several distinguished historians and journalists, who have challenged Haley's version of events, research methods, and source material. The first skeptical account came only months after the book's British publication, on 10 April 1977, in an article entitled "Tangled Roots," by a British *Sunday Times* journalist, Mark Ottaway, who had investigated Haley's sources in Gambia. This has been followed by many since.

Haley was in good company. Harriet Beecher Stowe, Thomas Dixon, and Margaret Mitchell had all felt forced to establish their authorial credibility. Harriet Beecher Stowe provided her critics with a *Key to Uncle Tom's Cabin* (1853), citing all the sources on which she had drawn for the novel, to prove she did not merely have a gothic imagination (though a century later Ishmael Reed would accuse her, in *Flight to Canada* [1976], of stealing material from slave narrator Josiah Henson). Thomas Dixon offered to hire a committee from the American Historical Association and then pay a thousand dollars to anyone who could prove an error in his fictional celebration of the Ku Klux Klan, *The Clansman* (1905). Margaret Mitchell wrote thousands of letters to readers and critics that refute, with scholarly reference, claims of historical errors in *Gone With the Wind* (1936). Haley always promised to publish *My Search for Roots* to establish his sources; he never did, though the two-hundred-page manuscript is in his papers at the University of Tennessee. Unlike his predecessors, however, he faced serious and lingering charges that have never been satisfactorily refuted.

First of all, many historians and literary critics found *Roots* wanting in historical accuracy and believable characterization and dialogue. Leslie Fiedler took Haley to task for creating a Kunta Kinte who is suspiciously like Malcolm X, whose autobiography Haley had written; for euphemizing Africa(ns) and vilifying the American South (erners); for obfuscating the polygamous sexuality of Muslim Mandinkas and, unbelievably, keeping Kunta Kinte a virgin until the age of thirty-nine; and finally, for presenting sexual passion always as evil and thus with considerable salaciousness. In the *Black Scholar*, five black intellectuals attacked the TV version as "A Modern Minstrel Show," "an electronic orgy in white guilt," and "an electronic *Uncle Tom's Cabin.*"[13] Critics on the left condemned it for presenting Juffure as "a chocolate-box version of [blacks'] history," the Gambian village "looking a little too much like 'Club Mediterranean'" or "Avalon." Its very commercial success and popularity (particularly with white readers and audiences) suggested a lack of political integrity in an author who was courted by *Reader's Digest* and commercial television companies. It is interesting to compare Haley's fate with that of later writer Alice Walker, who was attacked by African American intellectuals because of her (albeit uneasy) collaboration with blockbuster film director Steven Spielberg.[14]

To this day, *Roots* is ignored by most serious African American critics and writers; in studies of African American autobiographical, historical, and fictional writing, it is either absent or consigned to a grudging mention or footnote.[15] The soft-focused idealization of Af-

rica and African ancestors, the extremely patriarchal tone and character of the families depicted, the Horatio Alger–like story of enslaved
poverty to bourgeois success, and the sentimental, even utopian ending to a complex story all go some way to explain why scholars rarely
discuss the work. But they are not the main reason.

PLAGIARISM, INVENTIONS, AND INACCURACIES

Of greater seriousness are the plagiarism charges laid against *Roots*,
two of which resulted in court cases. In 1977, Margaret Walker took
Haley to court alleging he had copied his plotting from her novel
Jubilee; the case was dismissed. In a BBC program, Walker told her
interviewer that Haley had used her and fooled people. Claiming she
would have won her case had her publisher backed her, she called
Roots "a great hoax and fraud compounded on all American people."
In 1978, white novelist and folklorist Harold Courlander and his publisher, Crown, accused Haley of copying roughly eighty passages from
Courlander's novel *The Slave* (1967). Haley maintained to a skeptical
judge that he had never heard of *The Slave* but that strangers had
given him notes as he went round the country lecturing. The night
before Judge Ward delivered his decision after the five-week trial,
Haley capitulated, signed a statement to acknowledge the inclusion
of some of Courlander's material in *Roots*, paid a hefty sum of
$650,000, and managed to escape public disgrace. On 4 July 1989,
the *Voice* reported that Haley was facing a further court case, this time
from Emma Lee Davis Paul, an African American woman who had
grown up in the Deep South and claimed that her work *The Bold Truth*
was "lifted" for *Roots*. Haley might well have argued—but significantly
did not—that he was part of an intertextually rich black tradition.
Henry Louis Gates Jr. has pointed out: "Many Black authors read and
revise one another, address similar themes, and repeat the cultural
and linguistic codes of a common symbolic geography."[16] It seems
that Haley was reluctant to see himself as part of a black continuum
(even if it might have let him off a few hooks). Perhaps he wanted
to stand alone, to receive acclaim as the one writer who had uniquely
told the story of his whole race. Perhaps he clung to his belief that
the story of others was being told through him and that "plagiarism"
was thus irrelevant.

It has been no easy matter for journalists and critics on either

side of the Atlantic to raise questions about Haley's integrity in relation to *Roots*. Charges of racism are easily laid against any white writer
who challenges the authenticity of *Roots*, in view of the work's importance to African American pride and heritage. Mark Ottaway, the
British journalist who wrote the first skeptical article, recounts an
uneasy history with the work and Haley himself. He was visiting
Gambia, by invitation of an airline, just before *Roots* was to be published and televised in Britain. A seasoned investigative journalist (of
the famed *Sunday Times* "Insight" team), he read the book on the
plane and, once arrived in Gambia, smelled a few proverbial rats. Using Gambian archives, British colonial records, the Lloyd's shipping
register, and interviews with the national archivist, Ottaway discovered a great many discrepancies in Haley's account of the area. The
greatest discrepancy was the historical inaccuracy of Haley's depiction of Juffure as an isolated village: "Far from being a remote Eden
untouched by white civilization, the real Juffure was a white trading
post surrounded by white colonialisation. . . . Insofar as the inhabitants of Juffure were involved in slave trading it was not as victims
but as collaborators with the whites, helping them capture slaves from
further up the river."[17] The other major discovery made by Ottaway
was one potentially more embarrassing for Haley: the fact that the
so-called griot who revealed to him so movingly that Kunta Kinte was
his ancestor was no griot and was in fact a well-known Gambian playboy, drummer, and opportunist who told the African American writer
what he wanted to hear about his lineage.

In the article, Ottaway quotes replies made by Haley to questions
he posed about his discoveries. Haley never refuted any of his points
but argued instead for the "symbolic truth" of his story. He is quoted
as saying: "This book is also symbolic. I know Juffure was a British
trading post and my portrait of the village bears no resemblance to
the way it was. But the portrait I gave was true of nearly all the other
villages in Gambia. I, we, need a place called Eden. My people need
a Pilgrim's Rock." In a *Sunday Times* reader's letter responding critically to Ottaway's article, Ms. Dagnija Innus brushed aside the historical inaccuracies: "Haley *has*, as was his purpose, given his people
their Eden . . . their Pilgrim's Rock. All the research you may care to
undertake into the facts cannot remove *that* fact."[18] Haley attacked
Ottaway for demeaning his research (focusing on the short length of
the journalist's sojourn in Gambia). He sought and was granted the

right of reply in the *Sunday Times*; he never availed himself of this. Ottaway found the whole business disturbing, especially when hearing Haley denouncing him on the radio and receiving critical reviews from all sides of the political spectrum that appeared motivated by racism. He did not take the matter further. In a letter to me, he admitted, "Frankly, I found my brush with racism sufficiently upsetting to wish to leave the can of worms where it was."[19]

CRITICAL ATTACKS AND SILENCES

It was many years later, after Alex Haley's death in 1992, that an American journalist took up the baton and delivered an even more devastating blow to Haley's reputation and integrity. This time, the article appeared first in the New York paper the *Village Voice* and then was reprinted in an abridged version in the very *Sunday Times* that had featured Mark Ottaway's piece some sixteen years earlier. Investigative journalist Philip Nobile, who, of course, knew Ottaway's article, had followed the court cases and reputation of Haley over many years. He claimed that the cases already cited (Walker, Courlander, and others) were by no means the only plagiarisms, and he threw in for good measure other works Haley admitted to copying—*Travels of Mungo Park* as well as Shirley Graham's *The Story of Phillis Wheatley*. Nobile's explanation was that Haley (as he euphemistically put it) "was a writer of modest talents, as a number of editors would say, who required enormous editorial support," the manuscript extensively revised, rewritten, and probably partly written by editor Murray Fisher.

He went on to say that, although Haley's authorship was questionable, the accuracy of his historical research, the authenticity of his reports of trips to the Gambia, and the revelatory discovery of the griot (so movingly described in the book's final chapter), indeed the veracity of the ancestral lineage he claimed for himself, were all thrown into severe doubt by the researches, questions, and discoveries of historians, journalists, and critics who checked his sources and interviewed his editors, collaborators, and friends. These included distinguished figures such as southern historian Willie Lee Rose, Harvard professor Oscar Handlin, and British journalist Mark Ottaway, as well as Nobile himself, a prize-winning journalist known for his literary detective and antiracist publications. Also listed were genealogists

Elizabeth Shown Mills and Gary Mills, the latter of whom writes in support of the white supremacist Southern League, a body that would doubtless find considerable pleasure in exposing *Roots* as fraudulent. Nobile claimed that those who had bothered to examine Haley's research materials (especially audiotapes) in the Alex Haley Papers, opened in February 1993, shortly after his death, discovered so many distortions, inaccuracies, and bogus research claims that there was only one possible conclusion: "Haley invented 200 years of family history. All of Haley's ripping yarns about his search for Kunta Kinte and his 10-year struggle to write *Roots* were part of an elegant and complex make-it-up-as-you-go-along scam."[20] He repeated many of these charges, and added more, in a BBC TV program broadcast in Britain in 1997.[21]

So have the revelations damaged Haley's reputation? Hardly at all. Despite the plagiarism cases; the articles by Willie Lee Rose (1976), Mark Ottaway (1977), Gary Mills and Elizabeth Shown Mills (1981), and Nobile (1993); and Haley's death, which might have opened a few more minds and mouths, his position as revered writer and chronicler of his race's history remains intact. And there are surprising silences surrounding Haley and his famous work. Few critics of southern writing bother to discuss *Roots* at all, and even when they do, there is no mention of the controversy.[22] Philip Nobile, who might have expected to receive considerable feedback on his 1993 article and 1997 BBC documentary, met a wall of silence. No one seriously disputed his facts; many people, African American as well as white, privately told him they accepted his conclusions but did not wish to take them further. The Pulitzer Committee has never discussed whether to withdraw its 1977 prize from Haley; Nobile believes that its all-white male composition at the time makes the current mixed-race and -gender committee especially sensitive. The BBC program will not be broadcast in the States, and it is said that such an explosive program, fully airing the controversies surrounding Haley and his work, could never have been made there; even in Britain its findings made little stir. It seems that *Washington Post* editor and 1977 Pulitzer Committee member Ben Bradlee's words still apply: "Nobody wanted his ass."[23]

THE BLACK "GONE WITH THE WIND"

Another reason for critical unease with the work lay in its populist affinities with other well-known, best-selling works set in the plantation South. Many commentators, black and white, have noted the irresistibility of the antebellum South and slavery as subjects for popular fiction and film. Writing in 1978-79, both Leslie Fiedler and Willie Lee Rose located *Roots* as the culminating text in a line that began with *Uncle Tom's Cabin* (1852) and continued with Thomas Dixon's trilogy, especially *The Clansman: An Historical Romance of the Ku Klux Klan,* and Margaret Mitchell's *Gone With the Wind.* Of the four, Fiedler argues: "Rooted in demonic dreams of race, sex and violence which have long haunted us Americans, they determine our views of the Civil War, Reconstruction, the Rise and Fall of the Ku Klux Klan, the enslavement and liberation of American Blacks, thus constituting a myth of our history unequalled in scope or resonance by any work of High Literature."[24] Rose sees the group in similar terms: "They have given a vocabulary to American mythologies and demonologies that is generally understood at home and abroad."[25]

Roots is rarely seen as unique; most critics recognize its origins in earlier plantation epics. Afrocentric critics were unhappy about its formal and narrative links with *Gone With the Wind* and also with its willingness to simplify and modify African experience and cultural forms within a Western vernacular literary tradition.[26] Apart from its obvious affiliation with Mitchell's novel, Joseph R. Millichap calls it "a contemporary *Uncle Tom's Cabin,*" and *Time* called the TV version "middle-of-the-road *Mandingo.*"[27] Fiedler noted that *Roots,* like its famous predecessor, was accepted by the majority audience as "a new, revised secular scripture leading to its rejection by literary critics."[28] It may be that Haley's rejection by cultural critics, especially black critics who might have been expected to welcome it (however reservedly), stems both from its huge popularity with the majority white audience and from its association with a series of texts known for their patronizing, racist, or exploitative presentation of black history and experience.[29]

In a different context, Toni Morrison speaks of the problem of the slave narrative's relationship to the white "master narrative." Acknowledging the popularity of the narratives and their importance in influencing abolitionists and converting antiabolitionists, she concludes: "The slave's own narrative, while freeing the narrator in many ways, did not destroy the master narrative. The master narrative could make any number of adjustments to keep itself intact."[30] If one turns to *Roots*, it is possible to justify Morrison's pessimism. Jack Temple Kirby believed that *Roots* had "administered the *coup de grace* to Margaret Mitchell's ghost" and that no one would be able to "resuscit[ate] . . . the Grand Old South from now on."[31] A brief look, though, at the endless repremieres, rescreenings, media coverage, sequel and spoof novels, and TV miniseries of *Gone With the Wind*, not to mention such series as *Beulah Land* and *North and South*, suggests that Morrison's point about the master narrative's adjustments stands firm. In popular mythology, *Roots* has been received as a response to and rejection of the plantation epic saga, but it has not supplanted it. It has adopted and adapted the rules of the genre so that it may legitimately be read as the black *Gone With the Wind*: a family saga, a survival and success epic, with a structure that begins in an Eden-like innocent, formal, and ordered society (Juffure—the equivalent of the plantation novel's "glorious days before the War") and proceeds to the Paradise Lost of the Middle Passage and enslavement (for which, read the Civil War and loss of the plantation), followed by gradual restitution of black pride, self-worth, and economic and social order (read redemption of white supremacy). Working within the terms of the master narrative, it could be argued that Haley does not seem to have escaped its structure, parameters, and thus ideological power.

And if this is true of *Roots*, it is doubly so of the sequel Haley began before his death and that was completed by David Stevens, who also wrote the TV miniseries screenplay.[32] *Alex Haley's Queen: The Story of an American Family* purported to recount the story of Haley's father's line, as *Roots* had his mother's. Apparently written by Stevens from boxes of Haley's notes and conversations with him over years, the book traced the Haley line to a white ancestor in eighteenth-century Ireland, whose anti-British son flees to the New World and becomes a kindly slave owner and friend of President Andrew Jackson. In a fortuitously complementary manner to *Roots*, Haley senior turns out to have come from mixed-race stock, love child of one of Tennessee's first planters and sturdiest female slaves, and thus to combine some key elements of southern history missing from the earlier work: for instance, miscegenation, slave women's specific experiences, and the figure of the tragic *mulatta*. Even more doubts are cast over Haley's veracity when it appears that his maternal and paternal ancestors between them covered the full spectrum of slave and postemancipation experiences.

AFRICAN AMERICAN AUTOBIOGRAPHY AND HALEY THE GRIOT

For a derivative and in many ways pedestrian account, *Roots* received extraordinary international acclaim, large readership and viewing figures, and intertextual circulations. Some published accounts of *Roots*, as well as the critical silences, imply that its enthusiastic reader-viewers are a quiescent mass of disempowered consumers who have passively bought this commodity from a white-dominated cultural industry interested only in profit. This reductionist view refuses to explain the enormous appeal of *Roots* to a wide variety of consumers of most ages, races, genders, and nationalities, who have actively used *Roots* as a cultural resource to generate a variety of (often contradictory) meanings and pleasures. This is surely what John Fiske calls a "producerly" text—an accessible book and TV series that may be understood within the dominant ideology but that, containing limitations, gaps, and contradictory voices, is open and amenable to popular production.[33] It must also be seen (as I argue about Maya Angelou, in chapter 6) in the context of the powerfully reciprocal relationship that exists between African American writers and their black and white audiences.

Roots operates intertextually within the generic codes of the plantation epic master narrative. But this is not all. It is also a kind of autobiography, implicitly for the most part, then, for the final three chapters, explicitly so. (The last line of chapter 117, which has recorded the birth of a boy to Bertha and Simon, reveals, "The baby boy, six weeks old, was *me*" [615].) It is curious that, of all the genres Haley and his publishers claimed for the work (faction, nonfiction, part historical fiction), at no point did they name it after that most characteristically African American form, autobiography. As Selwyn R. Cudjoe points out:

> The Afro-American autobiographical statement is the most Afro-American of all Afro-American literary pursuits. . . . [It] remains the quintessential literary genre for capturing the cadences of the Afro-American being, revealing its deepest aspirations and tracing the evolution of the Afro-American psyche under the impact of slavery and modern U.S. imperialism.[34]

As Cudjoe and many others suggest, black autobiography is not read as personal statement or exploration but as communal expression of a collective experience and unconscious. Toni Morrison gives one of the clearest statements: "The autobiographical form is classic in Black American or Afro-American literature because it provided an instance in which a writer could be representative, could say, 'My single solitary and individual life is like the lives of the tribe; it differs in these specific ways, but it is a balanced life because it is both solitary and representative.'"[35] The complications often experienced by writers around this notion of representativeness are demonstrated by Ernest J. Gaines's *The Autobiography of Miss Jane Pittman*. Although it was published as a fictional autobiography, many readers believed it to be a real memoir. A *Newsweek* editor, asking Gaines for a photograph of Jane, was shocked to learn she was fictional, not real, though in fact Miss Pittman was inspired by the writer's real Aunt Augustine.[36]

Roots shares many characteristics of African American autobiography. Much of the narrative follows the themes of slave narrative (the aboriginal autobiography). It follows the trajectory of those "deliverance" narratives that Henry Louis Gates Jr. claims were most common in early African American autobiography, and it shares the "captivity narrative" (with its pattern of bondage, flight, and freedom) that James Olney claims is the prototype of American autobiography by women and minorities. It covers that thematic triad common to southern black autobiography, from Olaudah Equiano and Booker T. Washington to Malcolm X: literacy, identity, and freedom. It also follows one man who—like Frederick Douglass and other male slave narrators—becomes epic hero and race representative bearing eye/I witness to the sufferings and fortitude of the race. Like many earlier African American autobiographies, it is written with simple clarity, in order to be both didactic and inspirational. The book ends with an account of the funeral of Alex Haley's father, attended by "members of the seventh generation from Kunta Kinte." Haley hopes "that this story of our people can help to alleviate the legacies of the fact that preponderantly the histories have been written by the winners" (639).

And, as I have already argued, like slave narrators of the mid-nineteenth century, *Roots*'s author had to go on the defensive over authorship. Following in the slave narrators' footsteps, Haley toured the country telling his story to delighted and awe-struck audiences (on campuses rather than in abolitionist groups). Unlike those narratives, Haley's work was not published with many printed endorsements of white editors and abolitionists; on the other hand, it was produced with the heavy financial and moral backing, and continuing loyal support, of white patrons with international clout, such as *Reader's Digest* and *Playboy*.

Henry Louis Gates Jr., writing of the way in which "African American writing arose as a response to allegations of its absence," focused strongly on black *voice* as "a voice of deliverance from the deafening discursive silence which an enlightened Europe cited as proof of the absence of the African's humanity." In five of the earliest eighteenth-century slave narratives, he noted the repeated figure of the voice in the text (mainly the trope of the talking book, usually a Bible read aloud by a white master), which proved to the slave his own silenced and negated humanity. In order to challenge the "received correlation between silence and Blackness," the slave has "the urgent need to make the text speak, the process by which the slave marked his distance from the master."[37] This voice was one of deliverance and redemption, signifying a new order for the black.

A "CALL AND RESPONSE" EPIC

In Haley's *Roots*, the griot performs this function of offering the voice of deliverance and redemption. In the book's final chapter, the writer recounts his meeting with the griot, who recites for him the ancestral history of the Kinte clan "as it had been passed along orally down across centuries from the forefathers' time" (629). Significantly, it was recited "as if a scroll were being read." Haley, moved deeply that this was his ancestors' story, bawled, feeling as if he was "weeping for all of history's incredible atrocities against fellowmen," and then got on the plane and decided to write a book (632-633) This book, not just an account of his ancestral history, "would automatically also be a symbolic saga of all African-descent people." The relationship here between the spoken word, the printed text ("scroll" and book), and the uncontrolled bawling bear out Gates's point that "the very *face* of the race . . . was contingent upon the recording of the Black voice."[38] Or, as Toni Morrison says, "To enforce its invisibility through silence is to allow the Black a shadowless participation in the dominant cultural body."[39]

It should be recalled that *Roots* was published fortuitously in the bicentennial year (many years later than its publisher's deadlines required), with a dedication in its frontispiece: "as a birthday offering to my country within which most of *Roots* happened." The symbolic importance of such timely "participation in the dominant cultural body" cannot be exaggerated. It should also be recalled that Haley, while researching his family history, had spent many years on the lecture circuit, acquiring a considerable reputation as a storyteller and race chronicler. Speaking of Haley's "monologue" to campus audiences, Michael Kirkhorn says: "Through his lecturing, Haley has created an oral tradition of his own. The story of his ancestry is so intimately Haley's own story that Kunta Kinte seems almost his contemporary; bits of the narrative are threaded through his conversation."[40] In recent years, the African American oral tradition has been at the forefront of critical writing. The modes of oral communication developed by slaves who were forbidden to read and write—work song, group secular, spiritual, field holler, folk tale, blues song—have been understood as crucial formations of black literary culture. Houston A. Baker Jr. reminds us of the first definition of *vernacular*: "adj: *Of a slave.*"[41] The key element in this oral culture is "call and response," or "antiphony," in which the African American poet is empowered (like a black preacher) by the response he receives from his people. Call and response, according to Henry Louis Gates Jr., reenacts "the drama of finding authority through communal voice."[42] Toni Morrison echoes this when she speaks of black fiction needing to have "the ability to be both print and oral literature . . . so that the stories can be read in silence, of course, but one should be able to hear them as well." For her, of primary importance is "the affective and participatory relationship between the artist or the speaker and the audience."[43]

With Alex Haley and *Roots*, this relationship of call and response has been extraordinary. The success of the work, on the lecture circuit, in literary form, and on TV, and the lasting fame of its writer are surely models of that "communal voice," that "affective and participatory relationship" to which black writers and critics aspire. Whether or not Haley's Gambian griot was a cynical trickster exploiting a gullible black American, or a knowing colluder in a convenient myth, the fact is that *Haley himself* became the closest anyone has ever come to being an African American griot.

Even allowing for her romanticization of his quest, Mary Siebert McCauley's biographical study offers insights into Haley's persuasive and seductive ability to secure white patronage and finances, arouse enormous prepublicity excitement about his project, and then sell it and himself, ensuring his own personal wealth and international fame. Haley revered the African griots as living archives of oral history, and he emulated their techniques. After charming at a party the cofounder of *Reader's Digest*, he was invited to speak to her editors. McCauley describes the meeting: "Haley with his soft, accented Tennessee baritone voice, and with his low-key, boy-like shyness played griot for three hours as the editors listened spellbound."[44] When he recounted, in lecture hall or interview, the dramatic experience of spending ten nights lying in his underwear on a rough board in the cargo hold of a ship sailing from Liberia to the United States, to empathize fully with Kunta Kinte's sufferings (an apocryphal story, according to some critics), he described the despairing contemplation of suicide at his inability to identify with his ancestor. "Just a millimeter from dropping into the sea," he heard voices from nowhere calming him; he reports that these were the voices of his ancestors telling him to go on with his quest and his writing. This story ends with Haley returning to his ship stateroom and bursting into "a paroxysm of tears that lasted three or four hours."[45] This visceral response is characteristic of a man who believed he was "a conduit" for a story that was willed by his ancestors and his God. Although he denied comparing *Roots* with the Bible, he certainly saw himself as part of a great oral tradition that includes Homer's *Odyssey* and the Bible. And, most significantly in terms of American culture, he identified himself as a southern storyteller. Referring to the South as "one of the richest areas in the country for stories," he asked rhetorically, "What's more generic to the South than the old folks sitting on the porch telling stories?"[46]

Indeed, the whole story of his search for roots, involving extravagant amounts of international travel, false trails, sudden revelations, self-dramatizing epiphanies, and moments of profound despair and great euphoria, itself constitutes a modern epic tale. Haley constructed himself as both epic hero and African American griot, whose "quest" (a word he and McCauley use repeatedly) came to symbolize that of all black America, indeed the whole of multiracial America at bicentennial time. Against the weight of this, reinforced by Haley's carefully orchestrated lectures anticipating and following publication, magazine articles, and international promotional trips, is it any wonder that the accusations of historical and factual inaccuracies, plagiarisms, and stylistic lumpenness have fallen on stony ground? Haley the griot provided a powerful link between ancient bard and contemporary rapper. As Willie Lee Rose said, "*Roots* had gone where grass roots are, and on some things the general public does not care for an expert opinion."[47]

SLAVERY, RACE, AND AFRICA: THE BLACK AND WHITE ATLANTIC

Experts have offered carefully euphemistic opinions. During the 1997 BBC exposé, a notable journalist, Charlayne Hunter-Gault, argued that since there was such a dearth of information about African American history, and because artists who tackled the subject had to bear a huge burden of responsibility, there was "room for licence here"; after all, *Roots* had "awakened the sleeping psyche of generations . . . who had been portrayed by and large as victims." Henrik Clarke, a teacher of African history, also defended the work to a television audience: "For people short of heroes, sometimes we take the best we can get and sometimes exaggerate them a little beyond what they deserve to be. We don't always expect other people to understand this who have excess of heroes and excess of achievers." So, either through defenses of this kind or through their silences, African American intellectuals have—for the time being—secured Haley's reputation and the longevity of his work. *Roots* has been largely let off the critical hook; it seems racist to elaborate on the book's use of stock characters, stilted dialogue, plantation novel stereotypes, and history-by-numbers, as well as the miniseries's tired Hollywood clichés and idealized treatment of Gambian and slave family life. Since as both literary and televisual work it has many aesthetic weaknesses and resorts to the most conventional of formal qualities, it is easy to dismiss as facile fodder for a mass audience that knew little and cared less about African American and southern history. And yet the story it tells, and the clear, simple direction it follows, can be said to chart and invite political, social, and racial identification and resistance, albeit registered at a personal, familial level. Its autobiographical call-and-response structure (clumsy and sentimental as it is) does address us as active thinking citizens, whatever our color or nationality.

The story of slavery—in Toni Morrison's memorable phrase, "not a story to pass on"—has been passed on by a man who opportunely exploited the fascination Americans have for black oral culture, the southern storytelling tradition, the stock plantation epic, and the family-and-success saga. In a year when America was looking backward and forward, eager for new versions of its history and myths for its future, Haley the griot, the right man in the right place at the right time with the right product, gave it what it wanted. The existence and constant circulation of *Roots* (and *Queen*) undoubtedly opened doors to other African American artists, scriptwriters, and filmmakers responding to a national and international thirst for narratives about black life and culture. Haley's voice—on the lecture circuit, in the autobiographical nonfiction/fiction, and via the medium of TV—spoke in the first person (albeit imperfectly and unreliably) to huge audiences on behalf of a still largely silenced race.

However, in terms of thinking through representations of slavery, race, and Africa itself, does this griot's grassroots text offer a radical or conservative agenda for African Americans and other readers and viewers? *Roots* is imbued with an Afrocentric vision that has been culturally dominant since the 1960s. Afrocentrism, or what Toni Morrison calls American Africanism, has been seen as "a cultural and ethnic awareness [African Americans] have collectively constructed for [themselves] over hundreds of years . . . a cultural umbilical cord connecting [them] with Africa."[48] Alex Haley himself, speaking to Mary Seibert McCauley, traced his search for roots to the early 1960s and talked about blackness. "'Black is beautiful.' . . . [When I finished *Malcolm X*,] I began to hear about this whole exotic Africa thing and Africa as the motherland which had that sense about it, a sense of ancestry really in the sense of being the symbol source of Black people."[49] The emphasis throughout *Roots* is on establishing where the characters and author came from and celebrating the strong ties and especially *familial* links across continents and between generations of African Americans. This is curious in view of the fact that both book and TV series record a catalog of family and generational ruptures and discontinuities and that it is now clear Haley was economical with the truth in relation to his own genealogical "quest."

AN "AUTHORITARIAN PASTORAL PATRIARCHY"

Although Haley's search for his own roots was a protracted one, dependent on establishing a complex series of links between his grandmother in Tennessee and the Gambian village where he claims to have found his ancestral tribe, it slid quickly into something "typical" to all African Americans and thus the story of all. Haley said of *Roots:* "[It was] right out of my grandmother's mouth, and it turned out that what was coming out of her mouth is the story of all of us."[50] He was happy to share his ancestor: "Now because of *Roots* many Blacks have said that Kunta Kinte, my forebear, has become their ancestor. And why not? Ancestrally every black person has the same pattern."[51] Confusingly, too, not just blacks. Haley goes on to say that all of us, black, brown, white, and yellow, share "a desire to make this symbolic journey back to the touchstone of our family." His assertion was certainly correct in that one major consequence of the work's success was a huge rise in the number of people of all backgrounds making genealogical searches for their own roots.[52] National news magazines ran stories on how to research the family tree; letters and applications to use the National Archives soared. Gambian tourism began to explode, as African Americans traveled to Africa to find *their* roots.[53] *Newsweek*'s cover story on that symbolic date 4 July 1977 was "Everybody's Search for Roots."

This roots-mania was focused specifically on family history, as queries at the National Archives demonstrate, and the emphasis on family appears to have drowned out other major themes. The miniseries producer, David Wolper, asked: "Do you really think that the image of Blacks fighting on the streets is more progressive than a strong, powerful family image of a Black family held together in love, honor and courage?"[54] Michael Blayney described *Roots* as a "a child of the seventies" in the way its sentimental treatment of the family deflected attention from political concerns "toward heroic feats of individual characters," allowing white as well as black sympathy with the extinct "noble African." David A. Gerber underlined this interpretation of *Roots* as backward-looking, conservative text in his emphasis on its concern with family and—at a time of massive destabilization of family life—emphasis on "the triumph or survival of family ties amidst those forces which threaten them." In discussing the rise of the postmodern heritage industry, David Harvey argued that

> the preoccupation with identity, with personal and collective roots, has become far more pervasive since the early 1970s because of widespread insecurity in labour markets, in technological mixes,

credit systems, and the like. . . . The television series *Roots* . . . sparked a wave of family history research and interest throughout the whole Western world.[55]

He went on to note the irony that tradition is now "preserved by being commodified and marketed as such. The search for roots ends up at worst being produced and marketed as an image, as a simulacrum or pastiche."[56]

Haley's avowed intent was to bring people together, to speak of universals—and to do this through the family. In a *Playboy* article in March 1979 he argued, "I think that we as people—and I am talking about the world—badly need uplifting. We all have lineage and forefathers."[57] His book would offer "uplift," and furthermore he would go against the tendencies of the day and avoid "the use of obscenity and what [he'd] like to call corpuscular sex in writing" (i.e., no explicit sex scenes). Compare the endings of *Malcolm X* and *Roots* to observe the softened tone of the later work: in *Malcolm*, the final consideration is of X's role as "demagogue" and his pleasure at the thought he may die having helped "to destroy the racist cancer that is malignant in the body of America."[58] At the conclusion of *Roots*, Haley wallows in sentimental reflection on his "Dad" and all his ancestors who now "watch and guide" "up there."[59]

This emphasis on continuity through the family was praised by critics. James Baldwin, reviewing *Roots* in 1976, called it "a study of continuities, of consequences, of how a people perpetuate themselves, how each generation helps to doom or helps to liberate the coming one."[60] Cornel West, though never mentioning *Roots*, argued that such emphasis was a radical necessity for the black community, whose very survival is at stake. For him, black Americans' foremothers and forefathers created "powerful buffers to ward off the nihilistic threat, to equip Black folk with cultural armor to beat back the demons of hopelessness, meaninglessness, and lovelessness"; these were primarily religious and civic institutions sustaining "familial and communal networks of support." West claimed that these networks had broken down irretrievably, replaced by the dominating cultural industries, and he argued for a new *"politics of conversion"* through a "love ethic." The example he cited was *Beloved*, but it seems to me *Roots* is a better example of this *"politics of conversion"* at work—its accessibility and popular impact have been undeniably greater than the infinitely more complex and brilliant later novels.[61]

However, without reference to *Roots*, British critic Paul Gilroy use-fully challenged what he calls "Americocentric obsession with fam-ily." He objected to the pervasive symbolic projection of "race" as kinship and the fact that black Americans see the *family* as "the ap-proved, natural site where ethnicity and racial culture are repro-duced."[62] Arguing that this idea of black nationalism is dissociated from the politics of contemporary Africa, judging racial authenticity instead by "restored access to original African forms and codes," he saw those definitions of authenticity as defined by ideas about nurturance, family, fixed gender roles, and generational responsibili-ties. In his view, this "authoritarian pastoral patriarchy" leads to an interpretation of black politics and social life as a crisis solely of black masculinity that can be solved only by instituting forms of mascu-linity and male authority. Such forms resist more diverse, indeed femi-nist, symbols of political agency and change and kinds of antiphony that move away from cultural roots (fixed places and families) to cul-tural routes (flows of black popular culture, best exemplified for him in musical performance culminating in hip-hop).

This argument is useful in rethinking the whole plantation novel tradition, from the conservative and white supremacist epics of *The Clansman* and *Gone With the Wind* through to *Beulah Land*, the nov-els of Frank Yerby, and indeed *Roots* and its sequel, *Queen*. In rela-tion to Haley's best-sellers, this reading leads us to see the focus on male-dominated family, and Muslim familial continuity rather than racial fragmentation and discontinuity, as reinforcing a nostalgic and historically soft-focus patriarchal Afrocentrism, damaging for any radi-cal African American and black Atlantic agenda. The "authoritarian pastoral patriarchy" of Juffure, translated as it is to America through the tormented figure of Kunta Kinte, whose threatened masculinity is the key problem of his enslavement, may be read as celebrating a very restricted patriarchal version of idealized black social and fam-ily community. Haley the African American griot offered a bland, universalized, sentimental version of America's racial past that ob-fuscated religious and national differences and thus allowed *everyone* to dig for roots. This may well account for the work's huge popular multiracial, international success. It allowed European reader-viewers to revel in this saga of specifically *American* slavery and race history and to decry American racism and injustices, while also feeling that Haley's own triumphant success reassuringly suggests the smooth progress of his race. It enabled white British readers and audiences to weep their way through this story while resisting, until very recently, the recognition of a black Atlantic agenda that foregrounds the central British role in the slave trade and the nation's shabby national agenda on race. It also explains why Haley and his *Roots* are now regarded as culturally dubious by many historians and journalists and indeed a considerable embarrassment to key African American intellectuals.

SO, SHOULD WE CELEBRATE "ROOTS"?

Yet, in terms of a black *and* white Atlantic and a transatlantic flow of cultural exchanges, it is hard to dismiss *Roots* as having served a merely conservative cultural purpose. If we think of the lasting, if somewhat tired, heritage of *Gone With the Wind*, which has kept alive an ideologically more dubious image of the black and white South, it is churlish not to celebrate the success of a work that offered an alternative version of southern history and a countermyth of slavery. America had long needed a black *Gone With the Wind*, especially at bicentennial time, when the nation was being redefined and rededicated. In that first decade after the civil rights revolution of the 1960s, *Roots* was the ideal text, capturing the national imagination with its populist, upbeat narrative and style and its epic celebration of black pride, identity, and community. Other African American writers, such as Frank Yerby, Margaret Walker, Ishmael Reed, and Ernest Gaines, had produced works on the plantation theme, but Haley alone shared with his white predecessors Harriet Beecher Stowe, Thomas Dixon, and Margaret Mitchell a capacity to create a new myth for his times, and one that challenged and shifted—even if it could not overturn—the terms of that master narrative.

The iconic status of *Roots* gave a global audience a very different South, albeit one conservatively located in patriarchal American Africanism. It gave the American nation and the circum-Atlantic world a very *southern* fascination with, and flair for, genealogy and ancestral roots. And reparation, too: in 1998, Louisiana Cajun lawyer Walter Perrin issued a legal challenge to the British government, demanding an apology for the "ethnic cleansing" of French Acadians from Nova Scotia, Canada, in 1755. A fellow Cajun said, "I watched the re-run of Alex Haley's *Roots* on TV. I thought: hey what about *my* people?"[63] As Alice Walker said of the recirculations of her own family history: "We have the capability to connect to absolutely everyone and everything, and, in fact, we are all connected. . . . I discover that my family is like any other family in the world of our same class. When I write about my family, about things from the South, the people of China say, 'Why, this is very Chinese.'"[64]

Finally, Haley's family and community were black, with whites pushed to the margins and often shown in demonic (albeit caricatured) light. The ruptures and discontinuities of "his" ancestral line were demonstrably driven by the economics and politics of a slave system that was shown to be a shameful blot on American democracy and world history. In terms of recording, and giving imaginative life to, the long circum-Atlantic history of slavery, *Roots* deserves its success. Whether Alex Haley himself should be revered and celebrated is perhaps a different matter.

4

NEW ORLEANS, "AMERICA'S EUROPEAN MASTERPIECE"

The South of popular imagination is a rural rather than urban place. The South's best-known works—from *Gone With the Wind* to *Roots*, from Faulkner's novels, early blues, and country music to the Waltons— confirm in global imaginations a South of plantation, farm, and small town. The tone is rustic, nostalgic, parochial. Of course, the tensions between regions, between new city or large town and the plantation or small community, pervaded southern fiction, autobiography, and film throughout the nineteenth and twentieth centuries. But the "moonlight-and-magnolias" southern myth often led readers and audiences to romanticize or demonize the South as a site devoid of urban complexities and sophistications. Celebrated world centers—New York City, Los Angeles, and Chicago—are all geographically far removed and seem light-years away from their pale southern counterparts. And with the growing late-twentieth-century importance of the tourist industry, industrial, progressive cities such as Atlanta or Birmingham failed to make international imaginative impact by comparison with older towns conscious of their heritage, such as Charleston, Savannah, and Natchez. There is, however, one place that has long held a reputation as a crossover site for heterogeneous nationalities and ethnic and racial groups, a hybrid city that is both international in stature and ambition and rich in those historic and cultural associations that are music to the tourist industry's ears.

New Orleans is the single best example of a southern city that has profound historic and creative links with Europe and that reverberates through European culture. For tourists familiar with southern history and culture through music, film, and popular novels, New Orleans delights because it is both familiar and exotic: recognizably European in its English tongue and its French and Spanish ambience and cuisine; recognizably North American with the comforts of a streamlined airport, Superdome, convention hotels, and strip clubs; but also deliciously other because of its African and Caribbean peoples, music, and food. And, in recent years, through its increasing promotion via film, TV movie, novel, and advertisement, New Orleans has become a celluloid cliché, represented as it is predominantly through the French Quarter, an area that looks remarkably like a film set:

> sternwheelers, ferries, freighters, iron grillework, courtyard apartments, the Pontalba apartments, balconies, St. Louis Cathedral, courtyard restaurants, Jackson Square, strip joints, jazz funerals, horse and carriages, redneck policemen, crabs, shrimp, crawfish, Dixie beer, questionable politicians, Victorian mansions, voodoo, spanish moss, sex, violence, Bourbon Street, Creoles, Cajuns, the St. Charles streetcar, cemeteries, the Superdome, the Royal Sonesta Hotel, the Royal Orleans Hotel, Café du Monde, Mardi Gras, swamps, fans, French accents, Southern accents, prostitutes, fountains, magnolias, black children dancing, and Lake Pontchartrain.[1]

It is also the decadent city of our wildest dreams, as John Kennedy Toole's protagonist Ignatius O'Reilly describes it: "This city is a flagrant vice capital of the civilized world[?]. . . . This city is famous for its gamblers, prostitutes, exhibitionists, anti-Christs, alcoholics, sodomites, drug addicts, fetishists, onanists, pornographers, frauds, jades, litterbugs, and lesbians, all of whom are only too well protected by graft."[2]

So New Orleans is repeatedly presented, and represents itself, as a tourist city of consumption, pleasure, gothic horror, and grotesques, rather than as a city of considerable economic and social significance: the second-largest port in the United States, a shipbuilding and commercial center for offshore oil exploration and production, headquarters for the major multinational petroleum and chemical plants along the Mississippi River up to Baton Rouge, and a major university and convention city. Most memorable and most often repeated are images of an amazing mixture, a wild and somewhat out-of-control mélange of cultural experiences and phenomena: "the melting-pot within the American melting-pot."[3]

A natural hybridity and impurity are the very qualities that have characterized New Orleans throughout its history. For a start, it is a city founded in 1718 by the French on land already populated by Native Americans, transferred to the Spanish, restored to the French, and then sold by Napoleon, as part of the 1803 Louisiana Purchase, to the American government. Then there is the contradiction of a city that boasted a huge slave auction market and yet hosted the country's largest antebellum community of *gens de couleur libres*, many of whom had fled there from Haiti. As a result of all this, there has been semantic confusion (continuing to this day) over the term *Creole,* at different periods used to signify indigenous people of any race, white upper-class French and Spanish citizens, and French-speaking blacks. For these and other reasons, New Orleans has enjoyed a cosmopolitan and heterogeneous development that is reflected in its racial mixture and attitudes and its various cultural forms.

Known from its earliest period as "Paris-in-the-Wilderness," in the mid-nineteenth century it was called "the American Paris," and in the 1990s it is described in tourist literature as "America's European Masterpiece."[4] In 1968, Walker Percy called it "a most peculiar concoction of exotic and American ingredients, a gumbo of stray chunks of the South, of Latin and Negro oddments, German and Irish morsels"; historian Gwendolyn Midlo Hall argues that New Orleans "remains, in spirit, the most African city in the United States."[5] It is known for its relaxed style and ability to absorb multifarious cultural influences. Although this relaxation is often overstated (nowhere more so than in tourist literature), in its art, foodways, and music there has been a long tradition of fusion and hybridity that makes the city most appealing to both the U.S. visitor and the foreign tourist.

A MELTING POT IN THE MELTING POT

The term *melting pot* is particularly appropriate to New Orleans, for this city—often referred to as "the culinary capital of America"—is rarely discussed without recourse to culinary metaphor. Here cooking is an art form, food a "cuisine," and whatever else characters in New Orleans–based fiction, film, or tourist trip do, they certainly feast. The legend has it that the good and righteous go, not to heaven, but to the big kitchen in the sky. In tourist brochures, advertisements, film, and fiction alike, "Fat City" offers endless gustatory experiences to its inhabitants and visitors. New Orleans stories are almost bound to feature one of the well-known restaurants (Antoine's, Arnaud's, Brennan's) and often enough a recipe or two, while romance and murder alike are most often organized around the meal or drinks table.[6]

In addition, the city's characteristic and most famous dishes are notoriously eclectic, heterogeneous mixtures that speak of the city's mixed colonial and ethnic histories and conflicts. Its three best-known mixes are gumbo, jambalaya, and café au lait. The first two testify to that exciting fusion that is the best aspect of New Orleans life. Gumbo is a seafood or meat soup made with okra or filé (powdered sassafras leaf, as taught by the Choctaw Indians) and is often used to describe other kinds of New Orleans cultural mixtures; most notably it is the title of a famous 1945 collection of Louisiana folktales compiled by Lyle Saxon and others. "Gumbo" (from *gombo*, the African word for okra) is defined as meaning "EVERYBODY TALKS AT ONCE," while "gumbo ya-ya" is explained as a pejorative term for a gathering of gossiping women.[7] Jamabalaya is a combination of rice, onions, oysters, shrimp, ham, sausage, or other seafood and meat, with garlic and salt; reflecting the city's many ethnic origins and ingredients, "a bit of everything," it has come to stand for the city itself.[8] Ishmael Reed tasted jambalaya and immediately understood why it has "achieved the status, through lore, of a holy food . . . Hoodoo food. Syncretic: Spanish, African, Native American, French—adaptable to all cultures."[9] So, in the most optimistic and positive self-presentations, New Orleans culture can be seen to be regionally unique because of the very syncretism that is symbolized and best expressed through its cuisine.

More problematic, however, in terms of syncretism, is the city's world-famous drink, café au lait, which, together with the beignet (a kind of doughnut), features in virtually every cultural representation of the city. New Orleans's Café du Monde uses a chicory/coffee mix that is dark-roasted and double-dripped, then tempered with hot milk. A drink enjoyed in the city since the early nineteenth century, café au lait has metaphoric associations that are more problematic than those of gumbo and jambalaya. Rather like the West Indian "calalou," café au lait is a New Orleans term for mixed-race peoples, especially the famous nineteenth-century quadroons (one-quarter black). *Gumbo*

Ya-Ya documents the complicated business of nineteenth-century Creole courtship, including careful family investigations into possible "skeletons": "Even that really unmentionable consideration must be investigated; was there any possible trace of *café au lait*?"[10] Anne Rice's historically precise novel set in the 1840s, *The Feast of All Saints*, refers repeatedly to café au lait as the white term for quadroon, and there is a case of a white supremacist judge hearing cases in 1957 against white and black musicians, Kid Thomas and others, playing together and thus breaking segregation laws. His verdict? "We don't want Yankees coming to New Orleans mixing cream with our coffee."[11] This trope of mixture, then, is rarely simple or innocent, especially within New Orleans culture. Miscegenation is such a fraught and politically sensitive issue in the city's history, and throughout both its slavery and postemancipation periods such an unresolved area of conflict and difficulty, that it is not surprising that "mixing it" becomes such a sexually and racially loaded phrase.

In terms of mixing, the most significant event/metaphor for New Orleans is Mardi Gras, ideally that "gay time" festival in which people may enter "the utopian realm of community, freedom, equality, and abundance."[12] Mardi Gras (a festival that is shared by many Catholic cultures and is even better known in Latin American than North American culture) has long been celebrated and advertised within New Orleans as a festival in which that utopian realm is achieved, when all citizens and visitors are equal, allowed to *laisser les bons temps rouler*, to indulge in sexual, culinary, and alcoholic excesses free of censure, prohibition, or arrest. Tourist literature and TV programs feature large "the greatest free show on earth," and novels and movies set in the city often begin or culminate with the Mardi Gras processions and festivities. The majority of these emphasize the celebrations as the public expression of a basically hedonistic, mixed-up, democratically minded city, Mardi Gras open to and enjoyed by all, "a way of dreaming with others."[13] Lafcadio Hearn is only one of many outsiders to the city to be intoxicated by its hedonistic and yet poignantly short-lived charms:

> The night cometh in which we take no note of time, and forget that we are living in a practical age which mostly relegates romance to printed pages and merriment to the state: and the glorious night is approaching . . . and the blue river is bearing us fleets of white boats thronged with strangers who doubtless are dreaming of lights

and music, the tepid, perfumed air of Rex's Palace . . . who will dance the dance of the Carnival until blue day puts out at once the trembling tapers of the stars and lights of the great ball.[14]

Some of New Orleans's commentators have, however, been more brutally truthful about Mardi Gras's utopian charms. Elitist social groups that, in the late nineteenth century, began to invent archaisms such as "krewe" and references to English literary nomenclature still exist to privilege particular social groups and exclude undesirable races and social groups from the most prestigious carnival events. Immediately after the Civil War and emancipation, the Irish used Mardi Gras as "Get Nigger Day," invading Negro neighborhoods to shoot and murder. Carnival became a defiant stand for white supremacy (the Negro gorilla king was crowned at the Comus ball) and for Catholic supremacy (the Jewish Baron de Rothschild was denied entrance to Comus and Proteus elite balls formed in 1882). The Confederate flag had flown from every balcony and rooftop. Mark Twain blamed what he saw as the antidemocratic nonsense of Mardi Gras's kings, knights, and krewes on Walter Scott, and writers from Walker Percy to Ishmael Reed have commented on its many discriminatory practices, especially against black participation.[15] Until the now notorious December 1991 Mardi Gras Ordinance, instigated by the city council to desegregate carnival parades, there had been no mixed black-white float in the city parades, and only one predominantly black float, Zulu, was allowed on the parade route. It is a measure of the superficiality of the melting pot, and the fragility of the racial mixture, that the ordinance—far from bringing all citizens together around a truly mixed carnival—led to three long-established "krewes" (Comus, Momus, and Proteus) disbanding their parades altogether rather than desegregate, and only one major krewe, Rex, integrating; even then, sex discrimination was allowed as a concession to the traditionally all-male parade. "Gay time" mingling and the ludic "Bottoms up!" transgressions of carnival time cannot obscure the many problems and conflicts that exist in this southern city that—despite its boasts of being the City That Care Forgot—does not forget that easily. As Joseph Roach reminds us: "In an ethnically complex and divided city . . . carnival tradition asserts and enforces historic claims of entitlement, priority, and exclusivity. . . . At carnival time, race serves as a master trope for a broad spectrum of exclusionary designs and practices: classism, anti-semitism, sexism."[16]

NEW ORLEANS AND EUROPE

While racial and ethnic divisions continued to scar New Orleans's sociocultural life, the European connections remained romantically mythified:

> In 1717, she was a mere flicker in the eyes of the French. A year later she was christened on the banks of a great river—a Creole princess born in the new Louisiana Territory. She lived among the Choctaw and Chickasaw; explored dark shadowy bayous; lazed on sun-drenched shores; and battled flood and disease. She knew swaggering pirates; and scarifying voodoo secrets. The Spaniards adorned her with architectural splendors; but her proud French Creole origins were apparent everywhere. She warmly welcomed the fun-loving Cajuns who came in 1763, gifting her with incomparable zest. She discovered in herself a natural instinct for soul-stirring music; her cuisine was truly exotic. By the time she became an American citizen in 1803 she was quite famous, as Europeans flocked to her door. That little waif on the waterfront was named New Orleans, and she grew up to be the European Queen of the Mississippi.[17]

These words, from a tourist pamphlet, remind us that in contemporary discourse the most extravagant language celebrating regional characteristics is often to be found in promotional literature. All those French terms—most notably "Vieux Carré" for French Quarter—remind us strongly of the city's foundation in the unpromising swamps by the Frenchman Jean-Baptiste le Moyne, Sieur de Bienville. The resolutely feminine creature evoked here is a reminder of that other tourist city, Paris, which is known to be "the West's most seductive city . . . 'essentially a city of pleasure and amusements.'"[18] When it comes to Paris and New Orleans, the license and decadence of both are always enlarged within the imaginations of repressed Puritan Anglo-Saxons, on both sides of the pond.

Of course, Paris and New Orleans are not alone in having their imaginative geography configured in terms of the sensual body. Urban spatiality has become "recharged with multiple sexualities, eroticisms, and desires. . . . [Cityspace] is literally and figuratively transgressed with an abundance of sexual possibilities and pleasures, dangers and opportunities."[19] In terms of North America, the South is especially so. As Diane Roberts points out, white writers and commentators from the earliest colonial days have eroticized the South and seen it (in

Bakhtinian terms) as the nation's grotesque body, its "domestic Orient."[20] Even in its earliest preslavery narratives, the South was represented as a female body "to be penetrated, ravished, exploited and impregnated, a landscape of breasts and genitals displayed for the 'use' and 'enjoyment' of the European coloniser"; with slavery, the South became eroticized because of the association of Africans with sexuality. New Orleans, with its large slave market and quadroon balls (where free women of color were chosen by wealthy white planters as formal mistresses, *plaçées*), is seen again and again as the most "oriental"—meaning sexually secretive—city of the whole South.

And in twentieth-century literary texts, film, and advertising, that oriental flavor keeps recurring, expressed in obsessive focus on, and analysis of, such aspects of the city's history and character as the system of plaçage, Storyville, and sexual license, as well as images of the city as a continuing site of forbidden, clandestine desires and sinful pursuits. No wonder Joseph Roach sees New Orleans as representing "the nation's libido," as becoming a feminized "ludic space, the behavioral vortex, for the rest of the nation."[21] It is significant that Storyville in particular, that licensed prostitution district of turn-of-the-century New Orleans associated with Buddy Bolden and Louis Armstrong, has proved a topic of international fascination for cultural producers of all kinds.[22]

Today, despite the designation of southwest Louisiana as "America's Caribbean Coast," tourist literature and journalists' articles tend to yoke New Orleans firmly to its *European* rather than other cultural and racial roots. The New Orleans Tourist and Convention Commission refers to "America's European Masterpiece." The Windsor Court Hotel boasts a decor of seventeenth- to twentieth-century art and antiques, with a "decided emphasis on works which depict Windsor Castle and the Royal Family life"; it offers "afternoon tea in the informal atmosphere of Le Salon." (Indeed, the hotel's owners, the Anglophile Coleman family, of German-Jewish origin, bizarrely erected a statue of Winston Churchill near the river and were rewarded by being made honorary British consuls).[23] A 1990s Virgin brochure proclaims New Orleans as "A VERY AMERICAN FRENCH CITY . . . The street names will give you a clue—we have hotels in RUE DAUPHINE and RUE DECATUR—a far cry from the usual West 34th Street!" Europeanness still carries the main burden of historical weight and profundity, the very associations that are seen as central to New Orleans's "difference." And indeed, that sense of history is real enough, a factor that draws European tourists to the city and sets it apart from postmodern hyperreality. Umberto Eco claimed that, after visiting the "recreated New Orleans" in Disneyland, he welcomed the "real city": "[It] represents a still intact past, because the Vieux Carré is one of the few places that American civilization hasn't remade, flattened, replaced. . . . In New Orleans, history still exists and is tangible."[24] Echoing these sentiments is southern critic Lewis P. Simpson, who sees New Orleans as a typical postcolonial *southern* city, in which southerners live "in the anxiety of an unresolved tension between memory and history" and thus "live in the historical actuality of the modern world rather than in the illusion of a 'postmodern' world."[25]

And who can blame the commercial sector for marketing New Orleans as European? From the nineteenth century, it is the Vieux Carré's French Catholic Creole culture and lifestyle, infused and enriched by African cultural influences, that have attracted writers and visitors—from Mark Twain and Lafcadio Hearn to Zora Neale Hurston, Jewell Parker Rhodes, and Fatima Shaik. All have sought that combination of what Lewis Lawson claims Walker Percy liked, "an Anglo-Saxon seriousness of purpose and a Mediterranean mellowness."[26] Mellow yes, and wicked, too. As early as 1848, when Walt Whitman visited, Justin Kaplan claims it already had a reputation as "the wickedest city in Christendom," and even Tennessee Williams expressed shock at the sexual freedoms he witnessed when first visiting the city where he lost his virginity and that would later become his spiritual home.[27] James Baldwin's preacher stepfather left Louisiana partly, according to biographer James Campbell, "because his puritan soul recoiled at the prospect of New Orleans, with its vaudeville associations, as a new-world Sodom and Gomorrah," and the Sodom and Gomorrah image is one gently cultivated in tourist literature, amply explored in fiction and film.[28] Tourist leaflets call it the Big Easy, the City That Care Forgot, where you should *laisser les bons temps rouler*, a city of "naughty entertainment and an ongoing celebration of the joy of life."[29] A British journalist drew on all the familiar clichés in her enthusiastic endorsement: "New Orleans is a study of contrasts: of saints and sinners, of hot cuisine and cool jazz. A frenzied party town by night, the only place in America where it's legal to drink on the streets."[30] Often, northern characters or references remind us strongly that it's "a different language down here."

This "different language," all this wickedness, was often associated with its foundation as a *French*, thus feminized, city, one associated with "feminine" frivolity and pleasure-loving naughtiness. Tourist brochures refer to it as "the Queen of the Mississippi" and "the Queen City," a "carefree lady [with] a fabulous flair for gracious entertaining." Grace King, a Protestant writing of her native city as early as 1895, saw New Orleans as "not a Puritan mother, nor a hardy Western pioneeress . . . simply a Parisian" who was "tyrannical in her loves, high-tempered, luxurious, pleasure-loving."[31] Thirty years later, in his *New Orleans Sketches*, William Faulkner noted many of the same qualities, though for him this Parisian lady was a "courtesan, not old and yet no longer young . . . [who] lives in an atmosphere of a bygone and more gracious age . . . a courtesan whose hold is strong upon the mature, to whose charm the young must respond."[32] In 1962, novelist Hamilton Basso, who was born and lived in New Orleans through the 1920s, described the city as "'a Creole version of the Left Bank,' claiming he had 'Paris in [his] own backyard.'"[33]

However, despite its literary celebration as French, or more generally a "European Masterpiece," it is sometimes unclear which part of Europe it most resembles. Because of a certain promiscuity of national styles, it has been compared with other port cities or other tourist haunts. Simone de Beauvoir wrote of the two-story houses that remind one of France or Spain: "They have the serenity of Anjou or Touraine, but the balconies in wrought iron painted green remind you of Cordova or the iron window grilles of Arab palaces; an Andalusian warmth pervades the silence. Here the exotic is no longer Mexican or Indian; it is French."[34] John Kennedy Toole's epigraph to his comic novel *A Confederacy of Dunces* comes from A. J. Liebling's *The Earl of Louisiana*:

> New Orleans resembles Genoa or Marseilles, or Beirut or the Egyptian Alexandria more than it does New York, although all seaports resemble one another more than they can resemble any place in the interior. Like Havana and Port-au-Prince, New Orleans is within the orbit of a Hellenistic world that never touched the North Atlantic. The Mediterranean, Caribbean and Gulf of Mexico form a homogeneous, though interrupted sea.

And although the African American "Creole" presence is widely celebrated in terms of music and cuisine, there is a far stronger European flavor to the city's literary culture and promotional materials. I suggest that New Orleans, now a major convention and gambling city, markets itself as European, and particularly French, both in order to emphasize its sophistication, old-world dignity, and charm, precisely to avoid the racy, criminal associations of port cities, and in order to downplay the influence of Afro-American culture via the Caribbean (not to mention that uncomfortable part of New Orleans's slave history). For predominantly white U.S. and European tourists, analogies with North Africa, Marseilles, and the West Indies may prove a disincentive to visit; a Parisian-style Catholic bohemian jewel set within a puritan Protestant nation is probably easier to sell to the international tourist and convention set.

NEW ORLEANS ON THE LITERARY MAP

This New Orleans, defined in terms of exoticism and "difference," has long been featured in cultural representations of many kinds. From accounts by nineteenth-century British and American travelers such as Fanny Kemble, Harriet Martineau, William Thackeray, Fanny Trollope, and Mark Twain to those of the city's most celebrated resident artists such as John James Audubon, Walt Whitman, Louis Armstrong, Lyle Saxon, and William Faulkner, New Orleans's dramatic and romantic history, architecture, and art forms have become familiar cultural reference points. New Orleans appears repeatedly in song, film, advertisement, and moody photograph/poster.

But it was a *dramatic* text that noticeably accelerated this process of audience familiarity with images of the city. The huge worldwide success of Tennessee Williams's *A Streetcar Named Desire* (1947), and its subsequent film version (directed by Elia Kazan, 1951), placed the city firmly on America's postwar cultural map. One critic argues that *Streetcar* started the process that has led to the city becoming "shrouded . . . in a literary mystique that for many, both residents and outsiders, has replaced the reality."[35] In Britain, the play's title is alluded to in advertisements (Lotus cars, for example), newspaper headlines, even a murder report. When British tourist Adrian Strasser was murdered in the city in April 1993, reporters made much of his enthusiasm for the film *The Big Easy* and especially of his murderer's origins in the rundown subdivision "Desire."

Blanche DuBois's famous journey on the streetcar "Desire," which transferred to "Cemeteries" and stopped at "Elysian Fields," has confirmed the city's literary trajectory as one linking desire and death, the romantic and gothic. Those colorful subjects of nineteenth-century New Orleans history—the "basket girls," plaçage, miscegenation, the Black Codes, Congo Square rituals, yellow fever plagues, Marie Laveau and voodoo, Jean Lafitte the pirate and the Battle of New Orleans, the riverboat, and Storyville—have remained favorites of popular genre fiction. Indeed, New Orleans–themed genre writing is a staple of bookstores on both sides of the Atlantic. A typical example of the extravagant local color in which the city is often saturated is this cover blurb from a popular romance, *Bayou*:

> The passionate saga of a plantation family whose fortune was built by slaves and destroyed by mixed blood. . . . Where four generations of the Leblanc dynasty bear the curse of unbridled power over the bodies and souls of the slaves. . . . Where the Leblanc men and women pursue their forbidden lusts in exotic octoroon balls, opulent New Orleans salons and sweltering marshlands. . . . Where Carita Leblanc, the ravishing new plantation mistress, uncovers the secret world of mixed blood and deep-seeded [*sic*] guilt and is driven to an act of unspeakable violence—hurling this once proud family into scandal, ruin and murder.[36]

Racial struggles, miscegenation, and conflicts within the city's distinct ethnic and racial groups all feature in New Orleans's literary and dramatic heritage, from the skeptical late-nineteenth-century pens of George Washington Cable and Alice Dunbar-Nelson, through the literary experimentations of the 1920s *Double Dealer* literary magazine and the 1930s Black Unit of the Works Progress Administration, to the 1970s Congo Square Writers' Workshop, and the 1980s–1990s renaissance of New Orleans–based writers from Sheila Bosworth and James Lee Burke to Poppy Z. Brite and Kalamu ya Salaam.

The exotic and chaotic mixtures of peoples, languages, religions, and social practices within a relatively insular yet culturally vibrant city have attracted writers and provided them with ample literary fodder. Unusual among southern cities, this is one that has developed a memorable literature about itself, producing classic texts that keep the city alive in international culture: Kate Chopin's *The Awakening* (1899), E. J. Bellocq's *Storyville Portraits* (1912), William Faulkner's *Absalom, Absalom!* (1936), Louis Armstrong's *My Life in New Orleans* (1955), Tennessee Williams's *Streetcar* and *Suddenly Last Summer* (1958), and John Kennedy Toole's *A Confederacy of Dunces*.[37] Women writers have made a major contribution to this literature. Gender issues have always been at the heart of the city's most fraught and interesting historical crises, and those literary forms that have always attracted women readers—the romance and the gothic—lend themselves readily to the city's lush excesses. In the final decades of the twentieth century, women played a significant role in putting the city on the literary map, from Pulitzer Prize–winning Shirley Anne Grau and celebrated Ellen Gilchrist to the detective fiction writers Julie Smith and Chris Wiltz and gothic romancers Valerie Martin and Jewelle Gomez.[38]

ANNE RICE, NEW ORLEANS, AND EUROPE

By the end of the century, Anne Rice had become the most spectacular New Orleans literary success story. Not only did she bathe the city in literary glory through her fiction, but she also became a major asset to New Orleans tourism through her public tributes to its beauties, her purchase of several grand houses in the Garden District, and her welcoming of fans as visitor/worshipers. She has been referred to as "the best spokesperson for New Orleans," its "writer in residence," who has made more literary use of the city than any other and whose First Street house became one of the most recognized and photographed buildings.[39]

Anne Rice's literary career began outside the city, in geographical exile and emotional trauma, and as a result her enchanted obsession with the New Orleans of her birthplace and later residence exudes nostalgic yearning and a deep sense of loss. While Rice and her husband were living in San Francisco, their six-year-old daughter, Michele, died of leukemia, and after a prolonged period of alcoholic depression, Rice wrote her first novel, *Interview with the Vampire*, in five weeks in an attempt to exorcise grief.[40] The novel focused on the story of Louis, a vampire, who—in a bold literary innovation—tells his tale to a young reporter. He has engaged in an existential quest for the meaning of his immortality, across two centuries and throughout America and Europe. He recounts a long series of erotic and violent adventures, as well as anguished relationships with other vampires, notably Lestat, who created him; Armand, the Parisian vampire whom he loves; and the five-year-old Claudia, whom he makes into a vampire.

The novel has been interpreted biographically as Rice's literary challenge to the finality of her child's early death, the parallels between Michele and Claudia readily acknowledged by the writer herself. It has also been read as a postmodern reworking of gothic and vampire fiction, as well as a contemporary fable about polymorphous sexuality, the marginalized and alienated outsider (in social, sexual, and racial terms), millennial panics, and especially the AIDS epidemic of the final decades of the century. *Interview* also drew on Rice's childhood memories of, and adult longings for, the Catholic, antipuritan, Europeanized city of her desire, New Orleans, a city that is drawn into transatlantic webs of personal connections and journeys.

The huge commercial success of this novel, its immediate sale of film rights, and its later triumphant 1994 film version, directed by Neil Jordan and starring Hollywood heartthrobs Tom Cruise and Brad Pitt, created a vast international following for the writer. It stimulated an Anne Rice industry that she has helped choreograph, through both a prolific output of sequels and series—the Vampire Chronicles, the Mayfair Witches sequence—and other historical, gothic, and erotic novels (the latter under the pseudonym Anne Rampling, after the British actress, Charlotte). Rice has also created a feminist literary controversy by publishing (what she insists on calling hard-core) pornography under the French pen name A. N. Roquelaure.

Anne Rice's fiction follows earlier New Orleans writing and film in defining the city through its Catholic rather than Protestant culture, one inflected by its multicultural waves of immigration, from France, Spain, the Caribbean, Ireland, and Germany. The daughter of Irish parents, she was christened Howard Allen O'Brien but changed her own first name to Anne; she later adopted her husband's family name. As a child, she lived between two very different social and ethnic groups, on the borders of the wealthy "American" Garden District and the poorer "Irish Channel" section of the city. Her novels all reflect that early formation as a marginal, hybrid figure who learned early in life how to cross borders. For her many enthusiastic readers, she evokes the city's cultural mixtures, luxuriant landscape, and damp and oppressively sensual climate, as well as its architectural extravagances, from the Vieux Carré in the Vampire Chronicles to the Garden District in the Mayfair Witches sequence. She draws knowledgeably on the city's topography and history and captures the romance and horror of a city built below sea level, existing on sinking ground and borrowed time. Her characters live and move between Europe—Paris, Renaissance Venice, the Scottish Highlands, London, imperial Rome—and North America, returning obsessively to New Orleans.

Rice's Europe is a dark, gothic space that haunts and troubles its American southern characters but also offers magical, liberatory ideas and imaginative sites unavailable within a North American Protestant culture. Her literary influences derive as much from film as from literature, but her early reading of European writers profoundly informed her style. She acknowledges the early influence of the Brontë sisters, Dostoevski, Flaubert, Dickens, and Nabokov and, in Berkeley, where she studied in the 1960s, of European philosophers such as Nietzsche, Camus, and Sartre. Critics see in the anguished concern with the human condition that pervades Rice's gothics intertextual references to romantic and gothic English writers from Lord Byron and Mary Shelley to Bram Stoker and Robert Louis Stevenson, and Rice herself pays tribute to European influences Aristotle (for the importance of "spectacle"), Shakespeare (excitement and surprise), and J. Sheridan Le Fanu and Algernon Blackwood (horror).[41] Dickens's grotesques are explicitly referred to intertextually in several novels (most notably, the first Mayfair Witches novel, *The Witching Hour*); indeed, at a "Memnoch Ball" held at Anne Rice's home, one room was designated "Miss Havisham's Room," holding as it did a huge replica of the wedding cake enshrined by Dickens's doomed character in *Great Expectations*.

Indeed, Rice's main literary persona is one she defined early on as "a cultivated 'European' voice," while her two alter egos, Anne Rampling and A. N. Roquelaure, were felt to allow more "racy" literary play and generic experimentation. The novels are portentously prefaced with quotations from Julian of Norwich, John Donne, William Blake, W. B. Yeats, and E. M. Forster. Furthermore, there is a growing ambition in the writing, with the fifth volume of the Vampire Chronicles, *Memnoch the Devil*, pitting the Devil against God, in Dantean or Miltonic mode; a history of Christ is promised. But even more than literary texts, European films and directors feature large in her writing; movies are a greater passion in her life than fiction, as fans discover when they call her home Ansaphone message and are advised which recent movie to go see.[42] Given that Rice was a student on the West Coast in the late 1960s, it is no surprise that her inspiration derives from the films of Bergman, Fellini, Antonioni, and Truffaut, though tellingly the movies she repeatedly cites in interviews are romantic, erotic classics *Rebecca, Jane Eyre, The Bride of Frankenstein,* and *Gone With the Wind,* with a soupçon of postmodern chic, in *Angel Heart* and *Alien.* Her ambitious oeuvre attempts to break down the usual barriers between the European gothic and romantic traditions, the Hollywood vampire and gothic romance, and an existential, even theological concern with the meaning of human life and death. It seems Rice wishes to place herself and her native city within a noble tradition of European and transatlantic art and artists: "As Van Gogh found his inspiration in Arles, the 'lost generation' found theirs in Paris, I have found my aesthetic in New Orleans."[43]

Certainly, New Orleans should be grateful to Anne Rice. Her novels, and the film version of *Interview with the Vampire,* have created a whole new set of menacing, mysterious, and erotic associations for this city that thrives on its decadent reputation. Her Web site contains some of the most lavish personal advertisements the city has ever seen.[44] Tourist fans, many of whom had never visited the city before reading the book and seeing the film, were drawn to the sites in the French Quarter where Louis and Lestat had lurked, and then rode the streetcar into the Garden District to gawk at Anne Rice's Greek Revival mansion and her vast home and offices in the old St. Elizabeth's Orphanage. Besides, until recent years, Rice was always very open and generous to her readers and interviewers, assuring them that her own houses provided the actual settings she described in the fiction and encouraging them to attend book signings (to one of which she was delivered in a coffin), photograph her Garden District mansions, join the Lestat Fan Club, visit her doll museum, send for her "Commotion Strange" newsletters and "Kith and Kin" merchandise, and write, e-mail, and phone her at any time. This publicity savoir faire has certainly swollen the ranks of her Internet-using European following, largely among young and gay readers, and the demand for her books and films is huge. Her gay son, Chris Rice, looks set to cash in on this success by following her example of setting his first novel, the murder mystery *A Density of Souls,* in New Orleans.[45]

Rice's appearance of accessibility to the fans, together with a reassurance of her own personal saturation in and solemnity about the vampire myth, has proved a shrewd commercial move but also a potentially dangerous step. In the 1990s, like that other highly successful horror writer Stephen King, Rice found that life can imitate art only too uncomfortably: just as his novel *Rage* was found in a schoolboy's locker after the brutal school shootings that had imitated events in the story, so four Kentucky teenage "vampires" (one of whom had seen the video version of *Interview* more than twenty times) murdered two adults before attempting to drive South to Anne Rice's home.[46] Rice's eager weaving of her fans into her own fantastic web has dramatically declined as she grows more protective about her personal health, security, and privacy, and she (not to mention her fellow citizens) perhaps wishes to distance herself from those who take her fiction too literally to heart. Nevertheless, with the publication of various authorized and unauthorized guides to her work and its relationship to New Orleans and the brisk trade enjoyed by travel agents and book and record stores (Britain's pop star Sting recorded "Moon over Bourbon Street" in tribute to *Interview with the Vampire*), Rice has become the city's best-known writer and international publicist.[47] Her voluminous New Orleans–based body of fiction may well seal the city's international reputation in the twenty-first century, surpassing that of any other writer, including Tennessee Williams, and perhaps overtaking that of the city's other monumental cultural heritage, jazz.

THE BIRTHPLACE AND "AUTHENTICITY WELL" OF JAZZ

It is, of course, the *music* of New Orleans that is both most familiar and most globally celebrated. Whatever other associations Europeans may have with the city, it is as the "birthplace of jazz" that it will probably always be remembered. New Orleans music of all kinds is well known and celebrated in Europe, and France in particular has played a major role in keeping alive, through recordings and concerts, some of the greatest performers and performances. In Britain, where there is an informed and enthusiastic following, jazz and soul musicians such as Wynton Marsalis, The Dirty Dozen Brass Board, Fats Domino, the Neville Brothers, and "Dr. John" are sold out all over the country. The output of legendary songwriters and musicians such as Frankie Ford, Clarence "Frogman" Henry, The Dixie Cups, Allen Toussaint, and The Meters is so widely known and reproduced that it no longer carries the resonance of its native city.

Dixieland jazz, however, is a different matter, and for a certain generation of white male Englishmen it defined popular music in a way that has inspired their loyalty since the 1940s and 1950s. Many of them describe listening with delight to 1940s BBC Light Programme's "Jazz Club" after the football results, hanging around record shops, and sharing records with school friends and brothers. Several of them began to play jazz and entered enthusiastically into the 1950s New Orleans revival that swept Europe. New Orleans jazz musicians still find a very warm welcome when they visit Europe, coming from the "authenticity well" to play predominantly for white audiences. The annual jazz festival held beneath the Brecon Beacons Mountains in Wales has long been known as "New Orleans under The Beacons." In 1996, Woody Allen's New Orleans Jazz Band could have filled the Royal Festival Hall many times over, and obituaries of New Orleans jazzmen appear in the newspapers. British doyens inspired by the city's jazz after World War II, household names such as Humphrey Lyttleton, Lonnie Donegan, Chris Barber, Alexis Korner, Acker Bilk, and George Melly, are still playing from Manchester to Milford Haven before sizable audiences. In my hometown, Bristol, The Old Duke pub is a recognized center of live New Orleans jazz; in 1997 the controlling breweries were forced to keep it open as a jazz venue after a flood of letters objected to their proposed closure. Record shop owners and private collectors hoard and treasure precious "78s" and discuss historic recordings. Scholarship on blues and jazz, including the history of New Orleans music, by British enthusiasts such as Paul Oliver, John Broven, and John Chilton has been internationally revered. In 1995, the Manchester-based Oriole marching-band grand marshal Peter Horsfield was given a New Orleans–style jazz funeral and laid to rest in full regalia (bowler hat, sash, and brolly), accompanied by a thirteen-piece band in four-step shuffle.[48]

Following the lead of American rock singers such as Randy Newman, British and Irish musicians have recorded in and about the city. Paul McCartney, Van Morrison, and Elvis Costello know New Orleans well, and the Rolling Stones, who have long demonstrated their fascination for the city's charms, made it the focus of an album, a CD-ROM, *Voodoo Lounge* (1995), and a global chain of Voodoo Lounge club-restaurants.[49] Like others, the Stones have been drawn to the city's exoticism and eclectic culture, which invite a creative fusion and flow. Dave Gelly described New Orleans music as "so potent, so stirring, so irresistible," rejoicing in the fact it is "a natural hybrid . . . glorious impurity."[50] From non–New Orleanians, albums such as *Voodoo Lounge* and Robbie Robertson's *Storyville* (1991) and individual songs such as the Animals' "House of the Rising Sun" and Randy Newman's "New Orleans Wins the War" demonstrate the possibilities of interracial, interregional, and international intermixture. It is perhaps significant that *Coming through Slaughter*, the much acclaimed novel about the city's jazz pioneer Buddy Bolden, was written not by a New Orleanian African American but by Michael Ondaatje, a Sri Lankan who lives in Toronto.[51]

Nevertheless, despite this mixture and fusion of styles and origins, the major claim New Orleans has on the history of world music is its status as the "birthplace of jazz." This confers on it a quality of authenticity and purity that sets it apart from all other music-making cities (many of which have surpassed it in terms of commercial and popular musical success). It gives a historical solidity to New Orleans and helps explain its magnetism for European music critics and enthusiasts—even when the city's music is known only through recordings. Peter Linebaugh said, "The ship remained perhaps the most important conduit of Pan-African communication before the appearance of the long-playing record"; and Paul Gilroy discusses the movement of the slave ship between Europe, America, Africa, and the Caribbean as image of a redemptive return to the African homeland, through the modern circulation of ideas and cultural and political artifacts—"tracts, books, gramophone records, and choirs."[52] Without doubt, the jazz record and radio broadcasting became crucial not only in Pan-African communication but also, especially since World War II, in black and white Atlantic cultural dialogue and exchange.

It is one of the ironies of the diffusion of New Orleans jazz that the first gramophone record to sell a million copies was "Livery Stable Blues," an imitation of "hot" black jazz played in 1917 by the white Original Dixieland Jazz Band (soon to sink into oblivion). It is also ironic that, from being a subversive, vernacular urban "devil's music" in its early days, jazz quickly became identified as a mainstream cultural art form for international audiences. When, in the 1930s, Louis Armstrong and Duke Ellington traveled to Europe to escape American racial prejudice, they found jazz treated seriously, the jazz musician celebrated as artist rather than entertainer; Dizzy Gillespie has noted sardonically that "jazz is too good for Americans."[53]

There is no doubt that jazz is the greatest achievement of African

American culture, its major conceptual innovators all black; nevertheless, from the outset it was played by mixed-race and white musicians and mixed European form with African rhythm. It often suits jazz fans to romanticize the origins of the form, seeing it as a pure music that sprang from untutored, inspired black men living in a "birthplace" city that then brought "disciples" to hear and learn. Modern scholarship has, however, emphasized the complex evolution of jazz, deriving not from the segregation of races and thus pouring directly from the hearts and instruments of former slaves and their sons but rather from the assimilative, urban mix of races and styles, not to mention musical instruments within late-nineteenth-century New Orleans.[54] Jazz musicians still work with those European forms of bar lines, diatonic chords, chord sequences, and four-bar units of melody—all taken over from musical forms such as the march, folk song, and popular song that had arrived from Europe during the nineteenth century and already permeated the blues form that preceded jazz.

The "black Atlantic" cultural movement between North America, Europe, and Africa led jazz musicians such as Dexter Gordon to Denmark, Coleman Hawkins and Bud Powell to France. The "international language" that jazz provides is today derived from its truly international roots: "Jazz was always hybrid, always an inspired accident. Any search for authenticity or roots will be in vain."[55] Furthermore, New Orleans is a city in which musicians play with a number of different bands and individuals, often without special billing, preparation, or pay, in informal, shifting patterns that emphasize *performance* rather than appearance or recording. Throughout its history, New Orleans has combined dance with instrumental performance, inviting audience participation and response: "Come join the parade."

In this context, it is difficult (indeed futile) to search for authentic origins of black music, especially as it progresses further beyond those earliest forms and years. Paul Gilroy describes the bitter conflict between trumpeters Wynton Marsalis and Miles Davis: the former sees himself as custodian of "jazz tradition"; the latter espoused a creative "fusion." "The past is dead. Jazz is dead," Davis told an interviewer of Marsalis, and in his autobiography he wrote: "They got Wynton playing some old dead European music. . . . Wynton's playing their dead shit, the kind of stuff anybody can do. . . . I told him I wouldn't bow down to that music, that they should be glad someone as talented as he is is playing that tired-ass shit."[56] Gilroy's own argument, closer to Davis's than Marsalis's position (and making a strong argument for the importance of hip-hop culture), reminds the reader that music, preeminent in the diverse black communities of the Atlantic diaspora, has a history of "borrowing, displacement, transformation, and continual reinscription" that belies any model of fixity and rootedness.[57] Indeed, he suggests that in both literature and music, when African American artists moved to Europe (Jessie Fauset and Gwendolyn Bennett to Paris, Quincy Jones to Sweden, and Donald Byrd to Paris) the direction of black culture was significantly changed and reinvigorated—as with the revival of jazz as popular form in the early 1970s. The practice of antiphony involves new social relationships, meetings, and conversations "between one fractured, incomplete, and unfinished racial self and others."[58] And because music circulates and changes as it goes, it is impossible to place Africa as authentic, pure origin against the Americas of "hybridity, creolisation, and rootlessness."[59] The "chronotope of the crossroads" can describe a two-way traffic between African cultural forms and the political cultures of diaspora blacks over a long period. And, while one recognizes the creative fusions across a *black* Atlantic, it is also possible to see this creative transformation and dialogue as another crossroads: a *black and white* circum-Atlanticism that has both embraced and engaged with all kinds of African American music and also actively kept alive and reinvigorated the reception of musical forms. There are many European instances of this, but I wish to examine two specific British examples to illustrate this fruitful and complex reciprocity.

NEW ORLEANS JAZZ IN BRITAIN: THE KEN COLYER TRUST

On 18 April 1995, trumpeter Humphrey Lyttleton and the jazz-loving Conservative chancellor of the exchequer, Kenneth Clarke, unveiled a plaque outside the basement club Studio 51, Great Newport Street, London. It commemorated the musician Ken Colyer, who had played jazz there between 1950 and 1973 and who had died in 1988, too early to benefit from the trust set up in his name to care for him in his old age. That same year, the New Orleans City Council issued a formal proclamation: "BE IT PROCLAIMED BY THE CITY OF NEW ORLEANS that this Council recognizes 'The Ken Colyer Trust' and welcomes them to New Orleans."[60]

Ken Colyer is widely acknowledged to be the inspiration of the British New Orleans revival of the 1950s. He was first excited by 1940s recordings of Bunk Johnson, who was brought out of retirement to revive the great tradition of twenties musicians such as King Oliver and Jelly-Roll Morton and whose "78" gramophone records found their way to London's HMV shop counter. Colyer founded the Crane River Jazz Band to play "authentic" New Orleans music, and a dedicated group of followers gathered around them. In a perfect "Boys' Own" turn of events, the young Ken joined the merchant navy, hoping to land in New Orleans. The nearest port at which he docked was Mobile, Alabama, but he made his way to Louisiana and offered himself as the late Bunk Johnson's replacement in the residue of his band, led by George Lewis. He became leader and trumpet player for Lewis and then played trumpet with the Kid Orry Band; the only white British player in town, in one trust member's words he "thought like a coloured man."[61] He became something of a legend himself when he failed to renew his work permit on time; on Christmas Eve he was arrested, jailed for a night, and then deported.

Returning to England, he assembled a band of players who have since acquired high reputations, Lonnie Donegan, Chris Barber, and Monty Sunshine. The band had a short life, but it did manage to make a long-playing record from which the single "Isle of Capri" entered the Top Ten record charts. In 1988, when Colyer died at the age of fifty-nine, an "Early Day Motion" was passed in the British Parliament to praise his life and work. The Ken Colyer Trust was established by his friends, such as John Long, who had also bought Bunk Johnson records after the war and become fanatical about "pure" jazz. It began with £120 being put into a hat and by the mid-1990s had a turnover of approximately £40,000 a year from membership fees, concerts, sales of tapes, and memorabilia of various kinds. The Ken Colyer Trust Band is regularly booked at seaside meetings and theaters around the country, often playing alongside loyal friends such as Bilk and Kenny Ball, and it tours Europe annually, including Holland, Sweden, Denmark, and Germany. Ken Colyer's Band is credited by the trust with introducing American popular music to Europe after the war, and Paul McCartney (whose first band, The Quarrymen, played in the interval of a Colyer concert) agrees that it is owed a major debt by all popular musicians. The trust is committed to keeping New Orleans jazz alive, not only through performance and publications for devotees but also through educational and support programs for young musicians and students.

Every year, there is a trust trip to New Orleans, organized by a travel company, the Diplomatic Traveler, which takes devotees to the city of origins to meet musicians (including British-born players now resident in the city, such as Les Muscutt and Tommy Burton), to listen to authentic jazz, to eat and drink, and from time to time to play music as well. In both 1995 and 1996, the Trust Band played at the city's French Quarter Festival and appeared live on radio station WWOZ, hosted by British DJ Clive Smith. It has been welcomed by the city's musicians and audiences, though the Musicians' Union is wary of its playing for a fee; the hat has to be passed around each time. On every trip, the band members are met at the airport by the Eagle Jazz Band, which accompanies them with marching music from the concourse to baggage reclaim and the bus. The tour, costly and luxurious as befits a group of fiftysomething affluent white jazz buffs, offers an array of concerts, visits to record company headquarters and shops (especially Record Ron's, with the slogan "Vinyl lives!"), jazz dinners at the British-exile–owned Palm Court Café, jazz brunches, swamp tours, and trips around key jazz sites, from Storyville and Buddy Bolden's house on Perdido Street to the Hogan Jazz Archive at Tulane University and Preservation Hall, where traditional jazz is played nightly. The climax is the French Quarter Festival, which brings together traditional jazz bands and features jazz-related activities throughout a long weekend. In one of three unpublished but informally widely circulated "New Orleans Odyssey" accounts, a tour member described his trip to the Crescent City as "like a pilgrimage, to Mecca, long dreamt about and not to be forgotten."[62]

These trips are dominated by a particular group of white male Englishmen: middle class, financially comfortable, having repaid their mortgages and now with time on their hands, they cherish their long-standing record collections of 78s and LPs and turn up for reunions of the Colyer Trust at seaside resorts during the year, to play, listen, and parade. At Pontin's Holiday Camp, Sand Bay, Weston-Super-Mare, one delegate summarized the nostalgic emotional appeal: "We've been through it all—the marriages, the divorces, the kids, the successes and the failures, and we're here to relive that moment of optimism when everything seemed possible, when the whole world seemed as if it could be made to swing."[63] As well as aging and male, the trust is also overwhelmingly white. When I asked John Long, the oldest member of the trust, whether black Britons were interested in the trust and in New Orleans jazz, he commented:

> Very, very few. Strangely enough, it's something I've never thought about. I wouldn't like to say whether we've got a black member. Very rarely do they come to Pontin's [the regular festival]. I've seen some colored musicians at Blackpool among visiting bands. You can look on it two ways. I either look upon the music irrespective of color, which is probably a good thing. And then, people say to us, when they listen to our band and the Bunk Johnson/George Lewis aura about it, they say, "That's the blackest music we've heard for a long time." I find that amusing, but it's nice.[64]

On the trips to New Orleans, band members' wives accompany them (often under sufferance), usually spending their time not on the jazz-tour bus but visiting the Cajun cookery school, taking the tour of Louisiana plantation homes, and browsing around the antique and curio shops. By contrast, Nancy Covey, of the company Festival Tours International, leads a complementary trip to the New Orleans Jazz and Heritage Festival, including a Cajun Country Tour; these trips, focusing on the more recent New Orleans music trends of R & B, Cajun, and zydeco, have become very fashionable in recent years and attract women and men equally, often single people in their twenties or thirties.

The triumph of the Ken Colyer Trust Band's history was its invitation to perform in 1995 as a band (not simply with other musicians) at two French Quarter Festivals. John Long followed the example of the trust's namesake: "This man, inspired by the music, enough to make it his life's work, had gone to New Orleans and come back with the seeds of a revival which he planted in Europe to produce a very rich harvest. Our job in 1995 was to take the music back to New Orleans and hope for another revival." Long was not disappointed. He reports that "one coloured cab driver" praised the band for playing "real music, instead of that usual rap crap," and he quotes a retired journalist/photographer, originally from San Francisco, who followed the band around: "I have worked in 35 countries and I have to come to New Orleans to really learn about jazz from an Englishman." Band members were especially delighted to be praised highly by Harold Drob, who had recorded Bunk Johnson in 1946.[65]

There is an uncompromisingly nostalgic feel to all this. New Or-

Scarlett O'Hara beer mat, London pub, early 1990s.

"Frankly, I don't give a damn if my central heating breaks down — I've got 3 Star ServiceCare cover."

British Gas advertisement, 1990s.

VIVIEN LEIGH
CLARET

VIVIEN LEIGH
DRAPERY

Wax collector dolls of Vivien Leigh as Scarlett O'Hara, from The Paul Crees Collection, Bath, England, 1988.

The Elvis Shop, 400A High Street North, Manor Park, London E12 6RH. *Photograph by Helen Taylor.*

Yesterday Once More

PO BOX 1603, BRISTOL BS40 5YD. TELEPHONE: 01934 863327

PRESENTS

The GREATEST EVER
Elvis Week
at Hemsby

1980 - 2000
COME AND CELEBRATE TWENTY YEARS OF ELVIS AT HEMSBY*

4pm SATURDAY 16th SEPTEMBER 2000 - 10am SATURDAY 23rd SEPTEMBER 2000
AT PONTINS HOLIDAY CENTRE, BEACH ROAD, HEMSBY, GREAT YARMOUTH

**A MULTI MILLION POUND REFURBISHMENT HAS MADE THIS
CENTRE AN EVEN BETTER VENUE FOR AN ELVIS HOLIDAY**

TWELVE HOURS PER DAY NON STOP ELVIS ENTERTAINMENT

THIS WILL BE THE ULTIMATE TRIBUTE TO OUR MAN THE ONLY MILLENNIUM CELEBRATION FIT FOR THE KING

THE ELVIS HOLIDAY EXPERIENCE

ELVIS MOVIES, ELVIS QUIZZES, ELVIS KARAOKE, ELVIS DISCOS, ELVIS LINE DANCING, FOOTBALL, POOL CONTESTS,
TALENT SHOWS, ELVIS MUSIC FROM THE FIFTIES, SIXTIES & SEVENTIES AND MUCH MORE.

ALSO FEATURING THE STRONGEST LIVE ENTERTAINMENT LINE UP EVER COMPILED FOR AN ELVIS FESTIVAL

Suzi Quatro
Devil Gate Drive, Can The Can

Alvin Stardust
Red Dress, Pretend

The American Drifters
*Saturday Night At The Movies,
Save The Last Dance For Me*

Marty Wilde & The Wildcats
Rubber Ball, Teenager In Love

Herman Hermits
*Must To Avoid
I'm Into Something Good*

PLUS

THE ROLLING TONES, GARETH GRITTER AND THE GRITTER BAND, THE JETS,
MARK KEELEY'S GOOD ROCKING TONIGHT, THE FIREBIRDS, BLAST OFF, THE PREFECTS & THE ALLIGATORS

ALL IN THE MAIN LARGE BALLROOM

FROM ONLY £74 PER PERSON

ALL THOSE WHO HAVE MEMORIES OF ELVIS WEEK AT HEMSBY COME AND RELIVE THEM.
IF YOU HAVE NEVER BEEN DON'T MISS THIS ONE. ITS GONNA BE THE BIGGEST AND THE BEST. YOU KNOW IT MAKES SENSE.

ANY QUESTIONS TEL: 01934 863327

Advertisement for Elvis week, Hemsby, England, 2000.

SOUTHERN COMFORT.
ORIGINALLY POPULAR
AFTER SUNDOWN.
OR WAS IT BEFORE SUN-UP?

Southern Comfort liqueur advertisement in the British press, 1970s.

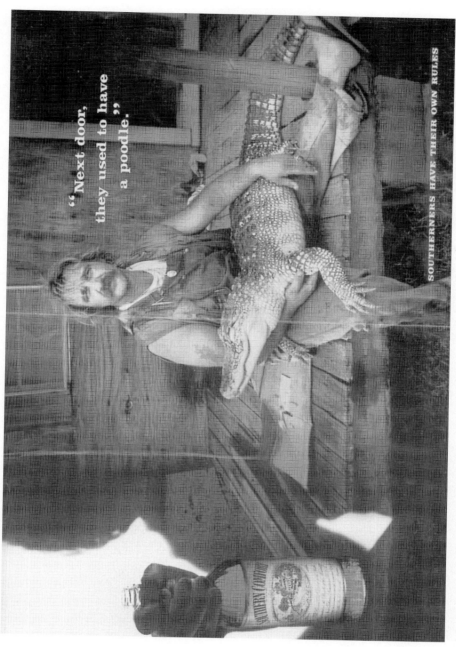

Southern Comfort liqueur advertisement in the British press, 1990s.

TAX-FREE SHOPPING FOR INTERNATIONAL VISITORS

Louisiana

The Louisiana Travel Guide brochure, Louisiana Office of Tourism, London, 1997.

Gathering of the Ken Colyer Trust, Pontin's, Sand Bay, Weston-Super-Mare, England, April 1994. *Photograph by Richard Smith*.

Poster for the production of Tennessee Williams, *Vieux Carré,* directed by Steven Pimlott, Nottingham Playhouse, England, May–June 1995.

Charlotte Emmerson as Baby Doll and Jonathan Cake as Silva Vacarro in Tennessee Williams's *Baby Doll*, Birmingham Repertory Theatre, 22 October–13 November 1999. *Photograph by Ivan Kyncl.*

Alex Giannini, James Black, Finbar Lynch, and Dion Graham in Tennessee Williams's *Not about Nightingales*. The 1998 production was a collaboration between two radical experimental theater groups, the London-based Moving Theatre and the Houston-based Alley Theatre, at London's National Theatre Cottesloe auditorium. *Photograph by Nobby Clark.*

Maya Angelou at Stirling Castle, Scotland. *Photograph by Charlie Crawford.*

leans music, like all popular music, has moved on from traditional "Dixieland" jazz, and it is significant that Long repeatedly uses that anachronistic term "coloured" and alludes to the praise of aging men. Anyone visiting the city today is struck by how little traditional jazz exists, outside the British-owned tourist haunt Preservation Hall (where music is played by very old men and women) and—in ersatz form—in tourist bars. An academic and musician, Michael White, gives illustrated historical lectures on it and deplores the fact that the rigorous demands of the music, especially daily practice, prevent young African Americans from developing the inclination or patience to learn. It is the museum piece, "preserved" in a hall and brought out at Jazz Fest time, compared with the very live and kicking (and more easily picked up and played) musical forms that have superseded it: rock, R & B, Cajun, hip-hop, and so on. The Colyer Trust musicians and members are not very interested in the racial and social history of this music or its evolution into other forms; their concern is with saving it as a pure music, undiluted and unhybridized.[66]

In the seventies and eighties, American cities saw a rash of developments of leisure-time zones for well-heeled local employees, tourists, and urban explorers: famous examples are the redevelopment of the once derelict port area of lower Manhattan into an upmarket tourist district, "South Street Seaport," Fisherman's Wharf in San Francisco, and Riverwalk in New Orleans. M. Christine Boyer discusses these projects in terms of that pervasive hankering after sanitized historical re-creations that characterizes the contemporary urban imagination. For her, nostalgia is "a sweet sadness generated by a feeling that something is lacking in the present, a longing to experience traces of an authentic, supposedly more fulfilling past, a desire to repossess and reexperience something untouched by the ravages of time."[67] In many ways, the Colyer Trust is locked into that "sweet sadness" that refuses to acknowledge the rich array of music that is now bringing New Orleans very much to the fore on the national and world scene. And as its most dedicated members grow old and less active, it may well be that the trust will die out for lack of interest from younger jazz fans.

Yet, given that many New Orleans musicians have welcomed the trust and indeed played with its band, there is something to be said for a transatlantic dialogue focused on a musical tradition that is disappearing fast from its original home. With the instant interactions and relationships possible through mass tourism and broadcasting, the parochial community of one city's musical heritage can now enjoy global scrutiny and publicity, while being appropriated and transformed in ways possibly unrecognizable to the originators. In the case of New Orleans musicians, it seems there is a relaxation, even excitement, about this transatlantic musical exchange, all the more surprising given that much European enthusiasm for black music comes from *white* audiences and players. Major record producer Allen Toussaint is one of those generous voices supporting the Ken Colyer Trust:

> I think it's the height of respect from those who could have latched on and loved any kind of music, grand opera if they wanted. But to choose to devote much of their lives to this kind of music, that's a lot of respect and a lot of love. . . . I can't quite put my finger on it, but something new is formed when something like this happens. If a group of those guys [are] playing some music from afar, . . . is that a duplicate of the music from afar? It may appear that way, but something else is going on which is creating something new. . . . I don't think the guys who're doing that [a British white band playing New Orleans music] are stopping the guys from New Orleans from doing that. It would be tough if the guys from New Orleans would just stop doing that and the only thing left was those guys over there. Well I would still glory them for doing such a thing, else it would be totally gone. I don't think they're whitewashing, they just fell in love. . . . And I think it'll breed something new in the future, whenever you cross some hybrids together. I like it, I like it.[68]

SISTER CITIES: NEW ORLEANS AND LIVERPOOL

Toussaint's notion of "cross[ing] some hybrids together" and creating something new in the future is at the heart of an initiative that began in the late 1980s, led by a few inspired individuals in two cities. The "New Orleans–Liverpool Sister City Programme" was designed to cross two hybrid cities in need of economic regeneration through cultural industries, and especially to bring them together through a combination of music and tourism.[69] The two port cities, each of roughly half a million people, were seen as sharing a maritime and cultural heritage, and both were racially mixed and historically linked through trade and commerce. From the 1980s, both cities had suffered accelerating economic and social decline, with rising unemployment, urban decay and crime, and declining inner-city population as families moved out for better jobs and education elsewhere.

Most significantly, both cities had developed an identity associated with popular music (New Orleans predominantly with jazz, Liverpool with the Beatles and the "Mersey Sound"), but despite their high international reputations, they had enjoyed few economic benefits: neither had a strong local recording industry, and local musicians had to go to bigger cities such as New York, Los Angeles or London to prosper directly from music production. In the late 1980s, individuals who had lived in and knew both cities tried to bring together both the expertise and common experiences of the two through a twinning strategy. As "global pop" was burgeoning at that period, many cities were devising local music initiatives to compete within an international music framework; Liverpool wanted to open up a market for its cultural industries and gain access to the U.S. college radio audiences and a share of the United Kingdom's American tourist market, while New Orleans wanted a strong foothold in Europe, with access to lucrative music festival work. Liverpool, which had then a very minimal tourist industry, wanted to emulate the American city's more sophisticated music tourist enterprises, while New Orleans was interested in adopting the British city's apparently successful relationship with the record industry. The southern city was ahead of its British counterpart in identifying tourism as the way out of economic decline, and Liverpool—having been awarded the European Union's highest funding category, "Objective One"—had appointed its first tourist officer.

By the late 1980s, in response to the rise of "global pop," cities such as Seattle, Austin, Sheffield, and Berlin were developing initiatives to sustain the independence of their local music scenes against the perceived colonization of the international music industry. The problem for Liverpool was that of sustaining local music production given an inadequate local market; for New Orleans, that of competing internationally without losing cultural identity. In this context, music entrepreneur Zane Branson, originally from Virginia but recently settled in Liverpool, prepared a document for the Department of Trade and Industry, North West Region, and the leader of the Liverpool City Council. "An American in Liverpool: A Perspective on Tourism" argued the case for making tourism, especially geared toward an American market, the "constant economic base" that would help it become "one of the major tourist destinations in Europe." This would be done through recognizing the city as the cradle of and primary influence on youth culture, a center of music and fashion that were then "exported to London together with all the credit."[70]

While avoiding any adverse or critical references to the Atlantic slave trade and England's unwholesome support for the southern side in the Civil War, Branson drew many connections (some politically dubious) between the two cities: from Liverpool's financial support of John James Audubon, New Orleans resident artist, to its flying more Confederate flags than in Richmond, Virginia, and its shipbuilding industry supplying the ships to fight the "War between the States." He did not spell out one of the most important subtexts of this proposal, the need for both to increase their revenue from and clout within the music industry and to lose the negative associations of high crime and violence associated with each city. Branson proposed a "Sister City" initiative following President Eisenhower's 1956 concept of international twinnings, one that has since resulted in approximately twenty thousand pairings. Branson envisaged a major Liverpool culture and music magazine that could be circulated abroad, specifically in New Orleans, which at that time ran the very successful *Wavelength* (edited by Branson's coenthusiast, Connie Atkinson). He also projected the idea of a "Liverpool Music and Heritage Festival" modeled on the New Orleans original, which attracts vast audiences, and he wanted to tie this in with another crowd puller, a Liverpool-style Mardi Gras. Musical heritage would link the two cities, and there would be exchanges of ideas, music, history, tourism, and trade.

The recently established New Orleans Music and Entertainment Association (NOME) welcomed this link, and in 1990 the cities' leaders (the mayor of New Orleans, the council leader of Liverpool) exchanged letters to confirm they were officially twinned. The letters mentioned their mutual long musical heritages; unfortunately, neither city had any money to set up an initial project. Liverpool voted £10,000 to fund the project, but the money was never released. Largely because of lack of funds, no official developments ever occurred, but in informal terms the twinning is said to have been successful. First and foremost, it enabled both cities to confirm their sense of themselves as *local* sites of music rather than part of an undifferentiated international music market. Because it was a grassroots, informal initiative, it created an intercity network of musicians, music industry personnel, city politicians and policy makers, and tourism workers. It attracted some publicity, boosted local pride and confidence, and enabled the exchange of information and data about international music industry norms and expectations. At one point, it looked as if large plans might come to fruition: Jim Green, owner of the celebrated New Orleans club Tipitina's, as well known in that city as The Cavern had once been in Liverpool, visited the Sister City to investigate the idea of building a club on the Albert Dock waterfront; since the recession was just beginning and capital costs were too high, the scheme never materialized. Joe Farrog, a black Liverpool community leader, visited New Orleans because of the twinning and bought a building in which he established a neighborhood gallery along New Orleans lines. He brought over Big Easy musicians, and for a while it was a success; it closed in the mid-1990s.

The Sister City link began with great ambition, "to establish a trade route that had been successful in the past."[71] Clearly, this noble aim has not been achieved, for the link thrived at neither an official nor a large-scale commercial level. Connie Atkinson and Sara Cohen argue that it foundered because of "lack of funding and economic chaos in city government," as well as inadequate funding and tourist policy.[72] The experiment highlighted many problems with such twinning endeavors, especially their funding and monitoring, and it served to emphasize the lack of understanding by city policy makers of the potential role of music and other cultural industries in urban regeneration, particularly through tourism. The most important effect of this endeavor thus remains informal and ad hoc, and for some of its supporters this has been wholly positive. Zane Branson and other enthusiasts had been anxious for the Sister City idea not to become bureaucratized but rather to be a person-to-person conduit, one that would grow organically rather than die amid the ceremony of chambers of commerce and mayoral visits. By all accounts, on a modest scale this ambition is beginning to make waves between the two cities. The Sister City project provides a further example of the potential for transatlantic relationships and networks to benefit the music and tourism industries in both countries and to develop expertise and commercial and social links that could work in the best interests of marginalized but culturally rich urban economies.

ADVERTISING NEW ORLEANS IN BRITAIN

In the final years of the century, a rather more lucrative and successful "trade route" than music encouraged transatlantic links and mutual interests: this time, advertising and publicity, allied closely to
the film and video industries. A key indicator of the rising significance of the city of New Orleans in global contemporary culture has
been its dominance in film and advertising campaigns. During the
eighties and nineties, suddenly New Orleans seemed to be everywhere—as location for movies, and in Britain as setting for a series
of advertisements. This was no coincidence. New Orleans had long
been a favorite location for movies, and from the earliest days of the
industry it hosted film crews in its historic areas. Films such as *The
Belle of New Orleans* (1912), *Jezebel* (1938), *King Creole* (1958), *WUSA*
(1969), and *Angel Heart* (1986) brought the city revenue and critical
and popular acclaim and opened the floodgates to many more productions, culminating in the hits of the 1990s such as *The Pelican Brief*
(1993) and *Interview with the Vampire*. By the 1980s, New Orleans
boasted a Board of Film and Television Production, and in 1987 it
initiated an annual Film and Video Festival. Large mansions in the
Garden District and hotels in historically interesting buildings were
already cashing in on existing film credits to offer the industry locations, cast parties, and other expensive trappings.

By the time Mayor Marc H. Morial came to office in 1994, there
was widespread recognition that the film and video industry offered
the economically ailing city its best opportunity for a major new
source of income. The mayor's Office of Tourism, Arts, and Entertainment was established to develop creative industries of all kinds—
the arts, film and video production, music, tourism, and new media
technologies. Within that, the New Orleans Film and Video Commission promoted New Orleans as a motion picture location and provided information on personnel, facilities, and services relevant to
filmmaking. With the slogan "Cameras Are Rolling on the River,"
publications and advice were offered in order to make filming as easy
and hassle-free as possible. "Forget the Red Tape!" the Commission
urged, handing out advice on hotels and bars, parking arrangements,
street and bridge closures, and interesting landmarks and film sites.
The commission was remarkably successful in attracting projects and
crews. Since Louisiana offered nonunion as well as union deals and

the city was well attuned to filmmakers' needs, there was no shortage of business. When the British advertising agency EURO RSCG went there to film a Peugeot "Mardi Gras" advertisement, it followed directly in the footsteps of a Heineken shoot (using the same plantation on which Heineken had filmed "Harmonica Fats" and—with a knowing reference—using the same actor) and was filming at the same time as four other commercials and two movies.[73]

In the decade during which I monitored British commercials filmed in the city, to my knowledge there were seven major campaigns made for British consumption only: Lotus and Peugeot cars, Levi jeans, Budweiser, Heineken and Southern Comfort drinks, and Lea and Perrins sauce. All drew on those now familiar associations of the city: excess, desire, good music, food and drink, a rich and wild nightlife, voodoo and eccentricity, carnival and serious partying. However, these associations underwent a certain shift between the sixties and nineties, and, in terms of the city's international reputation, it is revealing to focus on one prominent case study.

THE SOUTHERN COMFORT CAMPAIGN

The longest-running and perhaps best-known New Orleans–themed campaign in Britain is that for Southern Comfort. Its Stateside marketing and promotion make no connections at all with New Orleans; the product is said to be a rather downmarket, ubiquitous liqueur lacking what advertisers call "premium qualities" (associated with whiskies and bourbons). In Britain, however, the product was promoted differently, and it moved through several different incarnations. In the 1960s, it acquired a countercultural status through Janis Joplin's much publicized drinking straight from the bottle. But when the advertising campaign began in the 1970s, the "liqueur spirit" was aimed at a largely thirty-five-and-over female consumer group, who were targeted in color supplements and magazines through romantic, nostalgic moonlight-and-magnolia images of a riverboat on the Mississippi River, with a handsome white planter and his belle beside horses and carriages on the riverside, recalling the golden days of the Old South. At that time the bottle label, featuring Woodland Plantation, an old Louisiana sugar plantation near the meeting of the Mississippi with the Gulf of Mexico, described the drink as "Originated on the Banks of the Mississippi in St. Louis, Missouri, U.S.A." This campaign was consistent with images of the South familiar to magazine readers from southern romances and songs.

When the Louisville, Kentucky–based company Brown-Forman bought Southern Comfort in 1979, however, this older female drinker was ousted by a more lucrative market, the sweet-toothed eighteen- to twenty-four-year-old of both sexes, targeted mainly through cinema adverts. Thus the St. Louis connection was jettisoned in favor of a more modern, commercially appealing alternative: New Orleans. To reinforce that, the liqueur spirit label now claimed, "Originated on the Banks of the Mississippi in New Orleans, Louisiana, U.S.A.," its marketing literature telling a fanciful story about one M. W. Heron, a young New Orleanian barman, who perfected the recipe for what was to become "The Grand Old Drink of the South." The image of a fun-loving, hard-drinking city was introduced, during a period of new tourist promotion of New Orleans, as the place for the young and young-at-heart to go for a good time.

For the next two decades, the New Orleans connection was milked for its appeal to European drinkers. New Orleans was seen by the company as "a dream canvas" for marketing to work on, "a slightly seamy, bubbling, simmering cauldron of all kinds of activity—many races, many cultures, many foods and types of music revolving around late nights, partying and fun."[74] The company literature described the city as "the sound of a bluesman's horn, and gentlemen's laughter spilling out to fill the evening . . . a spirit of excitement and adventure. Out of this culture came a sound, a sound which personifies the very soul of the South, American Blues and jazz . . . a challenging mix of adventure and fun, food and drink, music and song." Until the early 1990s, Brown-Forman (UK), its parent company in Louisville, and the United Kingdom distributor IDV were happy to promote the liqueur invented in a New Orleans bar through images connected closely with the city. From the "Red Dress" cinema advert, which ran from about 1987 to 1992, the "Cop" advert, which ran briefly from 1991 to 1992, and the "Hurricane," from 1992 to 1995, with accompanying posters and magazine adverts, Britain was treated to a sustained blitz of New Orleans–based publicity. The city was both party and fun town ("the Big Easy") and also a fantasy space that appealed directly to the young drinker.

The first, hugely successful advert, "Rebel Spirit," did the trick for the company, selling the product in terms of "all the elements of edge, danger, sexual electricity, challenge and a strong heritage."[75] Because it appeared in the booming mid-1980s when young people were spending money on clubs and bars, competition was fierce. The Old South New Orleans of the 1970s campaign was spiced up for its new target audience with rock music, mixed-race dating, and a moody bar setting. To the strains of the Frankie Lyman song "Why Do Fools Fall in Love?" a poor white country boy is collected in a pickup truck by a black man, who drives him to his date's house in a clearly all-black neighborhood of New Orleans, where people stare at an unfamiliar white face. The shuttered doors open and a gorgeous mixed-race beauty emerges, in (dangerously sexy) red dress and shoes. They go to a New Orleans bar, where they drink and dance to a black band and then leave to stand arm in arm by the Mississippi, watching the riverboat *Creole Queen* sail slowly by.

The advert's suggestive final slogan, "Who are you mixing it with" (no question mark), ostensibly about young barhoppers' mixer drinks, alludes to the city's long history of racial tolerance but also of exploitative miscegenation. I say knowingly, because the whole tone and style of the film indicate a flirtation with the tabooed area of mixed-race dating, which has long been a fraught topic in the South and is still relatively rare even in laid-back New Orleans. The shadowy darkness in which the whole film is shot, the flickering light of the bar, and the alternating disappearance and reemergence of the woman's face from shutters and dark spaces all allude to well-worn demonologies of mixed-race liaisons, with their suggestions of secrecy and evil. And black and white New Orleans makes all this possible, indeed colludes with it: the black man's pickup delivers the white boy to his girl; the musicians and bartender provide drink and atmosphere; the riverboat recalls a slower and more gracious leisured age and reminds us of a historic South in which such a relationship would have been illegal, dangerous, and confined even more deeply to the cover of darkness. Indeed, that history and the racial tensions of miscegenation in the contemporary South caused raised eyebrows at the parent company. When the video was first run by the company's executive committee, one member said of the mixed-race dating, "That'll never play in Atlanta, but if you think it'll work in London, go for it." The committee did, however, insist on editing out one frame in which the white man stroked the woman's bottom.

The next cinema campaign, "Cop," was intended to build on this success but was racier and harder-edged. A collage of New Orleans nightlife, it reflected the tensions and eruptions of a night's work in the city by a young white male policeman and a white female bartender. The two lovers are shown in high-stress jobs, facing uncertain situations and people, sounds, and sights from 9:55 P.M. to the end of their shifts, 3:40 A.M., when they meet to unwind over a bottle of Southern Comfort. Director Tony Kay's New Orleans, with its slogan "Find Comfort in the City," plays on the drink's name to suggest a soothing rather than stimulating influence, creating a haven of tranquillity in a dangerous, fast urban space. The night's work—presented in very brief vignettes of bar and police department experience—is a bricolage of strange-looking people, streets, languages, and snatched dialogue, the whine of police sirens and the sight of fire, water hydrants pumping, an old toothless French Quarter character singing badly. A dramatic but tense soundtrack suggests a crisis to come. In fact, the music mellows to the lovers alone in a bar.

Not entirely to the agency's surprise, "Cop" was given a playing life of only six months. The Louisville parent company became uneasy about it, especially as in the early 1990s New Orleans was beginning to acquire a somewhat dubious reputation, with the highest U.S. murder rate (including a much publicized murder of a female British tourist in April 1992), which gave the company pause over associating its "fun" drink with the city. The "Cop" advert, "more aggressive and less friendly" than the backers had hoped, was described to me as having "overstepped the mark in terms of being on the edge and started to go for that sinisterness, tension, danger, seedy rather than just cool." A new company was commissioned for the next British installment. Brown-Forman was now very worried about too close a connection being drawn between its liqueur and the city of New Orleans, which was well known for its racial tensions and was feared could become a racial tinderbox. The firm wanted an upbeat, partying message, associated with a fun South rather than a dangerous city. It was 1992, recession had eaten away at young people's marginal expenditure, and Southern Comfort sales were dropping badly. A new, more innocent and cheerful image was required to boost the product.

Two successive poster campaigns were run, aiming to restore the "fun" brief, using tried and trusted images of the city. The first one focused on a "European feel" of balconies, white heterosexual couples drinking in the street to the strains of local musicians; the second, "Mardi Gras," was set in Blaine Kern's Mardi Gras World, the factory/museum where the carnival floats are constructed, and it featured a mixed-race group of musicians sipping their Southern Comfort to the slogan "MARDI GRAS. TWO WEEKS CELEBRATION. FIFTY WEEKS REHEARSAL."

Like all the later advertisements, the next cinema campaign, "Hurricane" (Autumn 1993 to late 1995), never named New Orleans but invoked it through clear references to this particular city. A hurricane warning comes over TV and radio, with weather commentators warning that this is a good night to stay home, no night to take a walk. But young New Orleanians stay at home for nothing and no one, so a young white man slings his guitar over his shoulder and moseys down to the French Quarter neighborhood bar, where it is business as usual; Dr. John—internationally famous New Orleans–based pianist/singer—plays with his band, and the young crowd joins in with "Everybody let's sing sing sing." The aim of the whole commercial was to convey cool; the agency's brief to itself was "laid back in the face of adversity . . . an idea that if something goes wrong you don't panic, you just say 'What the hell.'" In order to do this, as with the previous campaigns, the agency drew on familiar New Orleans signifiers: the French Quarter at night, neighborhood bars full of character and music, wooden shutters, ironwork balconies, heterosexual fun oiled by lots of drinking, spontaneity, and a sense of laid-back, guilt-free fun. As with other similar ads, music and drink are largely supplied by black musicians and bar people for the pleasure of beautiful young white people.

By the mid-1990s, the company no longer wanted New Orleans–themed ideas and wished to distance the product from a city that was receiving a bad press for violence and social problems.[76] In a series of posters brought out soon afterward, made originally for the Irish market, the focus on generic black southern music is explicitly linked with Southern Comfort, because the images are of individual instrumentalists, decontextualized, so the specific New Orleans link is lost. And, with the trend for violent and erotic movies begun by David Lynch's Wild at Heart (1990), the company decided to abandon New Orleans altogether. In a new venture for the late 1990s, it commissioned a series of vignettes of small-town and rural south Louisiana eccentrics, "Southerners Have Their Own Rules," including a "redneck" whose alligator has eaten next door's poodle, and a black woman living in a shack singing tunelessly the civil rights anthem "I Shall Not Be Moved."

In short, advertisers were drawn to New Orleans in the eighties and nineties at a time when the city was offering itself as a boom town for global TV and video industries. Its reputation as a city that flirted with various sexualities, danger, and decadence had been well established in genre fiction and film, and those images, as well as its reputation as a city in which good times roll, offered ideal aspirational material for young consumers of drinks (as well as jeans and zippy cars). As a more sober note intervened, with the British recession and also the divisions and conflicts of New Orleans itself—blown open by the 1991 Mardi Gras Ordinance—tarnishing its reputation as Party City, the campaign changed tack. It sought in rural south Louisiana a funky innocence increasingly hard to celebrate in a place that was beginning to resemble in too many respects other racially split, alienated American cities.

Cultural tourism has been crucial in bringing the whole South into line with other areas of the United States and a global economy that predicates economic survival increasingly on exploiting the distinctive, commercially viable elements of places. And, although the Sun Belt has benefited from its new industrial and commercial role within the American economy, many of its key cities are under threat from the vagaries of the marketplace and the many sociopolitical problems that can undermine their economic future, safety and desirability as residential and commercial centers, and reputation as cultural and tourist centers. Potential investors and tourists watch with horror the drug-related violence, schoolyard shootings, church bombings, and level of racial strife that seem endemic in many urban American areas, especially the South. Anyone who has visited a southern city is struck by the carefully worded instructions in hotel and tourist leaflets designed to keep visitors away from potentially dangerous neighborhoods, groups of people, and situations; even casual conversations with local residents will quickly come around to problems of safety and the perilousness of urban daily life.

New Orleans has suffered more than most southern cities from the vicissitudes of postwar developments. New Orleanians shrug off the fact that, for much of this century, the city has been said to be on the verge of bankruptcy, but in the decades during which it has looked to international tourism for new markets it has suffered deleterious setbacks. For example, the decline of oil and gas prices in the 1980s, the financial losses at the 1984 World's Fair, and the bankruptcy of the controversial casino in the 1990s all compounded the problems created by white flight to suburbia and the desperate condition of poor and drug-addicted blacks in inner-city projects. The sense of a city living close to the edge—resulting in a fabled capacity to party as if life depended on it and also a tendency toward extreme violence and corruption—leads cultural commentators too easily to demonize it and see it as that Bakhtinian "grotesque body," the gothic and hellish space of Anne Rice's vampires.

It is a space, moreover, that is described in racially inflected terms, for just as it was slavery and its legacy that gave the nineteenth-century city its gothic tone, so in contemporary New Orleans the impoverished and socially deprived black population is defined (implicitly in polite company, but only too often explicitly) as the problem, indeed the enemy within. Around New Year, 1994, the Italian granddaughter of Tyrone Power disappeared in New Orleans, having hung out in a seamy neighborhood with a black musician and probably swum to her death in the Mississippi. Her mother told the international press (without any evidence) that she may have been sold into the white slave trade or abducted for black-magic rites. It is no coincidence that the black musicians so beloved of white British jazz fans and advertising directors are old men, or better still, dead figures of mythology, rather than very live, younger music makers with a more politically challenging, in-your-face style.

For Europeans (as for others too), New Orleans is the nonpuritan American city of desire, pleasure, and excess. As well as the heart of darkness, it represents the return of the repressed, the gothic dungeon, a titillating, devouring, polluted, and diseased female body. Like Paris, it is a site of frivolity and consumption, associated with a colorful but violent history; like Venice, it is sinking into the sea, and its annual carnival is both a tourist's delight and a symbolic *danse macabre*. (For Britons in the late 1990s, this was especially true because of the appearance of a mysterious small-time supermarket bomber who labeled his bomb packages "Welcome to the Mardi Gra [*sic*] experience.") This is a city that is "not like other cities," as Stella Kowalski reminds Blanche DuBois, absorbed by a colorful history that provides fertile ground for its writers and filmmakers, as well as increasing numbers of tourists. In clichéd postmodern terms, it also lays claim to having bypassed history, memory, and social reality: the City That Care Forgot, the Big Easy, the Big Sleazy. The ultimate playground in Louisiana, what Ellen Gilchrist calls "The Land of Dreamy Dreams," it is also a city of racial violence, extreme poverty, high criminal activity, and police and underworld corruption. The French Quarter masquerades innocence, claiming to be clear of all this; for convention and gambling visitors and tourists, the quaint horse and carriage rides avoid the now badly deprived area named Desire. The original streetcar named Desire, which provides the most culturally resonant title of all New Orleans's fictional/filmic productions, is literally enshrined in a French Quarter museum but is also now a "virtual" streetcar that will carry one through the city's Web page.[77]

However, the city's fondness for its own mixtures and fusions is that quality that both reinvigorates its own culture from within and ensures crossover into other cultures. New Orleans's many long-established historical and cultural ties with European and other countries have been generously and enthusiastically sustained. In the last decades of the twentieth century, the city began to generate and encourage new scholarship in Europe, through conferences, festivals, and other forms of dissemination.[78] In 1999, the New Orleans Museum of Modern Art and Ordrupgaard Museum, in Copenhagen, staged an exhibition of the paintings French Creole artist Edgar Degas had produced in a hitherto-unknown five-month sojourn in the city in 1872.[79] Musicians such as "New Orleans Musical Ambassador" Lillian Boutté spent much time and energy drawing on the enthusiasm for New Orleans music in many European countries, to produce gospel and jazz concerts for schoolchildren as well as older aficionados. New Orleans can still capitalize on its reputation as "the authenticity well," the "birthplace" of a major art form. Pilgrim tourists seeking their musical "Mecca" will, if carefully cultivated, ensure its special place as tourist and convention destination, while Anne Rice aficionados will continue to flock to the Memnoch Balls and Garden District shrines. And the need to thrive as a new tourist urban space, to realize the liberating and lucrative benefits of international exchanges and fusions, means that New Orleans will use its reciprocal performances and relationships across the Atlantic in order to reinvent and recharge itself in the new century.

5

TENNESSEE WILLIAMS AND THE CONTEMPORARY BRITISH STAGE

A *Streetcar Named Desire* (1947), a play set in the heart of New Orleans's Vieux Carré, conferred on that city a romantic and erotic aura that remains to this day. It also launched its playwright, Thomas Lanier (Tennessee) Williams, onto an international stage from which he has never been ousted. One of the best-known dramatists of the twentieth century, Williams educated and excited theatrical and moviegoing audiences about the peculiar qualities of the South and southerners and thus was a key player in the cultural circulation of a complex, sexually and emotionally rich, and mythic modern South. And, though a proud and passionate southerner who adopted the name "Tennessee" and returned South obsessively in person and for his subject matter, this writer was no merely regional or parochial figure. Williams became a globally renowned name through his own internationalism and especially his close emotional and intellectual links with Europe.

A richly hybrid character, Williams made many transatlantic journeys, both literal and figurative. He boasted that he was composed of "a little Welsh wildness, a lot of puritan English and a big chunk of German sentiment ... a combination of Puritan and Cavalier strains."[1] Given his extraordinary capacity for itinerancy, there are many different travelers' tales about this writer. But here, I shall focus on the most significant international relationship the playwright enjoyed, with Britain, in order to explore the different ways one European country both embraced and helped shape the dramatist and his works.

In 1992, the Formula One car firm Lotus ran a glossy magazine advertisement. "A STREETCAR NAMED DESIRE" was its headline, above a sleek silver model with the registration "Esprit." That same year, an English tourist, Julie Stott, was murdered in New Orleans's French Quarter; her killer came from "Desire," the impoverished, crime-ridden district of the city. The British tabloid press relished the irony of the romantic, mythic "Streetcar" leading to a place that had become a derelict junkie's paradise.[2] *A Streetcar Named Desire* (1947) is a dramatic work of which most people have heard; it resonates throughout world culture and has taken on a life of its own. Philip C. Kolin calls it "the *Huckleberry Finn* of our theater," arguing that for Americans it embodies the whole spectrum of U.S. culture—with its playful allusions to major writers such as Poe, film stars like Mae West, populist heroes such as Huey Long, and cultural artifacts like Jax beer and cherry soda. And global capitalism has ensured that most of those allusions are just as familiar beyond U.S. shores. Elia Kazan's 1951 film version, with its extraordinary performances from T-shirted Marlon Brando and a quivering Vivien Leigh, came to embody the quintessence of a powerful American screen sexuality that has remained internationally iconic to this day. As Kolin put it, the play is "one of America's most significant cultural exports."[3]

Indeed, this cultural export goes far beyond *Streetcar*, for Williams has contributed, perhaps more than any other writer, to that irresistible popular myth of an iconic South as tragic, gothic site of desire and death. Although critics might claim that William Faulkner was the most revered southern novelist and Eugene O'Neill and Arthur Miller the most admired American dramatists, there is no doubt that the most passionate mass international responses have gone to the plays of Tennessee Williams.

Although there were ups and downs in this dazzling reputation, by the end of the century Tennessee Williams was hot news. In 1996, critic Brian Parker claimed that, fifty years after the success of his first major play, *The Glass Menagerie*, and twelve years after his death, Tennessee Williams's plays were "making a spectacular comeback, with major new productions for stage, television, and film on both sides of the Atlantic, and a confident new energy in academic discourse."[4]

Parker therefore explained this Williams revival in terms of the time lapse since the natural slump after a major artist's death; the death in 1993 of Williams's "tyrannical executrix," Maria St. Just, releasing for publication the playwright's vast, important archives; and finally, not least, "perhaps, a quirk in the zeitgeist that has made Williams's concern for losers more relevant to the desperate nineties than it seemed during the political euphoria of the sixties or the greedy materialism of the seventies and eighties." Parker's words suggest that Williams was being resurrected after a long period of neglect—and, in terms of theater and criticism, this may be true. Within popular culture and film, Williams never really went away and has become one of the most quoted and culturally appropriated modern writers.

A CHECKERED CRITICAL REPUTATION

This success is hardly a result of the plays' wide availability in print. As I write, there is not yet a definitive collection of the plays, the seven-volume New Directions edition notwithstanding; many of the lesser known are hard to obtain, and few of his plays are translated into other languages. This is surprising, partly because his writing was strongly influenced by non-Anglophone writers, notably Chekhov and Strindberg, and because he traveled, and was known widely, outside the States. His popularity has grown in large part from a handful of celebrated theater productions, but mostly from Hollywood film versions that have since become classic cinematic texts, notably Kazan's *Streetcar*, Richard Brooks's *Cat on a Hot Tin Roof* (1958), and John Huston's *The Night of the Iguana* (1964). The enduring success in film, television, and dramatic versions of his two masterpieces, *The Glass Menagerie* (1945) and *A Streetcar Named Desire*, consolidated his reputation. His bold treatment of controversial and dangerous subjects drew large audiences to theater, cinema, and TV productions and brought young people in droves into the theater (encouraged, at least in Britain and the States, by his long-standing inclusion in English and American literature school and college curricula). German students find his plays help them learn English; in Moscow, a production of *Streetcar* has been running for more than two decades. Some critics have even suggested that he has become "the voice of America."

However, Tennessee Williams suffered a checkered reception from scholars and critics. The nature of his subject matter, once seen as sensationalist, and the lurid revelations about his sex life in his own *Memoirs* (1975) have often led to a critical caution around, or dismissal of, the playwright as an anti-intellectual melodramatist. Former director of the National Theatre Richard Eyre told me, "The great misconception of Williams's work is that it's vapid and whimsical and camp and romantic or even sentimental."[5] Claude Coulon, French translator and director of Williams's plays, described the history of the plays' reception in postwar France, moving from critical hostility in the forties and fifties to high reverence in the nineties.[6] He explained the early negative reception in terms of critical misunderstanding of the nature of the works: in those decades the plays were produced naturalistically, thus dismissed as tastelessly sexually explicit and violent. Later, directors and critics managed to reeducate audiences and students.

The French came to understand what Williams's best interpreters have always recognized, namely, that he was primarily a poetic, symbolist, allegorical modernist rather than a realist or naturalist writer. And, as the subject matter, once so "torrid," increasingly appeared tame by comparison with that of postmodern theater and film, audiences and critics were able to examine the works in a calmer, clearer light. They came to appreciate Williams's penetrating psychological understanding of multiple sexual identities and forms of violence in personal and political life, as well as his ability to weave together a range of styles from the romantic, realist, melodramatic, and poetic to the surrealist, expressionist, gothic, and farcical. Timothy Walker, director of British fringe group Cheek By Jowl's 1997 production of *Out Cry*, suggested that audiences were ready for Williams's nonrealist, "elusive" style: "At the end of the century, in periods of enormous transition, people may look more towards the imaginative realm to make sense of things."[7] In terms of literary critical approaches to his work, the 1990s saw the publication of a collection of essays on the much discussed *A Streetcar Named Desire*, moving away from the old formalism and biographical obsessions, instead paying tribute to the play's thematic and theoretical complexities with new perspectives from feminism, Marxism, mythology, cultural/regional studies, reader-response theory, chaos and anti-chaos theory, perception theory, film aesthetics, and translation theory and practice.[8] This helped make him fashionable again within the academy, which had become suspicious of, and somewhat dismissive about, his great popularity.

WILLIAMS THE EUROPHILE

Tennessee Williams himself was a great Europhile, especially Anglophile. In this, he shared in the peculiarly southern sentimentality about British, especially English, culture. Moreover, Williams drew deeply on his transatlantic personal and professional friendships, as well as his reading in European poetry and drama. It is one of the ironies of this figure that he is said to have "reinvented the American stage" and to have written at least one play that is central in "the American cultural consciousness," but to have done so through intertextual responses to European poetic and theatrical models.[9] Williams himself declared, "I believe in Michelangelo, Velásquez and Rembrandt," and critics recognize influences from artists as disparate as van Gogh, Karl Huysmans, Strindberg, and W. B. Yeats.[10] Like other southerners, he enjoyed using Walter Scott ironically; he drew on English romantic poets Blake, Keats, and Shelley for visionary ideas and alienated, romantic characters; and he relied for his poetic intensity and melancholy on the symbolists and fin-de-siècle iconoclasts such as Rimbaud and Oscar Wilde. Time and again, not surprisingly since he was a poetic dramatist looking for role models, it is European rather than American writers who were his strongest influences. A voracious reader, he turned to writers who would empower him to write from his position as what Nancy M. Tischler calls "the archetypal outsider: a poet in a practical world, a homosexual in a heterosexual world."[11]

In an article about Williams's "creative rewriting," Gilbert Debusscher lists the fourteen main literary influences on the playwright: no fewer than twelve are European, and five are British. Of the three main influences, only one—the poet Hart Crane—is American. The other two are the Russian playwright Chekhov and the British D. H. Lawrence, both of whom offered alternative tones and preoccupations from the rather stultifying Ibsen-influenced realism of 1930s American drama in which Williams was apprenticed. Lawrence in particular is credited with freeing Williams to place the issue of sexuality at the heart of his plays and to insist on the liberatory force of sexual desire as well as the crippling and destructive nature of its repression.[12]

Given the weight of these European influences, it is perhaps not surprising that Williams's work has been understood and embraced so enthusiastically across the Atlantic or that this capacity to draw on European precursors is understood as one of his most original contributions to the American stage. Playwright Arthur Miller, struggling to write what would become *The Death of a Salesman*, was excited by the first production of *Streetcar*, claiming:

> [It] formed a bridge to Europe for me, to Jouvet's performance in *Ondine*, to the whole tradition of unashamed word-joy that, with the exception of Odets, we had either turned our backs on or, as with Maxwell Anderson, only used archaically, as though eloquence could only be justified by cloaking it in sentimental romanticism. . . . With *Streetcar*, Tennessee had printed a license to speak at full throat.[13]

Speaking at full throat, then, was the contribution this playwright made to the American stage, bringing together a rich European poetic-dramatic tradition to engage with southern, and indeed national, concerns that spoke to a world audience. From the early years, and in recent times (with a low patch during his difficult late years), Williams had, and continues to have, a very special relationship with Britain and the British dramatic audience. There was, of course, a golden era of film adaptations of the plays (many with screenplays by the playwright himself), when some of Britain's greatest, most popular film and theater actors played major roles in productions. I have already argued that this created a peculiarly special relationship between the two nations in the key casting of British actors in *Gone With the Wind* and its sequel, *Scarlett*. So, too, with the Williams canon. Vivien Leigh, who was the original Scarlett O'Hara, starred not only in *Streetcar* but also as Karen Stone in *The Roman Spring of Mrs. Stone* (1961); Elizabeth Taylor played Maggie in *Cat on a Hot Tin Roof*, Catherine Holly in *Suddenly Last Summer* (1959), and Flora Goforth in *Boom!* (1968). Laurence Harvey was John Buchanan in *Summer and Smoke* (1961), and Richard Burton appeared as Reverend Shannon in *Night of the Iguana* and as Chris Flanders in *Boom!* (1968), a version in which Noel Coward played the Witch of Capri. In 1976, Laurence Olivier produced, and starred as Brick in, a teleplay of *Cat on a Hot Tin Roof*, and Maggie Smith played Mrs. Venable in a 1993 TV version of *Suddenly Last Summer*. Since the early years, then, the cream of British dramatic talent has been centrally involved with the playwright's work and has brought a British (not to mention international) audience along with it.

Yet, as I have already suggested, this progression has not been straightforward. "Tennessee's time has come again," proclaimed the *Daily Telegraph* on 25 February 1997. The article, by Kate Bassett, traced a much documented curve in Tennessee Williams's fortunes: success in the mid-1940s with *The Glass Menagerie*, followed by a string of huge successes through the 1950s, dropping to a low ebb of creativity and commercial success in the writer's alcoholic and drug-addicted 1960s, ending with a short upsurge of dramatic productivity in the 1970s and an ignominious death alone in 1983 at the Elysée Hotel in New York City. It went on to argue that, more than a decade since his death, there was a considerable renewal of interest, the Williams renaissance described by Brian Parker. Bassett cited the British productions in 1997 alone: the Peter Hall Company's *A Streetcar Named Desire*, the Glasgow Citizens' *Cat on a Hot Tin Roof*, the Royal Shakespeare Theatre's *Camino Real*, Cheek By Jowl's *Out Cry*, and plans by the Chichester Festival to produce *Suddenly Last Summer* as well as Vanessa Redgrave's (then forthcoming) world premiere production of *Not about Nightingales*. With theaters up and down the United Kingdom, from Dundee and Mold to Bristol and London, staging many of the plays in the last decade or so of the century, it is easy to confirm Bassett's impression that, at both major national theater companies and regional repertory companies, Williams enjoyed a strong revival.[14]

"TENNESSEE'S TIME" ON THE BRITISH STAGE

Since the playwright's death in 1983, there has been a steady rise in the number of British productions. It comes as something of a shock to realize that, during Williams's lifetime, in a country where he had many friends and important theatrical contacts, Britain's most prestigious theater companies, the National and the Royal Shakespeare Company, staged none of his plays. The RSC's first Williams production, *Camino Real*, was mounted in Stratford as late as 1997. Peter Hall, the National's director during the sixties and seventies, rejected all the plays Williams offered him, feeling they would not work on stage; this was a great disappointment to Williams himself, since the young Hall had directed English premieres of his plays in the 1950s. It coincided with a transatlantic decline in the playwright's fortunes in his last decades, explained by American critic Roger Boxill in terms of the old-fashioned, backward-glancing nature of his subject matter. The British theater critic Nicholas de Jongh offers a different explanation for his absence from the British stage, one that recalls Claude Coulon's words about French reception. The form of the works demanded a stylized, symbolic staging, going against "the realist, austere, word-bound currency of English theatrical writing and the prevailing styles of theatre direction."[15]

In the late 1980s, however, everything changed. Peter Hall himself directed a triumphant production of *Orpheus Descending* as the debut play in his Peter Hall Company, with Vanessa Redgrave in the leading role. And after Richard Eyre became director of the National in 1988, some of the highest-profile and most commercially successful productions appeared there (including *Cat on a Hot Tin Roof* directed by Peter Hall, *The Night of the Iguana* and *Sweet Bird of Youth*). The American critic John Lahr joined a chorus of approval for these revivals. The measured enthusiasm Kate Bassett expressed in the *Telegraph* of 1997 compared starkly with one of its columnist's alarmist comments three years earlier: "Britain's National Theatre now seems far more at home with torrid American dramas of Tennessee Williams than it does with the plays of Shakespeare."[16]

It is easy to see why Williams has enjoyed such a strong renaissance in Britain. There is the obvious advantage of language; no translated edition is needed, and many American actors have been wooed to the British theater to perform in the plays. Then there is the existence of a particularly strong national subsidy for theater, a phenomenon that is renowned and envied throughout the world. The relatively well funded, critically acclaimed National Theatre enables risks to be taken with noncommercial dramatists and works. Although Tennessee Williams's work is not uncommercial as a whole, it is uneven, and successes are erratic and unpredictable, often depending on the reputations of the leading actors. As Claude Coulon says of Williams in France, "He is not a man of the boulevard."[17] In other words, the plays flourish away from Broadway and mainstream international theaters. Only in Britain do they receive major productions in high-profile repertory theater company programs (often including nationwide tours), which have the luxury of artistically refining the productions, rather than focusing mainly on box-office receipts. As with Arthur Miller, Williams's work has been kept alive, taken seriously by Britain's top directors, designers, and actors and allowed to accumulate a classic as well as popular status within the English theater.

Furthermore, it could be argued that British directors were less hostile than American to the later, more problematic plays of Williams and in the final years of the century began to give the playwright a wholly new theatrical spin. Plays ignored or underrated by U.S. directors, notably *The Night of the Iguana, The Milk Train Doesn't Stop Here Anymore, Out Cry,* and *Tiger Tail* were given new life on the British stage and excited new audiences in the whole oeuvre. *Chicago Tribune* reviewer Matt Wolf praised the English stage for taking "a far more adventurous approach to Williams than the American one, regularly scanning the writer's entire repertoire rather than sticking to the two or three sure bets."[18] For example, Williams's intensely autobiographical *Vieux Carré*, written in the late 1970s about the writer's days as a struggling young writer in New Orleans some forty years earlier, was usually a flop in the States but enjoyed modest success in English theaters.

In 1977, it closed after five performances in New York, but it was rewritten by the playwright, who then attended its first night, 16 May 1978, at the prestigious regional theater Nottingham Playhouse. After its run in Nottingham, it transferred to London's Piccadilly Theatre on 9 August, and in May 1995 it was revived at Nottingham to considerable critical acclaim. Its 1995 director, Steven Pimlott, suggested that the play's graphic sexual explicitness "over-stepped the mark" for American audiences (who were at the time of its first production still reeling from the shock of his *Memoirs*).[19] Pimlott believed there was little American tolerance for the fantastic and dreamlike "late phase" of Tennessee Williams; for him, the play not only illuminated—through the figure of the writer-narrator character—the early experiences that fed his whole career, as well as "the archetypes that later take many shapes and forms in his later work." Pimlott also stressed the vivacity and humor in the play: "He always finds the absurdity of the situation, and there's a wonderful humanity about it. . . . These characters hang in there, and don't go quietly into the dark. It's very exhilarating." The critic Robin Thornber, admiring Pimlott's production, compared the production with plays by European dramatists Gorky and O'Casey, in focusing on lodging-house low life "as a metaphor for the underbelly of a brutal society, scrutinising its quirky outcasts for signs of spirit and struggle in the face of degradation, despair and death." He went further, to suggest that a British audience may be "better placed to appreciate his exposure of the downside of the American dream than Americans themselves."[20]

THE PROBLEMS OF PRODUCING THE PLAYS

Not everyone agrees. There are some who argue that the sheer difficulty of staging those steamy southern dramas in cold northern European theaters is immense and that the most intractable problem is that of accents. In large companies such as the National, dialect coaches are hired, but this is impossible in small, cash-strapped regional companies. With or without coaching, some actors are more accomplished than others at American, not to mention southern, accents, and there is a further problem with the knowledge of audiences. Many theatergoers barely notice accents, or they make allowances so long as the acting style is convincing. But British audiences believe they know how southerners speak; ironically, their models tend to be Clark Gable and Vivien Leigh in *Gone With the Wind*, neither southern, the former making no attempt at an authentic accent, the latter succeeding somewhat fitfully. If not these two, British audiences imagine the heavy drawl or twang of the country or blues singer and so are disappointed with a lighter or less musical touch in the theater.

Maggie Smith is an interesting case in point. According to Richard Eyre, Smith has an impeccable ear for accents, which she reproduces to perfection. In the 1993 television production of *Suddenly Last Summer*, shown on both sides of the Atlantic, Smith's Mrs. Venable was criticized by the English theater critics, who said she did not sound southern; the U.S. critics heaped praise on her precise evocation of a (very particular, very unsouthern) New Orleans Garden District accent.[21] A New Orleans–based English professor told me he took a group of southern students to see a London production of *Cat on a Hot Tin Roof*; whereas the English newspaper critics said the actress sounded nothing like an upwardly mobile Mississippi girl, the students from Mississippi enthused that she had mastered brilliantly the tones of a country-club belle.

The training of actors on both sides of the Atlantic tends to produce very different kinds of interpretation. It can be argued that the lush, gothic, operatic richness of Williams's plays emerges best from an American "Method"-influenced improvisational style and that there is no way a British actor could come close to the perfection of a Marlon Brando's Stanley Kowalski. However, the predominantly classical tradition of the British theater schools young actors in technically expert delivery of lines, observance of the playwright's stage directions and punctuation, and ensemble work. Since Williams was acutely aware of the verbal subtleties and nuances of dramatic language and character interaction on stage, such actors have been ideally placed to follow his intricate stage directions to the letter.[22] For example, Clare Higgins, the Princess in the National's 1994 production of *Sweet Bird of Youth*, was compared favorably by several critics with Lauren Bacall, who had played the part on the British stage in Harold Pinter's 1985 production. Although Bacall was acknowledged to be a fine (screen) actress, Higgins was praised for a far greater quality of "vulnerability" and lack of sentimentality. Many who praised Higgins saw in this performance elements of her Shakespearean roles, notably Lady Macbeth and Cleopatra, which gave her gutsiness and terrible energy mingled with a fatal fragility: "She lets us glimpse the insecure human masquerading behind a monster's mask," said one, while another claimed that Higgins was "our stage's best exponent of erotic infatuation."[23] Clare Higgins explained this in terms of her own precise diction: "If you don't spit diamonds, you go off into this terrible sort of pseudo-poetic rampage of language that means nothing at all. Tennessee Williams really is about as difficult as Shakespeare, in his own way. The punctuation is so precise."[24]

The near universal critical enthusiasm for Clare Higgins was not matched by the reaction to Hollywood star Jessica Lange's portrayal of Blanche DuBois, in Peter Hall's 1996-1997 Theatre Royal, Haymarket, production of *A Streetcar Named Desire*. A huge commercial success, this production opened to mixed reviews, especially of Lange's performance. She had already tackled the part twice before to subdued reception, on the New York stage in 1992 and for CBS TV in 1995, and was clearly hoping to find—at last—a sympathetic reception for the part she adored playing. In the event, although audiences flocked to see her, critics regarded her Hollywood iconic status as a drawback to the performance. They complained she was too "drop-dead gorgeous" to play the role of the fragile, aging southern belle (many of them failing to realize that Blanche is only around thirty, whereas Lange herself was in her late forties). The predominantly male critics objected to the way she played the part as a survivor, with "a fragility of steel" and a "Hollywood sensibility." A British chauvinism seemed to favor the English actors, and one critic spelled out the subtext of many a review:

> Lange's delicate, pathetic Blanche . . . seems distant, opaque and brittle. It's as if she's performing to an invisible camera—and her lamentable projection would certainly be more at home on a film set.
>
> Compare her efforts to the work of [Toby] Stephens [Stanley] and his fellow RSC alumnus Imogen Stubbs, who plays Stanley's long-suffering and pregnant wife Stella. Here we see a conviction in text and character that makes the drama come alive, plus a technical dedication to movement, accent and behaviour that serves them, and us, well during the gruelling three-hour running time.[25]

To this critic, Lange's supremely theatrical performance was thus condemned as the inevitable result of Lange's own stardom. It was left to a couple of more perceptive critics to recognize that this superb actress was playing a self-consciously performative role. John Peter (in my view, entirely accurately) described Lange as "perform-[ing] her own life. . . . The audience (other people) is both essential and intrusive: you must impress it, but its sensibilities are never quite up to your standards and it usually leaves you in a superior, but wounded solitude." Or, as Shaun Usher put it more bluntly, "It is also an enormously histrionic performance, but then Blanche is an enormously histrionic woman."[26]

WILLIAMS'S BISEXUAL IMAGINATION ON THE BRITISH STAGE

Jessica Lange was not alone in relishing such a part as Blanche DuBois. British actors and especially actresses adore acting in Williams. A perennial complaint of talented British actresses is that there are so few meaty parts for them, since there are few successful female playwrights and still too few women's plays performed in British theaters. However, the Williams canon affords many opportunities and perhaps allows companies to justify taking on so little new work written by women themselves. Gore Vidal once claimed that actresses would testify that Williams had created the best women characters in the modern theater; his words were contested, however, by the *New York Times*'s Howard Taubman, who accused the playwright of portraying women as destroyers, sex maniacs, and disguised homosexuals, and Stanley Kauffman, who described his "viciousness towards women . . . [and] transvestite sexual exhibitionism."

In a 1994 series of interviews in the *Independent*, four top British actresses who had played recent roles in Williams productions described the pleasure of acting the playwright's female roles.[27] Frances Barber confirmed the fact that women are attracted to Williams's writing. For her, Williams understood women's propensity to be violent toward themselves: "We tend to turn upon ourselves and implode when unhappy. Williams understood that in an uncanny way." However, she enjoyed his characters' "large souls," arguing that "his women continue in the face of hell. The men don't." Sheila Gish claimed that playing Blanche DuBois changed her acting: "It freed me. Before that, I was a very English actor. It has informed everything else I've done. . . . The women's parts in his plays are the best parts. . . . Blanche is the single greatest part ever written for an actress." Lois Weaver echoed this, describing Williams's women characters as desiring subjects: "Their desire drives them. That was really shocking. Women who wanted sex and had their own desires." Clare Higgins went further, arguing that Williams did not separate men and women in the way most playwrights do, that his homosexuality allowed him to be nonjudgmental about women, get inside the mind of both genders, and give women a broader range than that of most writers.

All the actresses quoted here alluded to his homosexuality as an indicator of his sympathetic identification with, rather than objectification of, women and femininity. Higgins suggested that the character of the Princess, in *Sweet Bird of Youth,* was Tennessee Williams in drag, since he claimed he had made every speech she gives in the play. However, she said that her normal feeling—as an actress acting in male-authored plays—was to feel like a woman in drag, wearing high heels and makeup; with Williams's female parts, she saw the "drag" element as "a survival mechanism." Lois Weaver, who directed and played the part of Stella in a comic gay and lesbian version of *Streetcar,* claimed that Williams understood and empathized with women: "He understood loss and longing and displacement in a society that had no regard for women."

Blanche is often referred to as Williams's self-portrait, Williams in drag. Gay and queer criticism rejects such simplistic equation, rightly identifying the female characters as successfully projected facets of complex psychological and theatrical insights. Actors certainly relish Williams's bisexual imagination and see as part of his strength this cross-gender identification and understanding. Michael Oaks, a male actor who played the part of Blanche in 1991, defined for his audience the universal quality of the character that transcends a limited gender definition: "Try to personalize Blanche for yourself. Own her experience. For she is anyone who has ever suffered unjustly from a world gone suddenly wrong. She is the bag lady you scurry past on your way to work. She is every AIDS patient abandoned by a misunderstanding society. Blanche is you."[28]

"THE MILK TRAIN DOESN'T STOP HERE ANYMORE"

In 1994, a British production hit the headlines, intriguing audiences and critics alike. The Glasgow Citizens' Theatre, known for its radically innovative theatrical work and stunning colorful productions, staged the rarely performed *The Milk Train Doesn't Stop Here Anymore* (1962). The major part of Flora Goforth, a bitter, rich old lady in this "comedy about death," as Williams called it, was played by the six-foot, four-inch tall actor Rupert Everett, rendering the play—in one critic's words—"a monster of camp style with a gender-bending twist."[29] The Witch of Capri, as in Joseph Losey's film version, *Boom!* (1968), was played by a male actor, this time David Foxxe. The Citizens' had first opened its doors in 1969 with an unsuccessful production of the same play, starring Constance Cummings, and since then had developed a strong tradition of cross-gender casting. Its second production starred Everett, whose stage career had begun in its theater and who had gone on to become a matinee idol with film roles in *Another Country, The Madness of George III*, and *My Best Friend's Wedding*. Actresses as distinguished as the southerner Tallulah Bankhead and the British Hermione Baddeley and Elizabeth Taylor had already played the role of "the old Georgia swamp-bitch" Flora, while Everett had wanted to take it on for many years.

A good friend of Williams's literary executor, Maria St. Just, Everett tried to persuade her to allow this, but for a long time she resisted on the grounds that Williams's reputation must be protected, she did not like the cuts he proposed to the original script, and she suspected he was trying to send up the dramatist. St. Just agreed to the proposal just before her death in 1994, and the production was staged between 28 October and 12 November of that year, in a double bill with Noël Coward's *Private Lives*. Both plays were directed and designed by Philip Prowse, one of the key director-designers at Glasgow and a close friend of Everett's. The Coward Estate would give no permission for a gender-bending interpretation of *Private Lives*, but St. Just's death allowed considerable artistic freedom for *Milk Train*.

The play focuses on the last days of memoir-writing "Sissy" Goforth, who is dying of cancer on the Italian "Divina Costiera," where she is constantly preyed on by fortune hunters and finally by the gold-digging young poet known as "Angel of Death." This was a play that—despite a triumphant premiere in 1962 at the Spoleto Festival, Italy, featuring Hermione Baddeley—is generally dismissed as a critical and popular flop. A product of Williams's "Stoned Age" 1960s, and a depiction of what he referred to as "the deepening shadows of my life as man and artist," it is regarded as the meanderings of a playwright who had lost the script.[30] The Prowse-Everett version, designed to make the play come alive for contemporary, especially young, audiences, offered a fantastic, sculptural setting that moved from a signified Mediterranean site to a hospital ward, revealing Sissy to be in the last throes of dementia caused by AIDS. Philip Prowse's design recognized—as several critics did not—the hybrid symbolist-naturalist style that is the dramatist's trademark. His surrealist set, influenced (as perceptive critics understood) by Max Ernst, Giorgio De Chirico, and Damien Hirst, located the flamboyant heroine in a nightmare landscape of gray rock with a large tank containing a suspended sea creature. The melodramatic nature of the whole play was emphasized by the playing, then abrupt cessation, of canned laughter after comic lines.

Rather than a "drag" performance, Everett saw his interpretation as being about "a man who wants to be a woman," as a kind of "knock-on effect from the feminist revolution. We are not taking our conventional sexual roles for granted anymore."[31] The casting of a male actor as Sissy thus transformed the play into a metaphor for the physical and emotional disintegration in an AIDS-dominated generation, building to what one critic called "a company statement about sex and modern mortality."[32] Everett argued that he did not set out to convince the audience he was a woman; rather, he described himself as "a queen with dementia," a quality he has observed in people with AIDS. Playfully, he told an interviewer that he had modeled himself partly on Lauren Bacall, whom he met in Paris while filming *Prêtà-Porter:* "She was wildly camp and one day called me the wickedest woman in Paris." Reviewers were disturbed but reasonably impressed by the performance. Indeed, the confused terminology—"transsexual," "transvestite diva," "drag queen"—used to describe Everett's performance suggested critical uncertainty about what was being attempted. The *Financial Times* critic praised "one of those rare travesty performances where a man uses his physical and vocal force not to distort a female character but to intensify it," while the *Guardian's* critic dubbed the production "a fascinating failure," offering "a chill reminder of the spectre of AIDS—Goforth's demise is messy, bloody and undignified." The *Sunday Times*'s reviewer asked, "Ah, but is this acting? Or is this just a performance?" These are the very questions that, within a poststructuralist age, are germane to Everett's queer interpretation, since performative sexual identities have become a postmodern cliché. The reviewer's questions were also curiously dated, given the celebrated tradition of transatlantic postwar "drag" acting and gender switching in mainstream film, from the celebrated Tony Curtis and Jack Lemmon of *Some Like It Hot* (1959), through Mick Jagger and James Fox in *Performance* (1970), to Terence Stamp's *The Adventures of Priscilla, Queen of the Desert* (1994).

The production was expected to move immediately to London's West End, but nothing happened for three years. It then opened for a short run at the energetic and experimental theater the Lyric, in Hammersmith, and this time the production was a critical flop. The play was compared adversely with the great (earlier) Williams canon, and Philip Prowse's staging, though admired for its visually stunning qualities, was attacked for its sterile artificiality. Most damning were the reviews of Everett's Flora Goforth, accused of "self-admiring exhibitionism" and two-dimensional "simperings . . . and coldly grotesque hysterics."[33] It may be that the whole idea of this production had palled between Glasgow and London; it may be that the camp surrealism of the original had been toned down considerably to suit metropolitan audiences.

I did not see the Glasgow production, but I, too, was disappointed at the Lyric. Despite its dramatically beautiful surrealist set and costumes, the production had at its heart a cold emptiness and forced theatricality. In order to register the grim 1990s AIDS interpretation, the play needed to engage the audience—with either pathos or sensuous pleasure. Neither was achieved. There was little or no erotic charge between the desperate, dying Goforth and Christopher (Angel of Death); indeed, the latter was played disastrously as a rather dull, handsome young tourist on the make. The Kabuki theme, which recurs in Williams's plays, was absurd within the static pseudo-naturalism of the play and the use of popular music—from the Rolling Stones to Chubby Checker—merely gratuitous. Rupert Everett's Goforth was aptly compared by critics to a pantomime dame, Cruella de Ville, and David Bowie as Ziggy Stardust—or, in Sheridan Morley's apt epithet, "not so much La Dame aux Camélias as Auntie Mame on speed." The AIDS theme was spelled out with lumpen earnestness; as critic Susannah Clapp suggested, this is "a play about a painful encounter and about treachery, elements which are lost in a sandbagging production, eager to take Williams out of his closet and into the world of AIDS."[34]

The ambition of both Prowse and Everett to make Williams's play relevant to new audiences—especially younger movie- rather than theatergoers—paid off in terms of the massive press attention and publicity afforded to those innovative theaters, the Citizens' and the Lyric. This production's audacity in terms of gay and gender politics should, however, be put into the context of two earlier productions of another Williams play, *Cat on a Hot Tin Roof* (1955). In 1958, Peter Hall directed the British premiere of *Cat* in London, and because the Lord Chamberlain refused to give it a license on the grounds of its homosexual theme, London's Comedy Theatre was turned into a private club in order that the production could go ahead. Thirty years later, long after the demise of the Lord Chamberlain's office, the director Howard Davies staged *Cat* at the National's Lyttelton Theatre, at a point of high homophobia within the British government. Davies spoke of parallels he had found between 1950s America and 1988 Britain. *Cat* was first produced during America's McCarthyite period, and its focus on disaffected and dissident young men and women unable to express their subversive dissatisfactions compared ominously with late 1980s American and British society then in the grip of moral rearmament groups. Davies compared the character of Brick to the legendary figure James Dean, as well as other sensitive and androgynous

1950s male stars. At the time the National production opened, February 1988, the Conservative government had just passed into law the Local Government Bill, containing the now infamous Clause 28, which forbade the discussion or promotion of ideas about homosexuality within local authorities. This bill, opposed by a very wide spectrum of groups and individuals alarmed at the silencing of debate and information about such a crucial issue, was condemned as a McCarthyite move against gay free speech and autonomy. Critics were not slow to recognize in Davies's Cat a dramatization of the perils of suppressing truths about human sexuality and sexual ambivalence.

In 1999, the gay Spanish director Pedro Almodóvar won the Cannes Film Festival Best Director Award for *All about My Mother*, a film about theatricality, gender roles, and self-creation, focused around several dramatic performances of the play *A Streetcar Named Desire*. Like earlier theater directors, Almodóvar drew intertextually on Williams's histrionic, ironic, and tragic play for his focus on performativity in life and art, in order to examine the contemporary meanings of motherhood and mothering, desire, suffering, and death. As with Everett's *The Milk Train Doesn't Stop Here Anymore,* a post-AIDS, queer production brought a revitalizing European sensibility to bear on the questions Williams opened up so suggestively around gender and sexuality.

REDISCOVERING THE RADICAL TENNESSEE WILLIAMS

While issues of gender identity and queer politics brought Williams to new, younger, feminist and gay theater- and moviegoing audiences through the eighties and nineties, albeit with mixed success, British theater productions were also rediscovering other aspects of the political Tennessee Williams, attempting to rescue him from the reputation of romantic dreamer that had come to haunt (and date) him. Arthur Miller had long been a favorite of British audiences, recognized for his strong liberal humanist politics; Williams has been dismissed too often as the fey cousin. But in two 1990s productions on the London stage, a determined effort was made to rediscover a socially concerned, racially radical Williams, to give his work that sharp edge that has always made Miller a critical and popular success with mainstream audiences. Significantly, both involved a certain amount of archival research, as well as cooperation from Maria St. Just.

On 16 June 1994, The Lyttelton Theatre (part of England's National Theatre) saw the first night of Richard Eyre's production of *Sweet Bird of Youth*. This had been a long time coming, involving the director in a major rethinking of the Broadway versions of the play (especially Kazan's script) and a revision of the whole work by synthesis of various versions that existed in Williams's manuscripts at the University of Texas. In an essay written for the production program, Eyre described his process of preparation and revision: discussion with Maria St. Just, archival work, and redrafting. In the course of his research, he found a letter from the playwright to his then agent, Audrey Wood, typed in capital letters and describing the theme of *Sweet Bird*:

> IT IS ABOUT: THE BETRAYAL OF PEOPLE'S HEARTS BY THE SUBTLE PROGRESS OF A CORRUPTION THAT IS BOTH PERSONAL AND SOCIAL; THE TWO INFLUENCES—THE NATIVE POWER-DRIVE OF THE INDIVIDUAL AND THE FALSE VALUES WITH THEIR ACCENT ON BEING "TOP DOGS," ON FIERCE COMPETITION FOR A SUPERIOR POSITION—THAT DEFEAT THE POSSIBLE TRUE AND PURE AND COMPASSIONATELY LOVING RELATIONS BETWEEN PEOPLE.[35]

Taking his line from these words, Eyre planned his play script around a politically charged structure that edged the play away from melodrama and elegy and made it into a contemporary drama about the intersections of wealth, power, and fame.

The play is set in a hotel in St. Cloud, a small Gulf Coast town dominated by Boss Finley, racist and hypocritical politician, whose daughter, oh-so-white Heavenly, was raped and infected with venereal disease while in California visiting her boyfriend, Chance Wayne, an aspiring actor jailed on a drug charge. Heavenly's infection led to the need for a hysterectomy and thus to the loss of this southern belle's chances of motherhood. Chance returns to St. Cloud in the company of his meal-ticket patron, Alexandra Del Lago, Princess Kosmonopolis, an aging, addicted actress convinced she is truly washed up. Both cling together in a joyless haze of sex, alcohol, and drugs, she in a desperate attempt to regain some self-respect (which she does by the end), he in the hope that he can regain his innocence with Heavenly. The middle section of the play features Boss Finley's public appearance defending the random castration of a black man as a way of protecting white southern womanhood. Demagogue Boss's henchmen threaten Chance with similar castration because— like Finley's imaginary black rapists—he has violated white southern femininity. The play ends with Chance awaiting the bloody deed.

In most published versions of the play, the encounters between Chance and the princess (Acts 1 and 3) are separated out from the Boss Finley political subplot (Act 2), and the play ends with Chance acknowledging the arrival of the castrators, turning to the audience and asking for "your recognition of me in you, and the enemy, time, in us all." Richard Eyre believed that this division into three acts was not Williams's original intention and that it made no sense of the play. To him, divorcing the Boss Finley material from the rest of the play lost the central meaning, which is that "personal and social" corruption described in Williams's letter. He therefore restored the play to the *two* acts originally planned by the playwright, in order to bring together in each half those different corrupting influences and to show the fading playboy trapped between major forces of greed, embodied in the princess and Boss Finley.

He also sharpened up the racist political theme that Broadway versions had always obfuscated. In the production program, critic Christopher Bigsby pointed out that Williams began working on the play in 1955, the year after the Supreme Court ruling on school desegregation, and that for the playwright "the fact of racism was one more evidence . . . of what had destroyed his version of America: the victory of the powerful over the dispossessed." So, while Williams rarely included black actors in his plays and was hardly a sophisticated critic of racism, nevertheless he was fascinated by "the corruption which generates it."[36] Eyre incorporated Boss's racism within the main dramatic line and transformed the threatening castrators at the play's conclusion into Ku Klux Klan members with flaming torches. The final scene included the offer of a black waiter, Fly, to help Chance escape by the back way, signaling a Christian act of redemptive, racially integrated generosity. In the play script with which his actors worked, Eyre chose Williams's version of the ending, in which Chance escapes to join the princess in the getaway car; however, in the theater, he made Chance stay to accept his nemesis (though without the lyrical final words of earlier versions). By choosing his own preferred ending from various possibilities, Eyre defended himself by suggesting that the playwright would have approved. He quoted

Williams's laid-back (if tongue-in-cheek) response to Maria St. Just about a Moscow production's happy ending for *Streetcar*: "They're right, Maria. Blanche would have conned her way out of that mental home in a fortnight, and she'd have married Mitch."[37]

British critics adored this production, though few read it in the antiracist terms Eyre himself intended. The play was praised for its magnificent central performances, especially the "superb gladiatorial encounter" between Clare Higgins's "Raddled Monster of the Year," Alexandra, and Robert Knepper's "genuinely tragic grandeur" as Chance, as well as its "hot-house theatricality."[38] The production was compared several times to the film version of *Sunset Boulevard,* and (since critics and audiences were familiar with the sexually explicit and sexually adventurous playwright) its ability to raise to epic and tragic levels issues of love, sexuality, the ravages of time, and hollowness of ambition was much celebrated. Most critics ignored the racial subtext, though one lone voice, Carole Woddis's, felt Eyre had turned the play successfully into "a violent, radical indictment of southern racism."[39] John Gross, crediting Eyre with trying to bring out the play's political dimension, felt this was bound to fail because Boss Finley came across as a "complete cliché," his politics "simply one aspect of his complete nastiness." Alluding to Williams's *Cat on a Hot Tin Roof,* Gross saw Finley as "a monstrous Big Daddy," the play's emphasis remaining "resolutely personal rather than public."[40] Richard Eyre's attempts to make of Williams a more hard-edged political writer, redrafting the script as he did and refusing to see Act 2 as a separate element sandwiched between the "real" dramatic struggle, went unappreciated by a body of critics determined to see the Williams they knew and loved, rather than the social realist Eyre seemed to be proposing. This version of the playwright's work had to wait a few more years to emerge onto the British stage.

A WORLD PREMIERE

In 1998, there was a frisson around a production of an early play that had never before been staged. The world premiere of an apprentice work, *Not about Nightingales* (1938), was performed sixty years after it had won its writer a drama prize, the first play to bear Williams's adopted name, "Tennessee." Staged in the National Theatre's Cottesloe auditorium, it was a coproduction by the radical, experimental

Moving Theatre company and Alley Theatre, Houston; two years earlier, they had collaborated on a repertory season of Shakespeare productions in Texas. Having worked together on a British playwright
in the States, they agreed to perform an American play, and Vanessa
Redgrave, a leading artistic director of Moving Theatre, proposed the
play that she had read about many years earlier and finally secured
through Williams's executor, Maria St. Just.[41] The director was Trevor
Nunn, the new director of the National, succeeding Richard Eyre.

There was much excitement about *Nightingales,* not least because
British critics were thrilled that one of the nation's leading (and most
controversial) actresses had "discovered" it and decided to give it theatrical life. Vanessa Redgrave had known Williams since the 1970s;
he once described her as "the greatest actress of the English speaking
theater, bar none," and she had talked to him about the possibility
of performing his play about the John F. Kennedy assassination, *The
Red Devil Battery Sign.*[42] Both that play and *Nightingales* belong to a
very different Tennessee Williams than the one of popular reputation. *Nightingale*'s central protagonist, a young convict-poet, Canary
Jim, rejects the notion of writing a poetry of beauty, telling the prison
warden that—whatever he writes about—it will be "Not about—
nightingales" (a clear reference, of course, to John Keats's famous
"Ode to a Nightingale"). The situation evoked in this play is a brutal
world of male prisons in the 1930s. Characteristic of that decade's
drama, the play is based on a real incident that occurred in August
1938.

In Holmesburg, in Philadelphia, twenty-five prisoners who staged
a hunger strike over prison conditions were locked into a steam-
heated cell called "The Klondike." The heat was turned up, and after
fifteen hours of terrible suffering, four were found dead, their hearts
shrunk to half size through dehydration. Although there was a national outcry about the punishment and deaths, the whole incident
quickly became shrouded in a conspiracy of silence. Indeed,
Williams's first title for his play was *The Rest Is Silence,* and he dedicated it to the four dead men. The play reflects the agit-prop political and economic concerns of depression America, recorded in plays
by other dramatists better known for their radical agenda—Ben Hecht,
Clifford Odets, and Eugene O'Neill. It refers directly to Roosevelt's
New Deal, the approach of war and fascism, and the authoritarianism
within American society, expressing an urgent radical anger about

injustice that critics often complain is lacking in Williams's later, more allusive and symbolic work.

Williams's youthful writing was shaped considerably by The Mummers, one of many radical theater groups set up during the 1930s with which Williams worked at Washington University, St. Louis, and then by the University of Iowa playwriting course—itself strongly influenced by the Federal Theater Project, a socially concerned program working under the New Deal Works Progress Administration. During his early period, he wrote plays about such topics as a flophouse (*Fugitive Kind,* 1937), Alabama miners (*Candles to the Sun,* 1935), and tenement dwellers (*Stairs to the Roof,* 1945); but this was not the playwright of international popular reputation. The London premiere of *Nightingales,* staged in transnational collaboration with another radical theater company, made a refreshing change, since it showed audiences a different aspect of a passionate playwright's work and insights into his early development of character and dialogue. As Trevor Nunn described it, stylistically *Nightingales* pointed the way to the later, greater work, contrasting elements of "brutal human behavior and cadenced and perfumed language."[43] The production also pointed to a new relevance for the play in millennial thought. Despite the fact that it was based on a real incident, in his first stage direction Williams makes clear his intention to universalize the theme: "The conditions which the play presents are those of no particular prison but a composite picture of many."[44] Consistent with the revolutionary agenda of Vanessa and Corin Redgrave and the Workers' Revolutionary Party (from which the motivation for their theater company comes), the production program drew attention to violent treatment and appalling conditions of prisoners in late 1990s English jails. As with Howard Davies's 1988 production of *Cat,* which drew parallels between 1950s America and 1980s Britain, this play was staged not as a period piece but as a warning against contemporary brutality and authoritarianism.

Like Richard Eyre's 1994 production of *Sweet Bird of Youth,* this version was lovingly compiled from original drafts and sources at the University of Texas, Austin, this time by Vanessa Redgrave. The version of the play that was produced in March 1998 and was printed in its first edition by New Directions in the States and Methuen in Britain was a compilation of a script owned by Maria St. Just, as well as drafts and redrafts from thirteen folders. The playwright's penchant for making copious changes began early in his career, and it has posed an intriguing challenge, not just to scholars but also to theater directors and actors. So there was a sense of theatrical history in the making, as well as a refreshing sense that Williams was being represented not merely through the obvious canon.

The production was greeted with almost universal enthusiasm by London theater critics. Most of them expressed astonishment that such a play had been written by the (as they saw him) lyrical, romantic, "fey," southern gothic Williams, and they praised Vanessa Redgrave for prizing the manuscript out of the estate. But many of them agreed that the romantic subplot failed to work, unnecessarily complicating a powerful drama. As an apprentice work, it was described as "raw," "melodramatic," and "corny and creaky." It was compared by many to 1930s "B" movies, the spirit of James Cagney invoked frequently; the fact that prison dramas have become a cinematic and televisual cliché meant that the cast had to work against audience familiarity with an old story. However, the production was widely recognized as having elevated this apprentice work to the heights of a great radical event. The direction of Trevor Nunn, known for his brilliant choreography, ensemble work, and spectacular effects, was praised for transforming the play "from a Warner Brothers' prison screenplay into a passionate and moving drama of unimaginable brutality and human endurance, interspersed with moments of great tenderness."[45]

There was much admiration for Richard Hoover's stark monochrome set, in which everything in this "little suburb of hell" was shades of gray and presented a relentlessly noisy and oppressive steel edifice of prison cages, doors, corridors, and bunk beds, punctuated with agit-prop neon captions. The two actors playing the prison tyrants (Williams calls both "Mussolini")—Moving Theatre's Corin Redgrave as the cruelly charismatic prison governor and Alley Theatre's James Black as prisoner ring leader—were rightly praised for mesmeric performances. Nicholas de Jongh spoke for most critics and audiences when he proclaimed this was "one of the most remarkable theatrical discoveries of the last quarter century" and "one of the best theatre-documentaries." With words that echo the claims made for the play by Vanessa Redgrave and Moving Theatre, he said:

> With a cinematic structure, an almost Jacobean sense of horror and suffering, and poetic flashes of later Williams, the play remains unlike anything else he wrote.

> As a warning-message for end-of-century Britain and America, whose prisons remain reception-centres for institutionalised violence, cruelty and abuse, *Not About Nightingales* has hardly dated at all.[46]

I share the critics' enthusiasm. The sheer claustrophobia evoked within the small Cottesloe auditorium, with the relentless gray color of set, costume, and props, enclosed the audience in an oppressive, confrontational trap. The superb ensemble work of the two companies confirmed both the wisdom of transatlantic collaboration and the excitement of bringing to bear those two very different acting styles Richard Eyre outlined: classical training, which gave Corin Redgrave presence, verbal authority, and power, and psychological and emotional training, which made the American members of Alley Theatre convey a powerful and physically violent presence, as well as a bravura display of emotional and sexual humiliation and frustration. In late 1998, the production was transferred very successfully to Broadway as part of the British theater revival on the New York stage. This binational production was returning across the Atlantic new excitement to a forgotten Williams play, and a neglected face of the playwright.

THE TENNESSEE WILLIAMS BANDWAGON

At the end of the twentieth century, there was no sign of the Williams bandwagon slowing down on either side of the Atlantic, and, judging from the plethora of new productions of his plays, his popularity had become stronger than ever.[47] A new growth industry, however, developed in the 1990s in line with the international trend in cultural tourism. Suddenly, the very itinerant and restless writer who moved constantly through cities, states, and countries was adopted by two particular places that wished to claim him for their own. In 1986, New Orleans (spoken of frequently as his "spiritual home") launched an annual Tennessee Williams/New Orleans Literary Festival, and six years later, Clarksdale, Mississippi, his grandfather's long-term and his own childhood home, initiated the annual Tennessee Williams Festival.

These were shrewd commercial ventures, capitalizing on the Williams connection in order to increase middle-class tourism and thus cultural cachet for each chamber of commerce. There is a peculiarly southern way of going about these festivals: much emphasis on good food, drink, and social events, with music, dramatic productions, panel discussions with invited celebrities, and so on. Both festivals bring together local people who have memories of the playwright for a nostalgic session of "I Remember Tennessee." Both offer walking tours around key sites associated with the playwright: in New Orleans, his homes, favorite bars and bookstores, apartments where he got drunk, the route of the now defunct Desire streetcar; in Clarksdale the Episcopal church where his grandfather the Reverend Dakin was rector, Moon Lake, which appears in many plays, and the cotton plantation believed to be the model for Big Daddy's in *Cat on a Hot Tin Roof*. Small-town Clarksdale offers modest celebrations in the form of one-act plays performed by amateur and high school groups on front porches, as well as picnic box lunches and other community ventures. The New Orleans Festival is now well established, and with larger ambitions it draws together a reasonably cosmopolitan gathering of speakers and visitors.

The first festival was established by a shrewd group of New Orleans's cultural elite—broadcasters, journalists, and academics—to counter the increasingly philistine nature of the city's tourist attractions (drink, food, gambling) with an event that would generate intellectual excitement for both local people and the international tourists who flocked to the city in its warm, gentle spring. A surprising number of that elite had known the playwright (or knew someone who did), had researched, written about, or taught his work, and regarded him as one of the city's most important sons. New Orleans, as I have already demonstrated, has a long and honorable tradition of welcoming and nurturing writers, from Sherwood Anderson and William Faulkner to Ellen Gilchrist and Anne Rice.[48] Many locals regard Tennessee as one of their own and, although conceding that he could not help the place of his birth, can hardly forgive him for not dying there. He discovered himself as artist and gay man in this relaxed and pleasure-loving city and returned frequently, even buying a house in which he never settled: "If I can be said to have a home, it is in New Orleans where I've lived off and on since 1938 and which has provided me with more material than any other part of the country."[49]

The festival has become an extremely successful annual event, larger each time, organized with considerable enthusiasm and professionalism by the city's cultural movers and shakers, acquiring the kind of reputation that makes top people, restaurants, and hotels want to be associated with it. As befits a city internationally noted for its cuisine, the festival's panel discussions, lectures, dramatic productions, and readings are punctuated regularly by feasts prepared by the Madeleine French Bakery, Broussard's Restaurant (one of Tennessee's favorites), and the famous Monteleone Hotel, where the playwright liked to stay.[50] And while delegates buy souvenirs, drink Pimms cup courtesy of the Napoleon House bar, and munch birthday cake supplied by Omni Royal Orleans Hotel, they are annually regaled with reminders of Williams's faithlessness to his friends, his lies, unmailed letters, vicious behavior, and familial and sexual betrayals; at the same time, with tributes to his genius as writer, talker, thinker, drinker, and a man of the South, "one of us."

Despite all the open friendliness to all comers, the southern critics and literati believe at heart that "Tenn" (or "10," as he signed himself to friends, a pun made much of during the tenth festival) came from a southern culture and sensibility and thus is explicable first and foremost to southerners or those very close to them. Although there is much truth in this, the fact that Williams embraced a cosmopolitan and decidedly unparochial lifestyle, group of friends, and literary and dramatic influences means that nonsoutherners can bring to the study of his work and life perspectives that can only enlarge his reputation. The danger of institutionalizing such a festival (the same would apply to Clarksdale's) lies in its encouragement of an insular, protective attitude toward one's subject and a suspicion of newcomers and outsiders.

JOHN LAHR VERSUS LADY MARIA ST. JUST

During the 1995 and 1996 festivals, enormous hostility was expressed toward a woman whose name has emerged as a significant one in Williams's British theatrical history: his bosom friend, literary executor, and cotrustee of the Rose Williams Trust until her death in 1994, Lady Maria St. Just. Maria Britneva, an actress born in Russia, who married in 1956 the Morgan-Grenfell banking heir Lord St. Just, met Williams in 1948 and was an intimate for the next thirty-five years, until his death. He invited her to join him for first nights and holidays, stayed frequently as a house guest at her family homes in Belgravia and Wiltshire, England, and became godfather to her eldest daughter, Pulcheria. They wrote hundreds of letters to each other, selectively published as *Five o'Clock Angel*. He made her a trustee of his estate, allowing power of veto over productions and entrusting her with the care of his precious, hospitalized sister, Rose.

In a preface to the letters, director Elia Kazan described her as having a special place in the writer's life, providing "a loyal, because absolutely true, reaction" to his work, and being someone he could count on "when he was troubled or 'lost.'"[51] Dakin Williams, criticized for the decision to go against his brother's final wish to be cremated, argued the playwright's body should be buried because the two trustees, of whom Maria St. Just was one, had already made that decision before him.[52] St. Just herself died in 1994. The 1995 Tennessee Williams Festival was the first occasion for scholars and friends to discuss the significance of her unexpected death, and everyone was gossiping about an attack in the *New Yorker* on the recently deceased St. Just by critic and friend of Williams John Lahr.

Lahr began by quoting approvingly the claim that Lady Maria St. Just was "neither a lady nor a saint nor just," and he became increasingly vicious.[53] Although acknowledging her role in doubling the estate income to approximately one million dollars a year and bringing on board good British actors, he accused her of many crimes. So obstructive had she been to scholars and biographers that more than ten years after Williams's death there was still no edition of his letters or standard editions of the plays.[54] His library was unavailable; there was no publisher's schedule for his unpublished work; his journals still awaited publication. She stood accused of attempting to scupper Lyle Leverich's biography and of disapproving of any emphasis on homosexuality in productions (since she believed Tennessee was a lapsed heterosexual who would one day marry her). She repeatedly vetoed American productions of the plays, meanwhile approving selected British versions, and she tried to make an English playwright out of the very southern Tennessee. She was finally blamed for securing an unhealthy hold over Tennessee during the 1960s, his "Stoned Age" of sexual promiscuity and dependence on drugs and alcohol (all of which, Lahr claims, she abetted). It was this that led to Williams's great professional betrayal, the abrupt split with agent Audrey Wood.

The 1995 festival enabled Williams scholars to celebrate the removal of one of their major obstacles and also to welcome the forthcoming Leverich biography, which had been cleared by the estate shortly after St. Just's death. At various panel discussions, speaker after speaker condemned the adverse effect St. Just had had on Williams's production, research, and publication. Leverich, in measured tones, conceded her wit, charm, and responsible concern for Rose but regretted her role in blocking his biography to the last. He claimed that her objection to his work was that it might prove to be "pathography," revealing many of her own, as well as Tennessee's, peccadilloes. Had she not died, this authorized biography, quoting as it did so extensively from unpublished materials, would never have been able to be published.

Virginia Spencer Carr, currently preparing her own biography, *Tennessee Williams: A Life,* confirmed Leverich's stories and added her own, claiming that St. Just had tried to prevent key friends, such as Paul Bowles and Gore Vidal, from talking to her. Both biographers confirmed that St. Just had her own ideas about the authorized biography, insisting it should be written by a woman but one of her choice: she had engaged Margot Peters, acclaimed biographer of Charlotte Brontë. Virginia Carr noted that Peters was to be allowed to use only the quotations permitted by St. Just and as a result of such editorial control dropped out of the project. John Lahr himself reported that Peters screamed down the phone at Maria, "You have ruined Tennessee Williams! . . . You're ruining him! You're ruining his reputation! You're ruining scholarship for him!"[55] Carr continued with her own work, which will presumably now see the light of day.

It is tempting to see the hostility of American critics and scholars to St. Just as a result of a certain jealous resentment about the extent of her influence over Williams in life and his estate after death. She was, after all, a Russian by birth, English by marriage, who exerted extraordinary power over a southerner who perhaps relied too much on the kindness of strangers. It must be irritating to read her claims that she gave Williams the idea for the unicorn in *The Glass Menagerie* and the phrase "no-neck monster" in *Cat on a Hot Tin Roof* (besides Kazan's assertion that Maggie the Cat was the playwright's portrait of Maria herself);[56] even worse, to know that control over his published and unpublished manuscripts was solely in her hands. Dakin Williams was not the only one of the close circle to accuse her of fortune hunting and conspiracy (and worse) toward the trusting playwright. It is, therefore, interesting to examine her reputation across the Atlantic in the same period, to see if her influence on Williams was regarded universally as malevolent.

THE BRITISH PERSPECTIVE ON MARIA ST. JUST

What one finds in England is little but (public, at least) admiration and praise from the highest theatrical authorities. After her death, she was praised for her fierce defense of the writer's work and for her inspiration of some of his key characters, including Maggie the Cat. The *Times* obituary proclaimed unequivocally:

> Maria Lady St. Just will be remembered historically for her single-minded partisan promotion of the plays of Tennessee Williams. As his literary executor, she devoted herself to ensuring that they were presented in quality productions, by leading directors, with actors who were equal to his bravura poetic realism. She ensured that the years after his death saw not, as so often is the case, an eclipse but a renaissance.[57]

The *Guardian* claimed that Williams's "artistic heritage could not have been entrusted to a more vigilant administrator."[58] Five years later, homage was paid to St. Just in a dramatization of the Williams–St. Just letters by her friend and collaborator, Kit Hesketh-Harvey. In 1999 and 2000, the Red Pear Theatre Company staged *Five o'Clock Angel* in London and Antibes, France, putting the words of hundreds of the letters, as well as speeches from the plays themselves, into the mouths of two actors who depicted the four decades of friendship between this unlikely pair.[59]

St. Just had first met Williams at the home of Sir John Gielgud, and she was a close friend and respected associate of key people in the theater, from Sir Peter Hall, Sir Richard Eyre, and Ned Sherrin to actors such as Vanessa Redgrave (though she was loathed by certain actors such as Sheila Gish, who claimed that St. Just prevented them from playing certain roles, and by young directors like Howard Davies, who refused to flatter her). In the 1990s, Hall and Eyre were responsible for putting lesser-known Williams plays on the theatrical map and creating a vogue for his work in Britain; both had nothing but praise for St. Just. In the program for his 1994 production of *Sweet Bird of Youth*, Richard Eyre wrote an obituary note about her, in which he conceded her willfulness and imperiousness as literary executor, especially over permissions for performance, but described her as "a devoutly and indelibly loyal friend, an amusing, affectionate companion." Most pointedly, he echoed Elia Kazan's admiration for her taste: "I never knew her to be wrong about Williams's work."[60]

He especially praised her for agreeing to his proposed production of *Sweet Bird*; she had arranged to send five play drafts he had requested from the University of Texas Williams archives, and they arrived the day of her death. It was this kind of generosity she proffered to Vanessa Redgrave, when she produced the manuscript of *Not about Nightingales*. Furthermore, as I discussed earlier, despite standing accused of resisting homosexual elements in productions, just before her death St. Just agreed to Rupert Everett's request to perform as Flora Goforth.

Peter Hall agreed with Richard Eyre's assessment of St. Just's merits, arguing that she "was largely responsible for putting the Trust back into financial health and indeed developing [Williams's] reputation worldwide."[61] Both men conceded she was a woman of strong views, likes, and dislikes, who was thus regarded as a dangerous influence on the writer's work. They concurred over John Lahr's article, Hall regarding it as "a misrepresentation of a very caring person," while Eyre described it as "full of lies and half-truths, bile and pathetic attempts at post-mortem revenge."[62] Kit Hesketh-Harvey, who was hired to coedit the St. Just letters he later dramatized, agrees with the "revenge" motive. He explained that John Lahr had also been hired to coedit the letters but made the mistake of suggesting to a touchy Maria St. Just that they be performed, with actress Elizabeth Taylor playing St. Just. Lahr was unceremoniously fired, and vengeance emerged later in print.[63]

From a transatlantic perspective, the relationship between playwright and actress is a significant one. Williams was drawn to St. Just because of her vivacity and energy, as well as her ability to make him laugh and do small wifely tasks for him. However, he was also fascinated by her mixed European heritage, especially the Russian elements (however mythified, as Lahr claims). Calling her in his *Memoirs* "the furious Tartar," he loved being welcomed into her extended family, listening to her grandmother's and mother's stories of Russian life. Maria's mother, Mary Britneva, was a linguist who had translated into English Williams's favorite playwright, Chekhov. There is no doubt that Williams found in St. Just the appeal of the exotic, in terms of her Russian ancestry and also her English aristocratic marriage. He frequently visited her at her husband's ancestral Palladian villa, Wilbury, and took advantage of her contacts in the English aristocratic and theatrical worlds. Her fantasies about a possible romantic marriage with him, about her own background and acting talent, were little more than a flattering amusement or mild irritation for Williams. His cosmopolitan interests and friendships, as well as deep fascination with English life and theater (even to the extent of considering settling in England in the late 1970s), made St. Just a natural companion. There is no doubt that she smoothed his path into certain circles and provided useful mediation between Williams and key figures of the British stage.

The name of Maria St. Just arouses strong feelings on both sides of the Atlantic. It may well be that St. Just's favoritism toward the charming British directors who knew how to persuade or manipulate her really did tip the balance in favor of British productions during the eighties and early nineties. The directors can perhaps afford to be cavalier about the state of the scholarship, which was at the very least heavily handled and, in the case of Lyle Leverich, inexcusably roughshod. As the many accusations and counteraccusations surrounding an estate such as Sylvia Plath's demonstrate, the interests of executors and scholars are often miles apart. In St. Just's case, the bitter and defensive feelings on both sides of the pond have obscured an objective account of the extent to which Tennessee Williams's transatlantic friendships and theatrical dealings shaped and modified his southern themes and preoccupations and ultimately tranformed transnational understanding of the plays.

TENNESSEE WILLIAMS AND "THE HOT SOUTH"

Despite the plays' unevenness, the lack of critical attention paid to his fiction and poetry, and his neglect during the last decade or so of his life, Williams's work has held its own and grown in popularity. In Britain, he is now one of the most sought-after choices for "set texts" on examination curricula, and his strong appeal to school and college students has undoubtedly led to a wider demand for productions of the plays, including the lesser-known works that feature on few curricula. Audiences' evident enthusiasm for the smoldering South he seems to represent has without doubt led to a noticeably expanding market for other contemporary southern writers.

In chapter 1, I quoted Nancy Covey's characterization of the American South as a place of "heat." Indeed, the adjectives that are used repeatedly to describe Williams's plays, by directors, actors, and critics alike, suggest that he has played an important part in the creation of an emotional "Hot South": passionate, overblown, intense, operatic, melodramatic. Playwright John Osborne praised the work for being "full of private fires and personal visions and worth a thousand statements of a thousand politicians," while Richard Eyre claimed: "What Tennessee did—the whole southern thing—was to intensify everything, everything is hotter, the temperature is hotter, emotions are hotter, everything is more vivid, more dramatic. It's a wonderful soil for a dramatist."[64] Critics list with relish the various perversions included in any Williams play—incest, rape, alcoholism, repressed homosexuality, domestic violence, and cannibalism. These are now the staple of much film, theater, and fiction (and Williams's role in clearing the way for them is perhaps insufficiently acknowledged), but their impact in his theatrical productions is still powerful. For many directors and actors, the plays offer a raw emotional and sexual immediacy, with characters struggling between sensuality and puritanical guilts and repressions. Although the racial themes and subtexts of his work have only recently been foregrounded by directors experimenting with less familiar Williams themes, his insistence on the centrality and intense relationship of desire and death has done much to sexualize the South and southerners for an international audience, a sexualization that has opened the way for other writers, film directors, and advertisers. Vivien Leigh's mingled horror and fascination at the sweaty, T-shirt-clad southern icon, Marlon Brando as Stanley Kowalski, mesmerized generations of filmgoers, encouraging an appalled obsession with a steamy, gothic, earthy South that Williams productions on stage and film have served to mythify. So, while Arthur Miller saw *Streetcar* as "a bridge to Europe," for many Europeans the play, as well as many other Williams masterpieces, provides a bridge to America, especially to the Deep South.

The playwright's romantic radicalism—seized on by actresses looking for strong, feminist roles and progressive directors interested in problematizing gender roles and class and race definitions—made Williams a particularly appropriate playwright for millennial readers and audiences. A British critic once observed that no other American playwright had so shocked or alarmed theater audiences, and he has done more than most writers to keep alive in popular imagination an ambiguously gendered, luridly gothic, emotionally dynamic South. Recent productions have fed into that popular market for southern post-AIDS writers who deal with transgressive sexualities, such as Anne Rice and Poppy Z. Brite. But the tensions and arguments over the influence, for good or ill, of his British executor, Maria St. Just, on Williams productions and scholarship, and the special relationship with the playwright both exploited and flouted by key British directors and actors, demonstrate well the fraught quality of so many transatlantic cultural dialogues. And given the contested meanings of the South and Southernness that are constantly in play in American and British culture, the Williams revival is a reminder of how vital—indeed, hot—such meanings are in contemporary culture.

6

"A BLACK OCEAN, LEAPING AND WIDE"
The Ambition of Maya Angelou

The black American spiritual is sung in every corner of this world, and it's interesting that the writers of this great music are nameless "black and unknown bards" and in Wigmore Hall, or in the salons of France, in Germany in the opera house, in La Scala and in the country church just ten miles from my house, you can hear [sings] "Sometimes I feel like a motherless child. Sometimes I feel like a motherless child. Sometimes I feel like a motherless child a long ways from home. A long ways from home."

—Maya Angelou, BBC Radio 4, 1984

I'm a black ocean, leaping and wide,
Welling and swelling I bear in the tide.

—Maya Angelou, "Still I Rise" (1994)

It seems appropriate to end this book by focusing on a figure who, in her personal history and experience, her writing and performances, has embodied the very spirit of circum-Atlanticism. Maya Angelou, African American autobiographer and performer, has journeyed through all the spaces I have discussed—Africa, Europe, and North America—and engaged with them physically, politically, and emotionally in ways that allow her to claim herself "the dream and the hope of the slave."[1] Born in 1928, the southern great-granddaughter of slaves, Angelou moved from a traumatic and racially divided childhood, through a lifetime of heterogeneous work, relationships, and experiences, living on two continents and traveling to many more, to a position at the heart of America's establishment in the full glare of international media publicity. This trajectory has been motivated by an ambition to bring people together, bind racial and social wounds, and promulgate a Christian mission and message of love. Angelou, who insists on a very African and American southern courtesy, formality, and graciousness, has managed more than most to draw on African, American southern, and European culture and experience to produce a body of work that brings alive that triangular route to modern audiences. My purpose in this chapter is not to evaluate her writing from a literary-critical perspective but rather to examine the phenomenon she has become and to assess her significance in terms of a wider cultural agenda.

There are important parallels here with Alex Haley. Toward the end of the century, Angelou's reputation rose higher than Haley's, despite the fact that *Roots* remained the most popular and best-known nonfiction African American text. Angelou and Haley were near contemporaries who were both active in civil rights, both worked for Malcolm X, and became close friends over more than two decades. She never publicly criticized him, nor was she ever drawn into commentary on the controversy surrounding his work (except, perhaps defensively, by praising him highly). Angelou played the role of Nyo Boto's grandmother in *Roots*, for which she received an Emmy nomination, and planned to direct a TV series by the writer. He in turn was her enthusiastic cheerleader, claiming in the late 1980s that she had become "a legend" with what he admiringly called "Hollywood energy."[2] Indeed, their critical reception and reputation have many similarities. Both invested their personalities and personal histories in their work and its dissemination; both claimed for themselves virtually mediumlike qualities of writing for and on behalf of their race. They enjoyed huge popular success by writing best-selling works that were translated into other media, and they became darlings of the media and lecture circuits. Indeed, their published works acquired particular cachet and iconic status as a direct result of their dazzling personal appearances. Issues around generic definition have hovered over their "autobiographical" work, with questions raised about the "authenticity" and "truth" of their nonfictional accounts. Each writer is noted and conscientiously acknowledged in critical studies of literature and popular culture, but neither has been the subject of extensive serious critical scrutiny. In the case of Haley, I have already discussed publication silences because of the problems of his work's "veracity"; however, in the case of Angelou, there is a different story to tell.

It is useful to summarize briefly the career of this (as she dubs herself) "phenomenal woman."[3] Maya Angelou's life reflects the full range of black women's experiences in the twentieth century and encapsulates real and symbolic journeys across continents between races, classes, and genders. Born in 1928 in St. Louis, Missouri, she was sent south two years later after her parents' divorce. She and her brother, Bailey, were put on a train to Stamps, Arkansas, where their grandmother ("Momma") ran the local store. Her relatively stable early years in the racially segregated town were tragically disrupted by a return trip to live with her mother in St. Louis. The eight-year-old girl was raped by her mother's boyfriend, who was arrested and then released from jail and murdered (probably by her uncles). She blamed herself for speaking about the rape at the trial and, after returning to Stamps, ceased to speak for about five years.

Brought back to speech by a caring black woman, Mrs. Flowers, who introduced her to literature and encouraged her to read aloud, Angelou graduated from school and became a critical, independent thinker. She left Stamps a second time, to live with her mother in California. After a single sexual encounter at sixteen, she became pregnant and gave birth to her son, Guy. In California, then throughout Europe and in Africa, she worked at jobs as disparate as conductor on a cable car, cook, waitress, whorehouse madam, prostitute, driver, dancer, singer, actress, journalist, editor, songwriter, poet, autobiographer, performer, and university professor. She worked actively in the civil rights movement, appointed by Martin Luther King Jr. as northern coordinator of the renowned Southern Christian Leadership Conference (SCLC).

Beginning to write seriously only in her forties, she became an overnight success with the first volume of her autobiography, which described her childhood years, *I Know Why the Caged Bird Sings* (1969). This was followed quickly by four more volumes of autobiography: *Gather Together in My Name* (1974), *Singin' and Swingin' and Gettin' Merry Like Christmas* (1976), *The Heart of a Woman* (1981), and *All God's Children Need Travelling Shoes* (1986). She has also produced five collections of poetry (now together in *The Complete Collected Poems*, 1994), two essay collections, and several illustrated books and stories for children, as well as many song lyrics, screenplays, plays, and short fiction. She has traveled widely throughout the United States, working on both West and East Coasts, and lived for some years in Egypt and Ghana, rediscovering and interrogating her ancestral roots. She toured the world as part of the cast of *Porgy and Bess* (1954–1955), learned at least seven languages, and developed many international friendships, as well as overseeing multiple translations of her books. To complement this internationalism, she married or cohabited with a Greek American, "Tosh" Angelos; an African, Vusumzi Make; and a Briton, Paul du Feu (and possibly another national—she refuses to confirm this). In 1975 and 1977, she was placed on major national commissions by two U.S. presidents, Ford and Carter, and in 1982 became lifelong Reynolds Professor of American Studies at Wake Forest University, North Carolina. Her most visible honor was her choice, as first African American, and woman, to read a presidential inaugural poem. In 1993, for President Bill Clinton, she declaimed "On the Pulse of Morning," standing grandly before a place that, recalling the nation's exclusion of her race from the seat of power, she had described as "the cold marble steps / of America's White Out-House."[4]

This was perhaps the most prominent of many "firsts" for Angelou. She was the first black conductor on the San Francisco streetcars, the first black woman to write a Hollywood film (*Georgia, Georgia*, 1972), the first black woman nonfiction writer to reach the national best-selling lists (and to stay on them longest), the highest-selling black female writer in the world, and more. A southerner who, unusually for her generation of African American artists, returned to live and work in the South and who openly glories in her southern heritage, Angelou has developed a huge international reputation and popular following. And in the final decades of the century, Angelou's consummate abilities to become the performance artist for a hungry world media elevated her popular profile across a range of outlets higher than that of other, more critically acclaimed African American writers such as Toni Morrison, Alice Walker, and Gloria Naylor. She has been honored by universities and organizations across the globe. Although Angelou describes herself as a writer, autobiographer, and teacher, her admirers see her as a cultural icon. Phrases such as "a tower of strength, a dynamo of inner energy," "Six feet of talent and outrage," "like a diva," "a roguish Queen," and "America's unofficial Poet Laureate" all testify to the reputation of this figure who never divided her extraordinary life from her art and is recognized as having brought both together with considerable pizzazz.[5]

And with Angelou there is also a style that is exotically *southern*, one that nonsouthern interviewers comment on with both astonishment and relish: "Maya Angelou can roast a turkey of such honey-hued, crusted splendor as to weaken a vegetarian's resolve. . . . Angelou's home is a shrine to good food, good drink and good friends. You don't sit on the multitude of plump couches in her art-crammed,

shocking-pink living room, you sink."[6] Angelou's capacity for southern hospitality, especially cooking, has often been remarked on, and
her cornbread dressing recipe is available on various Web sites. This
towering woman has been seen as monumental in many ways, bearing an imposing and unforgettable presence that has proved a publicity godsend. The darling of the talk-show, newspaper article, TV
special, concert platform, and campus circuit, she acquired the kind
of cult celebrity status afforded very few writers, even in this media
age. Furthermore, this continued into her seventies, at a time when
most celebrities are long overlooked in favor of younger and prettier
models. Angelou moved from phenomenon to internationally renowned grand dame, elder statesperson, and wise woman. She was
encouraged in, and applauded for, her ambitious embrace of a
postcolonial status as circum-Atlantic—indeed world—spokesperson
on race, gender, and nation. She enjoyed the ear of presidents and
millions of readers and audiences everywhere. The late-twentieth-
century world was very much her oyster.

A CREOLIZED ANGELOU

So what kind of international figure did Angelou carve for herself?
Toward the end of the fifth volume of her autobiography, Angelou
reflects on her five years' domicile in Africa between 1961 and 1966.
"I knew that Africa had creolized me," she commented and noted
that she had "become something other, another kind of person" than
the rest of her touring acting company.[7] In these few words, there is
a recognition of the long process of transformation in Angelou during her time on the African continent and of the metamorphosis that
enabled her to become a writer who could speak across continents
for the different cultures she came to know. For Angelou, an accomplished linguist who always picked up languages easily and had a phenomenal recall of songs and poems, this process of "creolization" was
something that came out of lived experience but that needed to be
voiced through the subtleties and complexities of language. In the
late 1980s, she responded to an interviewer's question about whether
she wrote only for other blacks by saying: "I write in English, which
is not a language created for the black palate or tongue or teeth or
lips. So I'm using those tools, trying to make those tools fit a rhythm
which is really African and of Creole descension [sic] of African and

English. The person I'm writing for beyond myself is a person who can hear my melody."[8] Expressed poetically, this comes close to explaining Angelou's original contribution and the source of her enormous success, for she is describing a process of translation and use of language to bring together different tongues and cultures, in order to create a transnational discourse.

It seems that critics miss this point repeatedly. Whenever the issue of her African experiences and the Afrocentric writings comes up, critics are quick either to praise or to condemn her evocation of Africa and understanding of her adopted culture. Her sojourn in Egypt and Ghana is seen as a process of clarification, a realization that—in Brita Lindberg-Seyersted's words—"the African American is a different breed whose home is America."[9] Lindberg-Seyersted shares the widespread belief that her African experience gave Angelou a new wisdom, especially that Africa can never be the "home" to which any African American can return. Furthermore, the fact that for a black woman it is "very much a man's continent" makes it a problematic "home" for an emancipated woman.[10] But most commentators describe as a serious literary flaw the contradictions in Angelou's various insights about the African episodes. They therefore miss the importance of this process of creolization, which Angelou brings to bear in the later volumes of the autobiography and draws on in her readings and performances throughout the world.

The method Angelou uses in order to accomplish this is focusing fairly relentlessly on her own hybrid experiences. From the earliest days in which slaves struggled to express themselves despite lack of legal identity and personal freedom, autobiography and eye/I witness were ideal for African American cultural practices, from the blues to autobiographical fiction, precisely because of the need for artists to establish their right to speak at all. The slave narrative, from Sojourner Truth and Frederick Douglass to Harriet Jacobs, the postbellum and Harlem Renaissance autobiographical account, from Booker T. Washington to Richard Wright and Zora Neale Hurston, and the post-1960s political autobiography and personal essay, from Malcolm X and Alex Haley to Angela Davis and James Baldwin, all expressed the urgency of personal testimony as a crucial element in the survival and growing dignity of the African American. Angelou began to write in the late 1960s, after a prolonged period of political engagement with black politics and so was understandably caught up in that trend for foregrounding the personal as political—a revolutionary practice of both the black and women's movements.

Her first published volume of autobiography, *I Know Why the Caged Bird Sings,* followed in this tradition, recalling especially Richard Wright's hugely popular *Black Boy* (1945) and following the publication of Anne Moody's *Coming of Age in Mississippi* (1968). Though a major critical success and best-seller in the United States, it took time to be recognized outside its own country. This set the tone for Angelou's subsequent career as serial autobiographer. And acclaim for the first volume, leading as it did to demands for sequels and personal appearances by this woman already well known in show-business circles, began to put Angelou on the map. The unfolding saga of her extraordinary life seemed to confirm Angelou as a woman who embodied a representative black life within her diasporic journeyings. Her former husband, Paul du Feu, noted one example of this recognition of her status as representative. She was selected as a member of President Gerald Ford's 1975 Presidential Commission for the Bicentennial, regarded at the time as surprising because she did not represent a national or regional association or special interest group:

> Every other nationally recognised Black I could think of, with the exception of Alex Haley, was tied to a region. They were involved in regional politics like Jesse Jackson in Chicago or in entertainment like Sidney Poitier in Los Angeles. Maya and Alex Haley had been travelling the length and breadth of America for years. She had lectured the Mormon Elders in Salt Lake City, librarians in Michigan, tobacco factory workers in North Carolina, and Baptists in Harlem. And everywhere she went she probably spent ten hours in face-to-face conversation for every hour she spent on the lecture stage. It was a hell of a way to acquire an overview.[11]

Critic Kadiatu Kanneh pointed out that, in the 1990s, African American writers had a high profile as *"defining* icons of Black identity," and she argued: "The packaging of texts by Black women writers in contemporary terms relies on the foregrounding of authorial identity, on emphasising the race and gender of the author to signal authenticity, a kind of autobiographical force behind the text."[12] Surprisingly, Kanneh makes no mention of Angelou, arguing her case through Toni Morrison and Alice Walker, who both acknowledge autobiography as central to their literary heritage. But of the three of them, Angelou is the one who has gone on record as saying, "My major platform *is* autobiography," and has produced a negligible amount of fiction.[13] Many critics refer to her autobiographies as "autobiographical fiction," but this is not her own definition, since she argues that she writes "the truth" (Kanneh's "autobiographical force"?) and never theorizes about or problematizes autobiography as a form. She also frequently repeats her intention to try to live "the poetic life," indicating how closely linked she sees her quotidian and her writerly existence. Thus Angelou's daily routines, experience, thoughts, and very body provide the central focus of attention in a way no other African American woman writer has ever commanded.

Interviewers and critics galore find themselves compelled to comment on Angelou's bodily presence. British psychiatrist Dr. Anthony Clare, interviewing her on BBC Radio 4, asked if she was aware of being "a formidable woman," citing her height (six feet) as the first reason; in a long reply, Angelou discussed the conflicts about femininity inherent in her size, and her deliberate wearing of very high heeled shoes to enter a room as a "presence."[14] At the outset of his collection of interviews with the writer, Jeffrey M. Elliot speaks for many contributors when he calls her "in sundry ways, larger than life," and goes on to describe her "mellifluous southern accent . . . a voice caressingly seductive yet strong," saying that she has been called "'a giant among people,' 'a protean woman' with 'a spine of iron.'"[15] Thus Angelou's imposing size and apparent strength are read metaphorically, not simply by Elliot, and seen as awe-inspiring. Many interviewers express themselves nervous of meeting her, then relieved to find she is human.

Angelou herself invites such slippage between physical reality and moral or spiritual strength or weakness. Famously, the first volume of her autobiography opens with the young Maya's dream of metamorphosis into a pretty little white movie star, and throughout her writings negative definitions of black female beauty recur to anger and humiliate her. The autobiographies repeatedly describe people in terms of skin color, especially gradations of blackness. In a wide-ranging conversation with one of her contemporaries, writer Rosa Guy, the two women begin with a fascinating debate about "pretty hair."[16] Furthermore, she has spoken of the appalling physical symptoms she experiences when preparing to write (swelling knees, backache, swelling hands and eyes), and her work resounds with visceral responses to suffering and oppression: "It's necessary . . . to be tough enough to bite the bullet as it is shot into one's mouth, to bite it and stop it before it tears a hole in one's throat."[17]

"GLITTERING WITHOUT WISDOM"?

Perhaps inevitably, such charismatic celebrity invites skepticism and criticism. The relentless focus on the persona of Maya Angelou and her unique experiences have led some commentators to focus with a harsh lens on her life, practices, and predilections. There have been carpings about her grand manner, her inability to hear criticism, the lavish lifestyle, and mink coats and limousines that cosset her. British publisher Margaret Busby notes "the dissenting voices of those who think that fame has gone to her head, who accuse her of having too much ego and attitude, of 'wearing her ass high on her shoulders,' of being a diva who has come to believe her own hype."[18] The satirical British magazine *Private Eye* produced a parodic "Maya Angelou Diary," which wickedly captured that diva quality:

> There is an old African saying, never truer today than yesterday or the day before: "The stony path is best travelled with bare feet." Africa—my Africa—is rich in such wisdom. It is the heartland of beauty, the boiling-pot of spirituality, the very crucible of all art and literature. . . . The culture of Africa—simple, heartfelt, full of grace and hope—is everything that America's is not. And that is why I chose for my present homestead a dwelling in North Carolina with the deepest, bluest, longest, widest, most heatingdest swimming-pool you ever did see.[19]

There is a readiness to agree with her own ironic self-assessment that she "too often, glittered without wisdom."[20]

Angelou is a good example of an iconic figure whose high public profile has led to critical suspicion and neglect. True, she has been accused of "borrowing" another writer's words, though the case never developed into a plagiarism charge.[21] She has claimed (probably correctly) that other writers and critics were suspicious of her prolific output, especially in the 1970s. Ironically, she seemed excessively prolific to a British reading public, since her first volume, originally published in the United States in 1969, came out only in 1984 and was then followed in just three years by the other four volumes, which had been written over a period of seventeen years! And both her massive popularity and her very extraordinariness seem to flabbergast critics. In conversation with Dolly McPherson in the late eighties or early nineties, she claimed autobiography was not taken seriously or was dismissed summarily; she conceded (correctly) that American studies was beginning to accept it as a serious literary form, though in fact it was primarily women's studies and feminist literary studies that led the way, paralleled by renewed interest in slave narrative and other autobiographical writing by African and Native Americans.

I imagine, rather, that the uneven quality of the later volumes of autobiography, and her failure to produce a significant fictional work, diminished critical interest in her. Furthermore, the apparently transparent style and populist poetry and prose lead many interviewers and critics to describe her as a "natural writer." Angelou herself fulminates against what she sees as a devaluation of her artistry, usually going into considerable detail about how hard she works and claiming, "Easy reading is damned hard writing." To one adoring fan who assured her she had read one of the volumes in a single afternoon, Angelou frostily replied that it had taken her a whole year to write. Her well-documented admiration for chat-show host Oprah Winfrey (who made *The Heart of a Woman* an instant huge seller by recommending it through her personal Book Club, but is often sneered at as middlebrow) also raised intellectuals' eyebrows.

Angelou's mutually admiring friendship with Oprah Winfrey is not surprising, given their shared determination to be both accessible and populist. Indeed, Angelou's mantralike repetition of homilies, such as "We are more alike than unalike" and "We live in direct relation to our heroes and sheroes," can suggest the coziness of the Oprah talk show rather than the rigors of the academy. Many critics who praise some or all of the autobiographies find Angelou's poetry hard to take seriously. One spoke for many in calling the poems "tired and faded imitations [of late-nineteenth- and early twentieth-century poems] rather than fresh, new interpretations" and cruelly compared her imagery to that on a Hallmark card.[22] On the whole, literary-critical attention to Angelou's work (despite the adoption of *Caged Bird* as a required text in school and college courses) has been slight and most publication about her, in biographical, critical, and Web site form, sloppily hagiographical.[23] For many years, the only full-length study of the writer (albeit a solid and well-researched work by a scholar) came from the admiring pen of Angelou's close friend and neighbor Dolly McPherson. As with Haley, few commentators subjected her work to the theoretically and critically rigorous gaze that has been turned on Alice Walker, Ishmael Reed, Toni Morrison, and others.[24]

A VERY TRADITIONAL SOUTH

Of course, those other writers work and live at arm's length from the South, locating themselves within metropolitan urban cultural circles. Although many African American writers draw on southern material for their fiction and nonfiction and acknowledge its importance in their psychic and literary lives, most have tended to distance themselves from the region, and few settled there permanently. Maya Angelou is an exception, though even in her case this was after living in many different parts of the States and Africa. By residing in North Carolina and taking up a lifetime post as professor at a private, affluent, mainly white southern university, she returned to a region that is still regarded with suspicion by many black intellectuals but in which she feels more comfortable than any other:

> You'd have to see the South, it's so beautiful, you can understand why people were willing to fight and lose their lives for it, it's so beautiful. I do believe once a southerner, always a southerner. There's something in the rhythm, something in the pace. . . . There are moods that are particularly southern, and I feel sympathy for black people who have no southern roots.[25]

Her autobiographies are resonant with lyrical evocations of the texture of a southern childhood, growing up in a place of "light, shadow, sounds and entrancing odors," always underscored by that atmosphere she describes in Faulknerian terms as "pressed down with the smell of old fears, and hates, and guilt," and that southern accent that "recalled lynchings, insults and hate."[26] Her work fits easily within a long and very popular tradition of southern gothic, beginning with the Poe of her childhood reading and the slave narrators Nat Turner and Harriet Jacobs, through women writers who deal with subjects close to her own—Flannery O'Connor (the force of southern religion), Carson McCullers (profoundly marginalized and damaged folk), and Lillian Smith (racial and sexual transgression). The lush and warm embrace of landscape and community is celebrated without obfuscating the powerful white myth of the South, that

"region in the American fantasy where pale white women float eter-
nally under black magnolia trees, and white men with soft hands
brush wisps of wisteria from the creamy shoulders of their lady
loves."[27] More than African American male writers, Angelou acknowledges the power of the white southern myth, exemplified best by *Gone
With the Wind* but reinforced in a long tradition of southern films,
on the damaging self-concept of black girls growing up—especially
when they grew up to be six feet tall, lacking classic beauty, but with
large feet and a deep booming voice. And the profoundly segregated
section of the South that molded her character, that "flesh-real and
swollen-belly poor" hamlet of Stamps, Arkansas, becomes the prototype for a southern identity and character that provided the young
Maya with a respect for history, tradition, dignity in the face of racism, and an ironic stoicism embedded in deep religious faith.[28]

This version of the South—small town and close-knit, guided by
"mother wit [in which was couched] the collective wisdom of generations" and "customary laws" determining everything from rules
of cleanliness to the familial coded naming of adults—is presented
throughout Angelou's work as a fragile bolster against the chaos and
oppression of a white-dominated world.[29] The South of her childhood
was an old-fashioned, rule-bound, authoritarian place, in which "the
customs [were] as formalized as an eighteenth-century minuet," and
she and her brother read Shakespeare and nineteenth-century novels and poems by Edgar Allan Poe and Rudyard Kipling. Her grandmother's economic security shielded her from the worst of the
depression, and her grimmest childhood experiences took place outside the South (most notably, the rape). In her writing, Stamps becomes increasingly a mythic site of absolute security, dominated by
(grand)matriarchal power, authority, and wisdom, offering a long religious and moral schooling on which the adult Angelou can draw.
In many ways it reminds post-1960s readers of the rural, "enduring,"
communitarian South captured by writers Zora Neale Hurston, Jean
Toomer, and William Faulkner. Though the violent twentieth-century
history of the South is alluded to and features in some stock anecdotes, the overwhelming impression given of the region is of one still
recovering from and rejoicing in its slave past, religious and oral roots
and heritage, and rich traditions of fundamentalist religion, good
food, and family values.

Like a nineteenth-century abolitionist or black preacher, or a slave

narrative autobiographer, Maya Angelou is at her most lyrical in evocations of the slave experience and heritage of her people. But some-
how, twentieth-century black history is obfuscated or omitted from
her account. The Great Migration, the Harlem Renaissance, postwar
urban problems are alluded to (often through quotations from other
writers, such as Langston Hughes or Nikki Giovanni) but only in the
most general terms. Her most detailed, precise, and telling accounts
return the reader and listener to the horrors of southern slavery and
the loss of African origins. By apparently concluding her autobiography in the late 1960s, she avoided the complexities of the postwar
Sun Belt South and reverse migration, a story that produces a more
heterogeneous, postmodern South in which regional identity is less
clear and African American southern heritage melts into the muddled
homogeneity of an Americanized Dixie.

In this way she is at her most traditionally *southern*: thus she resembles not contemporaries such as Amiri Baraka or Toni Morrison
but rather Paul Laurence Dunbar and Alex Haley—and most of all,
southern Baptist preachers and singers with their insistent call-and-
response mode of delivery. It is an indication of how comfortable
Angelou is with her southern literary heritage, white and black, that
in conversation with critic and friend Dolly McPherson, she animat-
edly discusses Lillian Hellman's autobiography of growing up white
southern, *Pentimento* (1973), while McPherson compares Angelou's
"southern legacy" to that of the distinguished white writer Eudora
Welty, whose autobiographical *One Writer's Beginnings* celebrates the
King James Bible for providing "the South's writers-to-be" with the
"cadence" that lingered in their writings ("In the beginning was the
Word").[30]

"THE LITTLE ME WITHIN THE BIG ME"

The main quality that Angelou brought from her southern upbring-
ing was a somewhat old-fashioned, puritanical devotion to service and
education, invoked through ample biblical reference and allusion.
While her mother, Vivian, emerges from the autobiographies as the
feckless, reckless blues diva on whom Angelou modeled much of her
life and emotional roller-coasters, the stern but morally impeccable
grandmother Henderson made her the teacher she has become. The
blurb to her most recent essay collection, *Even the Stars Look Lonesome*,

describes Maya Angelou in all her different modes, as "Poet to the President, champion of the people, best-selling author . . . dancer, singer, film maker, activist, director, teacher, wife and mother," arguing that her unique experiences make her "one of the few people truly qualified to share her lessons of a lifetime." "Lessons" is an appropriate term, since this most recent prose collection from Angelou is the culmination of a lifetime's didactic writing, a kind of very high profile pedagogy. This may well have been prompted by Martin Luther King Jr., whom she met while working for the SCLC and both revered and loved (especially after his compassionate words about her jailed brother) and whose dynamic style is certainly discernible in her own performances.

In both her essay collections published in the 1990s, *Wouldn't Take Nothing for My Journey Now* and *Even the Stars*, Angelou is preoccupied with her customary questions: How is one to live well? How is one to respect others and at the same time love and respect oneself? What is the nature of the well-lived life? Her reflections on these issues, often repeating material from the autobiographies, are primarily directed at other women and at children, who can best empathize with, or be in awe of, her triumphs and mistakes (and reconstruct as audience the young Maya listening obediently to Momma):

Women should be tough, tender, laugh as much as possible, and live long lives.[31]

It is necessary, especially for Americans, to see other lands and experience other cultures.[32]

Mostly, what I have learned so far about aging, despite the creakiness of one's bones and the cragginess of one's once-silken skin, is this: do it. By all means, do it.[33]

The first essay collection is the more obviously didactic, the more steeped in biblical sayings, parables, fables, and moral messages. Preacher and teacher struggle for dominance in her discourse. Texts are taken from the Bible: "The Sweetness of Charity" begins with the New Testament's injunction that it is better to give than receive; "Style" reflects on the notion of turning the other cheek; there is much imagery about roads traveled, sowing seeds that fall upon arable land, and many reflections on faith and its testing. There is a preacherly tone of admonition, magisterially invoking abstract nouns to denote moral values: courage, love, virtue. Human types rather than named individuals recur: "the cruel person, the batterer, and the bigot" (34), "the complimenter" (40), "the timid sadist" (117). Her references are to the Bible, hymns, spirituals; the wisdom is from homespun and Christian tract. Usually, the essays demonstrate a quietly reflective faith that sustains and survives a hard and volatile life, but occasionally the visceral fundamentalist of Angelou's early childhood emerges to remind us of Angelou's insistence on the primacy of the body. She told one interviewer that no one could know "what demons [she] wrestle[s] with," and on another occasion she describes the knowledge of God's love: "[It] humbles me, melts my bones, closes my ears, and makes my teeth rock loosely in their gums."[34]

Her friend and mentor, James Baldwin, called *I Know Why the Caged Bird Sings* "a biblical study of life in the midst of death," and Harold Bloom explains the appeal of Angelou's work to American readers in terms of its reference to self within the paradigm of "the American Religion," originating in slaves' West African spirituality, which spoke of "the little me within the big me."[35] This emphasis on looking beyond the individual—indeed, to embracing the individual within an internationalist "big me"—further echoes the preoccupations of Angelou's preacher-mentor, Martin Luther King Jr., who "led a movement of the excluded that also 'widened the circle of the we . . . affirming a national American we and the solidarity of black people at the same time'" and spoke (as with his condemnation of the Vietnam War) as a citizen of the world.[36] And, in terms of theological philosophy, Angelou was also considerably influenced by Martin Buber. Buber was a Jewish mystical writer who, like Angelou, aimed at a broad reading public, drawing on the thinking of several other twentieth-century Jewish philosophers. His most influential work, *Ich und Du* (1923), developed a theory of dialogical relations between the self and other(s), stressing the mutually affirmative and spiritually interdependent nature of relations between the "I," another, and God.[37] It is easy to see why Angelou was drawn to such a socially responsible Jewish philosophy, since he echoed the concerns of her own people as an oppressed group who (like the Jews) could hardly afford to rely on individuality and the isolated self.

The adult Angelou drew on an eclectic religious and philosophical background, from the stern strictures of her somewhat orthodox matriarchal teacher, grandmother Henderson, the literary texts that coaxed her back into emotional health, the preaching of Martin Luther King Jr. and other African American spiritual leaders, and the moral and philosophical works she devoured as eager autodidact. Teaching the young key lessons is seen as fundamental to ensuring a just and righteous society. In an essay denouncing "Complaining," Angelou notes, "It is said that persons have few teachable moments in their lives."[38] Her grandmother, she recounts, caught her at each such moment between the ages of three and thirteen. Teaching moral lessons is a refrain in all her work (a woman teacher, after all, gave her back the gift of speech and taught her to read literature), and in her essays very often the point of the piece is a lesson learned, taught, or not passed on. For example, describing an art dealer's involuntary betrayal of his racism and then embarrassedly cutting off contact with her, Angelou regrets the lost opportunity for mutual "teaching" and uses the verb "to teach" four times in fourteen lines.[39]

The second essay collection repeats this preoccupation with teaching. Perhaps in tune with its emphasis on the last phase of life and the aging process, *Even the Stars Look Lonesome* is dedicated to children ("MY BRITISH CHILDREN . . . MY AMERICAN CHILDREN . . . AND ALL THE CHILDREN OF THE WORLD"), with whom the writer charges the responsibility "to eliminate warfare, promote equality, exile disease, establish justice and increase joy. In fact, to make this a perfect world." The teacher-lecturer tone recurs, with her insistent use of injunctions, "I suggest that . . . ," "I mean that . . . ," "I pray. . . . " This time she celebrates as great teacher her recently deceased mother, Vivien Baxter, who followed in the line of matriarchs best represented by grandmother Henderson. In a supermarket, where she aggressively denounces young women's inability to cook, Vivien Baxter is hailed as a "true teacher," something requiring not an academic qualification but "a calling" and "a bounty of courage."[40]

CHARISMATIC PEDAGOGY

In these words come together two of Angelou's central concerns: the notion of life as a series of lessons, and the idea of a moral or spiritual calling or vocation, which she sees as fundamental to her own and others' lives. In interviews throughout the seventies and eighties, Angelou reiterated her view that "we are all teachers and students, and people taught me who never even knew my name," while emphasizing the fact that life itself is a series of lessons from which the individual must learn.[41] She saw herself as a good teacher, teaching one simple, classical lesson: "I am a human being. Nothing human can be alien to me."[42] As for other African Americans, teaching has always had a political urgency for Angelou. Education—in its broadest sense—is about keeping a people's history alive, in order to prepare and strengthen them for the future. In a lively exchange between Rosa Guy and Angelou, both women (the former a keystone of the Harlem Renaissance, the latter of the civil rights era) discuss a generation "cut off from the past," with "no awareness of the struggle and their places in the struggle, and the inheritance which is theirs naturally of triumph, defeat, of the glory of struggling for equality and fairness which they have inherited by right from the people who went before them."[43] Their mutual alarm and horror at the younger black generation's casual disregard of its history of suffering and struggle are matched by their passionate concern for formal, informal, familial, and comradely education.

This sense of an urgent need for political and personal pedagogy is rendered more messianic by Angelou's conviction—a very *American* preoccupation—that everyone is called, and can always be persuaded, to aim higher. This gives both a moral urgency and a pious, even sentimental sententiousness to the essays, as well as to some parts of the autobiographies and poetry. Perhaps inspired by the example of Martin Luther King Jr., whose mantle she may subconsciously wish to don, she does not balk at the term *prophet* being used to describe her. Some critics see her as a kind of guru; Curt Davis, for instance, describes her as speaking "in the tongues of men and of angels."[44] This mixture of the spiritual and didactic can work well when the subject matter is familial or domestic, but it sits very uneasily on politically sensitive subjects.

For instance, "I Dare to Hope" is Angelou's defense of her decision to support Clarence Thomas's nomination to the Supreme Court. While acknowledging the specific reasons for the controversy over his appointment and his antiprogressive stand on many issues, notably race, she switches to that tone of utopian generality that characterizes so much of her writing. Quoting from Lamentations, she justifies her support in almost parodically clichéd terms, saying that she comes from "a people who had the courage to exist, to be when being was dangerous, who had the courage to dare when daring was dangerous, and—most important—had the courage to hope."[45] Similarly, when talking about "the chasm that exists between the sexes" within the black community, she issues a call for unity because of the shared heritage of slavery. Decrying the forgetfulness of this history, the "subjugated . . . memory" and "mutilation of memory," she urges brother and sister to come together. "Together, we may be able to plan for a less painful future. Separate, we can only anticipate further ruptures and deeper loneliness."[46] As in an earlier essay, when Angelou deplored the behavior of young blacks on the street and proposed the re-creation of "an attractive and caring attitude in our homes and in our worlds," a resort to vague hopes for future harmony and understanding rings somewhat hollow in the face of the desperate state of all America's ethnic minorities.[47]

Curiously, she decried the most famous multicultural metaphor for the United States, the "melting pot," for producing "a goo," and her most famous aphorism, "We are more alike than unalike," appears a mass of puzzling contradictions when she argues for the importance of travel in order that we may all understand precisely how *different* people are—in language, culture, and philosophy.[48] Acknowledging that travel does not necessarily prevent bigotry, Angelou opines that "by demonstrating that all peoples cry, laugh, eat, worry, and die, it can introduce the idea that if we try to understand each other, we may even become friends."[49] Such cracker-barrel philosophy diminishes the integrity of her mission.

And this is no quiet, private, subdued mission to be undertaken away from the glare of publicity. Angelou is part of that long and distinguished history of American orators, from the earliest Puritans through to Reverend Jesse Jackson. The ringing tones of the political orator, but even more the evangelical preacher—in the pulpit, at the public meeting and large rally, on TV and radio—became her forte. Growing up, she had thrilled to the preacher's voice and described it to Dolly McPherson as "going to the opera for me." Her own grandmother said she saw the young Maya as a future preacher, and so she became, trying to write down events in the form of a black minister's sermon, with a "beginning, a middle, and an end . . . [so each episode is] a level . . . always dramatic, but a level of comprehension like a staircase," offering gradual broadening of vision.[50] Her autobiographies describe various kinds of performance, which are related to convey small epiphanies or large revelations: a dramatic "revival" meeting, Momma standing up to white girls' impudence or a white dentist's racism, Angelou threatening her son's tormentors or walking out of an ambassador's party in anger at her flirtatious husband. She was schooled within a southern black oral tradition, in which the histrionic "roll of thunder" tones of the Methodist Episcopal and revivalist preachers, the store customers' "lurid tales of ghosts and hants, banshees and juju, voodoo and other anti-life stories," Mrs. Flowers's reading aloud of Dickens, and the wise saws and songs of her female relatives and close friends all taught her the arts of communication, persuasion, and (what I would call) charismatic pedagogy of her "tongued folk. A race of singers."[51] It often strikes interviewers as remarkable that this five-year-mute gawky black duckling turned into a singing, dancing, dazzling performing star. If one reads the autobiographies closely, it is soon apparent that performing one's life, thoughts, emotions, and problems was the model for all her artistic practice. Former husband Paul du Feu describes her technique in talk-show interviews: asked by the host about growing up as a black, poor single mother, she replies: "A diamond is the result of extreme pressure. Less pressure and you have coal, less pressure than that and all you have is *dirt!*"[52] Such a response, deflecting personal comment and engagement while generalizing about all human experience with aphoristic flair, would be recognized and admired by any southern preacher or teacher.

"GOING HOME": ANGELOU IN AFRICA

Of course, much of her southern wisdom, folkloric saying, manner, and style owe their origins to her African heritage, and specifically to the time she spent living and working in Egypt and Ghana. In terms of her life as an African American woman and writer, that five-year period in Africa was extremely significant. She did not go to Africa as a political gesture, nor indeed as a freedom fighter herself. She fell in love with African nationalist Vusumzi Make, lived with him in Egypt, and then realized she could no longer sustain a relationship with a patriarchal African and so moved with her son to Ghana. Her sojourn in Africa helped her see how American she was and how she could never really "go home." She claimed that since one's origins are "under your fingernails, in the bend of your hair," it is an illusion to imagine there is an ocean between where you came from and where and who you are.[53] However, for a woman like Angelou, the differences were crucial. Early in her relationship with Make, she learned what a restricted role the life of a revolutionary African man's wife would entail. While in London, at a lunchtime meeting with the wife of Oliver Tambo (then head of the African National Congress) and other African wives and professional women, she heard that many of them regarded themselves as "portable pussy," "wombs" rather than "wives."[54] According to her account, the women proclaim their own intellectual capabilities, political struggles, and spirit of survival, and they embrace, drink, and perform tribal rituals with one another. What this exchange amounts to is an elaborate performance of call and response, with the African women staging a little ceremony and then Angelou responding with tales of black American women's secret organizations and the life stories of American slaves—Harriet Tubman and Sojourner Truth. There is mutual entrancement, and Angelou comments that there, "in Oliver Tambo's English apartment, I was in Africa surrounded by her gods and in league with her daughters."[55] She recognized the significance of this harmonious and revelatory moment occurring at the crossroads of three continents: an African American among African women in an English apartment.

Maya Angelou claims to have been curious about, and hugely respectful of, Africa for many of the reasons shared by her revolutionary contemporaries. She revered its long history as a great, cultured continent, and she was caught up in its recent history of slavery, colonialism, and the earliest periods of postcolonialism (she lived in Ghana, after all, in the early years of independence). Her writings testify to an engagement with its ideological function in the Pan Africanist movement and its traditions of, and high value given to, religious practices, the family, and motherhood. Her criticisms, stemming largely from her treatment by men who tended to patronize, dominate, and misunderstand her, tend to focus on the day to day, on attitudes and styles rather than abstract political issues. What she admires about Africa is a grace and formality that she sees reproduced in the body of her grandmother and indeed in southern courtesies. She attributes her own normally soft voice to her grandmother Henderson's low tones, something she argues is African, not American. "Momma," however, had no idea she was a "culture-carrier"; for instance, she forbade Maya and brother Bailey to put their hands on their heads, a gesture (as Angelou learned in Ghana) that signified

West African mourning. The soft-spokenness and modest female drop-ping of eyes that are so often described as characteristic of the white southern belle are explained as African mores that became a central element in southernness.[56] For Angelou, this discovery of the Afri-canisms she had always assumed were black Americanisms was a plea-surable revelation, as was her renewed appreciation of the qualities of African Americans that the settled, ancient African cultures lacked and failed to value.

Her initial enthusiasm for all things African was considerably dampened by this lack of mutual fascination. Often, she found her-self the butt of simplistic and crude assumptions made about her people by Africans who readily revealed their prejudices against all Americans, making no distinctions of color or class. Through selected anecdotes, she points up Africans' ignorance of black America, such as a Ghanaian student accusing Malcolm X of being a white man, because of his pale skin, and University of Ghana vice chancellor Nana Nketsia pressing Angelou to admit that all Americans show dis-respect to mothers through the insult "motherfucker."[57] Different sexual mores and gender roles between the ethnic groups produce crises for this strong, liberated woman—notably in the expectations made of her as wife and the Africanization of her son Guy in ways that alarm his mother. "Black American insouciance" is the quality she found herself missing most in Africa—something she describes characteristically with a *physical* power, that quality of "audacious defences" just under the skin that can quickly "seep through the pores and show themselves without regard to propriety, manners or even physical safety."[58] This sense of a vibrant dynamism and volatility is the quality she finds in her mother, Vivian, and that strongly sug-gests the different rhythms of American life: what she calls "exhibi-tions of bravado, not unlike humming a jazz tune while walking into a gathering of the Ku Klux Klan."[59]

Angelou's African adventure, indeed her whole autobiography, comes to a climax in a cathartic meeting with the Ewe market women of Keta, in eastern Ghana. Just before her final departure from Af-rica, she is taken to the small town, where she is astonished to meet a woman who looks exactly like her grandmother. The meeting pre-cipitates a dramatic and emotional mutual recognition, in which sev-eral women are moved by her resemblance to another local woman. Angelou then learns that Keta, once a good-sized village, had been very badly hit by the slave trade, with every adult inhabitant killed or taken, and only a few children escaping into the bush. These children, having watched their parents set fire to the village and bash children's heads against tree trunks rather than see them sold into slavery, were taken in by nearby villagers. The women who rocked, moaned, and wept at the sight of Angelou believed she was descended from these slaves, and they mourned "Not for [her] but for their lost people."[60] The book, and entire autobiography sequence, thus concludes with everyone weeping together and Angelou joyfully proclaiming, "Despite the murders, rapes and suicides, we had survived." This apparent recognition of a maternal line allows the book to end on a decidedly optimistic note, the author claiming this "second leave-taking" was easy because her people "had never completely left Africa." Africa was sung in American blues and gospel, its color and rhythms modified, its spirit carried in the African American body.

This dénouement alludes to many other African American writings about the continent but most of all recalls the joyous ending of Haley's *Roots*. I have already noted Angelou's admiration for Haley and her acting role in *Roots*. As with *Roots*, the reader may be skeptical about the poetic coincidence of her historic meeting, at the very moment Angelou needed to leave and summarize her feelings about the continent. Cannily, she is careful not to follow Haley's claim to have found blood kin, and the close resemblances are credible within the context of a group of women trying to communicate across continents (they are initially puzzled about her inability to speak Ewe, then deeply impressed to have met "an American Negro"). I believe Angelou may have deliberately distanced herself from the neat epiphany of Alex Haley in Gambia, recognizing that too similar a revelation might raise readerly suspicions. "I had not consciously come to Ghana to find the roots of my beginnings," she says, but nevertheless she had "continually and accidentally tripped over them or fallen upon them in [her] everyday life."[61] And there is the key. It was through everyday experiences, working, performing the tasks of wife and mother, friend and socializer, that Angelou came to understand Africa and Africanisms and to track them back to her American home, where they could be reflected on, revised, and used in the later travels and writings. Nevertheless, since she usually captures her experiences with a light narrative touch, the solemnly triumphalist Keta meeting strikes a false note. The symbolism weighing on this episode seems too pat and proposes a forced holistic conclusion to the muddled ambivalences of her African experiences.

AN ANGLOPHILE ANGELOU

Although this final encounter describes some Ghanaians' fascination with her exotic American otherness and echoes the privileged treatment accorded Angelou by her African friends in high places, she claims it was exceptional. More usual, she claims, were Africans' distrust and misunderstanding (albeit in some ways justified) of black Americans. By contrast, in the other country she knows intimately, Britain, Angelou has always been seen as an exotic of a very different kind. Her otherness has opened doors and secured friends who have been an important bulwark in her writing life. It was no coincidence that she and other freedom fighters' wives felt more able to speak freely about their problems in London than they did on the African continent. Like other African Americans, Angelou found a personal welcome and intellectual freedom in Britain. She looked to Europe for inspiration, cultural allegiance, and personal support in the way of earlier artists and intellectuals such as Olaudah Equiano, Frederick Douglass, William Wells Brown, Harriet Jacobs, Nella Larsen, Josephine Baker, Claude McKay, Paul Robeson, and James Baldwin.

As with Africa, throughout the twentieth century, the image of Europe has changed radically within African American artistic and academic circles, and its popularity as refuge, home, and cultural model for black artists of all kinds changed in quality and intensity. Despite, and probably because of, its own long colonial past and shabby history of excluding and oppressing ethnic minorities and immigrants of color, Britain (or, at least, certain enlightened, liberal, intellectual British circles) has a tradition of sheltering, educating, and supporting black political and cultural figures and has remained an important site for visiting scholars, writers, and musicians. Transatlantic traffic is sustained because of London-based publishing houses and recording studios with access to world markets outside the United States, and many major British universities have close links with those publishers and with the American academy that has helped foster black culture. Before World War II, Britain and other European countries provided invaluable havens for Negro American artists, as well as transatlantic cultural stimulation for movements such as the

Harlem Renaissance and black modernism. Black writers paid tribute to their European cultural heritage, claiming that literature in English, from Shakespeare to Dickens, had shown them the possibilities of language and oiled their imaginations.

After the war, however, African American artists became impatient with their predecessors' Europhilia and tended to leave Europe behind in order to engage with the immediate domestic political and cultural crises facing their race. They may still have drawn on European models but now insisted on the primacy of black history and experience. Black Arts writers turned mainly to Africa, choosing for themselves African names and frowning on black artists who lived in Europe rather than engaging with the struggle. James Baldwin came in for such criticism and described the complexity of this moment: "I was forced to recognize that I was a kind of bastard of the West; when I followed the line of my past I did not find myself in Europe but in Africa."[62] However, this African heritage offered no simple alternative ("I had certainly been unfitted for the jungle or the tribe"), so the only alternative was to abandon both European and African "heritages" and write honestly from his own experience. This was the mood of postwar black writing and artistic practice, with many artists turning their back on European cultural hegemony, spending less time in European countries, and paying less lip service to its artists. Indeed, among African American women writers, few have lived or spent much time in Europe, and—unlike nineteenth- and early-twentieth-century writers—a mere handful have set novels in Europe or used European characters.[63]

Maya Angelou is an exception to this. Early in her career, she spent time in London, and she has visited frequently since. Ever conscious of her international readership, she pays extravagant tributes to British and other European writers she claims freed her, like Baldwin, to write about her own life. In one interview, she explained why a black girl in the South would fall in love with Tolstoy or Dickens. Her answer was that they educated her "about me, what I could hope for."[64] In May 1998, the newly formed "Friends of Angelou" organized a spectacular gala evening at London's Dorchester Hotel to mark the writer's seventieth birthday. Described by the *Evening Standard* newspaper as "a bit like a Royal Variety Performance—with Angelou cast as Queen," a body of distinguished guests, from writer Jean Binta Breeze and member of Parliament Paul Boeteng to publisher Carmen Callil and broadcaster Jon Snow, fêted the writer with song, poem, and speech.

The event was not merely a birthday party, however; it was also a fund-raiser for a charity in which Angelou had taken an active interest, the National Society for the Prevention of Cruelty to Children (NSPCC). Some seven years earlier, she officially opened the Maya Angelou Family Centre in Turnpike Lane, north London, to shelter children who (like her) were subjects of abuse. During the 1990s, she helped the charity launch a specialist service for abused deaf children and supported the NSPCC's 1999 "Full Stop Campaign" against cruelty to children. During the eighties and nineties, when child abuse of all kinds became one of the most politically sensitive issues in Britain, as on the other side of the Atlantic, Angelou's own description of child rape, both in *Caged Bird* and in media interviews and personal appearances, gave her and her work profound symbolic importance.

Angelou is a longtime Anglophile. For many years after the huge U.S. success of *Caged Bird*, she was puzzled and aggrieved that a country in which she felt at home did not seem interested in publishing her book. It appeared in Britain in 1984, after feminist press Virago's all-woman board recognized its brilliance and launched a publicity campaign supported by a warm letter of recommendation from the renowned writer, Angelou's good friend Jessica Mitford. The Mitford connection was important in bringing Angelou to England on a regular basis. They met through another London literary connection, Sonia Orwell, widow of George Orwell. Jessica Mitford (1917–1976) was Angelou's closest friend from the late 1960s until her death. They seemed, as journalist Natasha Walter put it, "the most unlikely pairing in the world," since Mitford was the sixth child of the second Baron Redesdale, raised in aristocratic splendor, the sister of Diana, who married the British fascist leader Sir Oswald Mosley, and Deborah, who became duchess of Devonshire.[65] Jessica had rebelled against her family in more ways than one, eloping at twenty with a fellow upper-class rebel and communist, and, after writing an early autobiography, became best known as an investigative journalist and socialist lecturer. The two women shared a sense of humor and imaginative determination (for instance, Mitford accompanied Angelou to Stamps, Arkansas, for a TV documentary and boasted to Ku Klux Klan protesters that she was the writer's mother), and this friendship undoubtedly consolidated Angelou's love affair with England, as well as confirming her conviction that human beings are more alike than unalike. The autobiography was an instant hit, especially after the writer herself appeared in London and went on chat shows hosted by British TV personalities such as Mavis Nicholson and Terry Wogan. Virago's Lennie Goodings describes accompanying Angelou to a reading at a predominantly black British venue, The Factory, in Paddington, where there was intense excitement: Goodings says it was as if the writer was "quenching a thirst," with people "falling to their knees" before her.[66]

Within four years, Angelou was a household name in Britain, with all five volumes of autobiography published by Virago, which continues to publish her essays and poetry. From her first visit to England, and especially after the publication of the autobiographies, the writer has been celebrated and hosted by many of Britain's white and black intellectuals. She has filled vast public halls up and down the country with her poetry readings, from the massive Liverpool Philharmonic to the cavernous Falmouth Pavilion. And she was guest of honor at a party to celebrate the election of Britain's first four black members of Parliament. Although she pulled out of the production before opening night, she composed lyrics for the London premiere of *King*, a musical based on the life of her friend Martin Luther King, and directed Errol John's classic Caribbean play *Moon on a Rainbow Shawl* for the mainly young, unknown cast of black British actors in Akintunde Productions, a company profiling the black arts in the United Kingdom for multiracial audiences.[67] *Caged Bird* is a set text on many British school curricula, as well as university American literature and women's studies courses. As I write, at the end of the century, Angelou has sold well over a million copies of her books for Virago's British, Canadian, and Australian and New Zealand markets and remains one of their three top-selling authors. Her success (along, of course, with that of other popular African American women writers) has without doubt inspired black British writers such as Jackie Kay, Andrea Levy, and Meera Syal, making their publishers realize there is a growing reading public for contemporary black writing.

Lennie Goodings believes Angelou relishes the special status she has in England and Scotland, where people delight in her style, extravagance, and glorious excesses. Furthermore, she claims the writer has a penchant for the English sensibility: "Maya likes the use of language—people speak very beautifully here, if less emotionally and spontaneously than in North America. She's very interested in the precision of language; for her it's about manners, not being sloppy in your presentation. She tends to move in very well-read circles and she enjoys herself."[68] It is no coincidence that her third husband (and, she claims, the love of her life) came from Britain.

Angelou's reverence for Shakespeare, Charles Dickens, and the Brontës led her to romanticize and idealize England and the English and to share the Anglophilia common to many Americans, especially southerners. However, she has also made an unusual and interesting transatlantic connection with Scotland (a nation with which, of course, there have been many different kinds of southern links). In 1997, the BBC and Scottish Arts Council invited her to make a program about one of her literary idols, Robert Burns. She had long been on record as admiring the eighteenth-century nationalist poet, whom she taught alongside Paul Laurence Dunbar: "Even though there was a century and an ocean between them I felt both men managed to reach into the mouths of their people and bring out the language, wit, pathos, need, and hunger, and put it all down on the page."[69] The BBC documentary *Angelou on Burns* made personal connections between the poets—both born in poverty, defenders of liberty, lovers of music, emotionally and sexually passionate, successful as writers and consequently nationally and internationally famous.[70] It also allowed Angelou to talk about her favorite theme, that human beings are more alike than unalike, to which she added a transatlantic spin: "The battle for freedom . . . from Birmingham, Alabama to Birmingham, Britain, from Dumfries, Scotland to Dunbar, Ohio . . . it is because of my identification with Robert Burns, with Wallace, with the people of Scotland for their dignity, for their independence, for their humanity, that I can see how we sing, 'We Shall Overcome.'" The program, focused on a celebratory Burns night of song and poetry, with Angelou emotionally connecting with Scottish music and words and paying special tribute to Burns's antislavery poem "The Slave's Lament" (written, as she argues, by a man who had never been to Africa or America or met a slave), gave a stylish new gravitas to her role as transatlantic cultural figure.

ANGELOU AS PICARESQUE HEROINE

So we come full circle to consider the creolized Maya Angelou of three continents, the writer who not only traveled widely but who used metaphors of journeying through her book titles and writings. Dolly

McPherson quotes Henry Thoreau's autobiographical *Walden* (1854), with its demand that each writer send an account of his life "as he would send to his kindred from a distant land," in order to compare Angelou's "geographical spaces." In Angelou's case, McPherson argues, these lands are "the self and the peculiar individuality of the self" that she probes so distinctively in a journey "to full selfhood."[71] This journey is defined very much in the terms of the improving and re-made life readers are familiar with from the Bible, *Pilgrim's Progress*, the nineteenth-century bildungsroman, and the blues song of re-newal, resurrection, and so on. It is a journey of self-improvement, a quest for wholeness, wisdom, the good life ("order out of chaos," as McPherson's book title suggests). Certainly the autobiographies are redolent with imagery of resurrection, survival, renewal, pickin' your-self up, dustin' yourself off, and tryin' all over again. As many have noted, there is a faintly innocent air in Angelou: refusing bitterness and cynicism, she renews her faith in human nature, in the strength of community and family, the goodness of individuals, the power of love. Despite all that happens to her (and she takes many knocks in a fairly wide ranging and daring life), she manages to "survive with style."

Angelou would clearly love to figure in a pantheon of great writ-ers, about whom readers would say, "that's the truth."[72] Besides emu-lating the moral strenuousness of the nineteenth-century novelists, she is said to have wished to become an American female Proust, ex-ploring her life through probing anecdotes, reflections on motivation, and so on. This latter wish is curious, since few modernist writers fea-ture in her list of heroes and sheroes, and she experiments very little with form. And for all her expressed desire to demonstrate progress to self-knowledge, the books endearingly describe a repetition of er-ror, minor insight immediately forgotten, disappointment followed by change of heart or plan. Most of all, the autobiography is a chronicle of a life lived by the seat of her pants, on her wits, surviv-ing and at times prospering, but all the time responding to the exi-gencies of present (often perilous) circumstances with imagination and shrewd self-protectiveness.

When Dolly McPherson describes her as "like a cunning hero-ine in a picaresque novel" and Françoise Lionnet compares her story to Defoe's *Moll Flanders*, they get closer to the form and tone than Angelou's own magisterial claims of Proustian depth.[73] This is a useful way of seeing Angelou's work, because it describes a life full of movement and journeys (the essence of the picaresque novel and also the black autobiography) and also because it explains the rather fragmented, anecdotal trajectory to her autobiographical writings. Journeys, be they of immigrant ships, slave ships, steamboats, wagon trains, or railroads, lie at the heart of American historical and mythic experience,[74] and the physical and metaphorical journeys that constitute the black Atlantic make up a major part of black autobiographical accounts. Journeys are never simple; for blacks they are often dangerous, involving flight from the perils of slavery, oppression, and punishment or (as with Alex Haley) quests far from home in order to rediscover lost origins and identities. They can also offer new promises, exciting and romantic possibilities. The journey to Africa is the most symbolically important journey for twentieth-century African Americans, while that to Europe bears cultural and historical weight that offered many blacks liberation from overt racism and discrimination.

In many ways, Angelou traveled farther than almost any other. She lived in many parts of the United States and spent many years touring a variety of countries, as well as living in both Egypt and Ghana—not simply visiting for research or lecture tours. She spent long periods of time in London and other British cities and counted British friends among her closest. At certain points in the autobiographies, she gives those journeys symbolic and sensual resonance (the "black ocean, leaping and wide"), and the moral and emotional force of her extensive travel hits home. At other times, the journeys yield little but fine travelers' tales, and the moral or political commentator's voice is lost.

What differentiates her writing from the autobiographies and essays of black male slave narrators and intellectuals, from Frederick Douglass and W.E.B. Du Bois to Ralph Ellison and Malcolm X, is her insistently gendered analysis of black experience. From the first anecdote of her first autobiographical volume, throughout her poetry, screenplays, interviews, and so on, Angelou's particular experiences as a girl, woman, lover, wife, mother, and female icon set her apart and provide new perspectives on black history. Critics have noted the considerable differences between male and female slave narratives, largely in terms of the relative emphasis on maternal ancestors, motherhood, female community, and sexual vulnerabilities. In women's narratives, the heroic, representative, objective masculine tones are replaced by an intimate, informal feminine voice. Angelou's autobiographies and essays are infused with anecdote about, and reflection on, female desire and sexual insecurity, and in the picaresque tradition Angelou recounts episodes of sexual indiscretion, accidental pregnancy, prostitution, impulsive marriage, and disillusionment and tension with the men she loves. In her case, these gendered problems are always complicated by class and race issues—such as all her mixed marriages, with a Greek American, an African, and a Briton, and her need to raise her son to ensure he understands his black heritage and prospers in white-dominated America.

For a woman, the issue of names is crucial. Anjelou was born Marguerite Johnson, her surname (as her son reminded her) bearing the slave name of her great-grandfather's white owner; her first marriage changed her name to "Angelos," which she glamorized for show business purposes to Angelou. But in many ways, unlike that of her male counterparts, her life as picaresque heroine of her own story is determined by emotional rather than political currents, and especially by her sexual history. As Brita Lindberg-Seyersted observes, "Chance and infatuation brought her to Africa, not a hunger for knowledge or a conscious search for roots."[75] And, given her predilection for attractive men and sexual adventures, the same applies to the many different journeys taken, jobs accepted, and homes established. In this way, Angelou's experiences speak directly, especially to women readers, and strike a chord with general audiences and admirers whose own lives have followed similar trajectories. The randomness and serendipity of her life have made her endearingly human to those many readers who can barely imagine what it feels like to have lived through so much.

On the other hand, she is no unequivocal feminist role model; Angelou's "womanism" is less consistent than that of other African American writers such as Alice Walker, and she claims less allegiance to women writers and the women's movement than some of her contemporaries. The literary mentors she cites are usually male, and she has supported causes very unpopular with other womanists: speaking up for Clarence Thomas, addressing the notorious Million Man March (to which the Black Muslims invited only men, urging Black women to stay home), and supporting Mike Tyson on release from jail, after his rape conviction. In the BBC program on Robert Burns, she defended the poet's wretched sexual conduct against the careful critiques, and defenses of his wife and mistresses, by several male scholars. She has also alienated feminists and womanists alike by openly criticizing male and female homosexuality, even though she had close gay friends such as James Baldwin, and gays were included in her inauguration poem's Whitmanesque listing of American types. In these ways, it could be argued that Angelou has proved herself acceptable to a reactionary, as well as liberal and revolutionary, reading and viewing public and, because of her political equivocations and apparent inconsistencies, has negotiated a blander, if broader, populist line than any previous African American cultural figure.

ANGELOU'S "PHENOMENAL" PERFORMANCE

It is not easy to know to what extent this apparently bland approach reflects Angelou's conscious political strategy to be conciliatory to the politically reactionary and racist, in order to win them around, and in Christian terms to insist on similarities between people rather than crucial and telling differences. The very versatility and flexibility that made her succeed in a bewildering range of jobs and creative forms have made of her a kind of political and emotional chameleon, a figure of mixed styles, political commitments, and opinions that made her an ideal fin-de-siècle media star. Certainly, she is always conscious of her position as a hybrid, diasporic figure, one whose "roots" have been replaced and redefined by her "routes"—routes that offer liberatory modes of human understanding across language, nationality, race, and space. In the third volume of her autobiography, *Singin' and Swingin' and Gettin' Merry Like Christmas,* Angelou relates a moving story about her late 1950s trip to Yugoslavia as part of the cast of *Porgy and Bess.* She visits a music store and asks to buy a mandolin. The storekeeper's wife bursts in with all her children, uttering the name "Paul Robeson." The whole family then proceeds to sing every word of "Deep River." Angelou, who has tried to communicate with them in Serbo-Croat, is extremely moved by this display and reflects that this music "fashioned by men and women out of an anguish they could describe only in dirges" would be for her and other slaves' descendants "a passport . . . into far and strange lands and long unsure futures."[76] This meeting is related with uncritical, heightened emotion.

It may be contrasted significantly with a similar incident in the final volume of the autobiography, at an audience in Cairo with President Tubman of Liberia, who asks Angelou to sing "Swing Low, Sweet Chariot."[77] Not only does the president join in with the spiritual, but so too do a large number of Americo-Liberians of the diplomatic community. Angelou is profoundly uncomfortable at this point, arguing that only South Africans of the Zulu, Xhosa, and Shona tribes who knew profound suffering could produce the appropriate sounds to communicate that "message of pain." Thus a claim to authentic song by professional African blacks seemed to her more dubious than that of white working-class Serbo-Croatians, an interesting and troubling class and ethnic distinction that reveals some of the complexities of the cultural trade routes trodden by Angelou's "travelling shoes."

Throughout Angelou's autobiographical and essay writing, and at times suggested in the sad cadences and bitter lines in the poems, we come close to the "heart of a woman" that is otherwise kept carefully guarded. In interviews, Angelou has suggested she has been "kind" about people in her life, especially those still living, and all too often the reader is left wanting more self-conscious reflection on the nature of autobiographical "truth," not to mention more emotional insights into her most intimate relationships. Like Alice Walker, she entered into mixed race/ethnic marriages that were often difficult for her black peers to accept and ultimately destructive for those partnerships (though none of those marriages was tested by marital residence in the South). But she offers sparse commentary on this sensitive area, and she communicates little about the sadnesses of her neglect by both parents and lovers.[78] It is surely significant that the book long promised about her complex mother has never appeared; Angelou's plans to write an annotated cookbook will include anecdotal but presumably no new analytical material about that figure.[79] What emerges fitfully, sometimes angrily, from the oeuvre is a self-protective wariness about the possibility of returning to one's origins and roots—be they the mother who had abandoned the "motherless child" or the nation of ancestral origin. In both cases the journeys back were fraught with difficulty. Returning to the mother's arms, the child Maya was raped by her mother's lover; returning to Africa as an idealistic "Revolutionist Returnee," the adult Maya is the object of husbandly betrayal, colonial suspicion, and ethnic marginalization. While the older autobiographer reflects ironically on the naïveté and absurdity of the younger self, nevertheless the tally of undeserved brickbats and perilous experiences amounts to harsh lessons learned by a woman all too open to the challenging and difficult.

Angelou's life quest has not been, as so many commentators blithely assert, simply one of self-discovery (even if the self is understood as representative of the race). Her ambition, which arises from an earnestly evangelical Christian, messianic, and pedagogic training and disposition but which undoubtedly owes a great deal to the moral earnestness of American feminism and womanism, has been to embrace the worlds she has known and from which she derives her own life and meaning: the Africa of her (particularly maternal) descendants; the Europe of her early reading, adult friendships, and loves; and the American South, which is her birthplace and home. And she has always been resolutely populist: "I never intended to write any dust-catching masterpieces. I want my work in people's hands, in their minds and their hearts."[80] Her autobiography to date relates no events beyond the end of the 1960s; the most exciting part of her life's narrative was over, and her political work had achieved the major success of putting women on the African American historical map and giving them a voice in the revolutionary struggle. As I write, Angelou is picking up the threads after thirteen years in order to complete a further volume of the autobiography, but she intends to finish her memoirs with the beginning of her publishing career.[81] She formed part of an influential group of women writers and performers who were rapidly upstaging their brothers in terms of publishing and media successes (something for which her early show business training had amply prepared her). As Sondra O'Neale claims, "Angelou bridged the gap between life and art, a step that is essential if Black women are to be deservedly credited with the mammoth and creative feat of noneffacing survival."[82]

It is said that her autobiography parallels that of other African Americans', in its "sense of geographic, cultural, and social displacement."[83] Unusually for an African American writer, Angelou lived on all three continents, experiencing work, domestic, and social lives that rounded out her understanding of the pleasures and constraints of circum-Atlantic relations, routes, and roots. Although her work is flawed and uneven, at her best, especially in the magical *I Know Why the Caged Bird Sings*, the historically important *Heart of a Woman*, and the finest poems that echo great blues lyrics, Angelou manages to capture the flavor of all three with an inspiring, liberating voice. Most significant, in her performances she has always proved the "phenomenal woman" who can manipulate "call and response" better than any other literary figure and emulate the power of the greatest blues and jazz divas. When she sings and chants her poetry; selects, and gives a whole new spin to, lines and stanzas from Robert Burns and Nikki Giovanni; transforms TV interviews into passionate revival meetings; brings mixed-race audiences to their feet; and enters a room as if she had "diamonds at the meeting of [her] thighs," Angelou performs her utopian vision of a creolized, symbolically unified triangular route between disparate continents and cultures.

EPILOGUE

> Despite the standardizing forces of global capitalism, despite
> the pervasiveness of our movies and music in Europe, the world
> does not yet run on an American plan. And what a good thing!
> For any cosmopolitan admirer of human diversity, transnation-
> alism poses a difficult dilemma: is it possible to be a citizen of
> the world, without flattening out that world in the process?
> —Robert A. Gross, Opening Address to the British
> Association of American Studies Conference (1999)

By the end of the twentieth century, politicians and scholars alike had
developed a healthy skepticism about many of the certainties that
were central to its worst tragedies: nationalism, authoritarianism, racial and ethnic classifications, and fixed definitions of class, gender,
and community. Moreover, there is a "flattening out" of the world
by transnational capitalism, with production, distribution, nations,
and peoples required to be mobile and flexible in response to mo-
nopolistic, multinational forces. While I do not underestimate the
many terrible consequences of our postcolonial, postethnic world, I
believe there are exciting, progressive possibilities opened up by this
new emphasis on hybridity rather than pure essence, movement and
mediation rather than roots and rootedness, and multiculturalist,
transnationalist, and globalist discourse. American studies scholars are
now rightly wary of using the term *American* because of the nation's
multiple identities and constituencies, and it is hard to refer to "the
South" or "southern" without needing to qualify and amplify what
kind of South/ern/er you mean.[1] No one could now write a book
called, simply, *The Mind of the South.*

In order to avoid glib generalizations about a very complex region and its culture(s), this book has focused on particular cultural
instances, through a metaphor of circling to suggest the constant
movements, reciprocal patterns, and interrelationships involved in a

circum-Atlantic human geography. Although there are global stories to tell, there are also specific, local ones, depending on the point at which one's lens is trained. My perspective has been that of a white British scholar who lives in England, knows the South fairly well, and has traveled some of those trade and cultural routes, from the United States to Africa. Over the three decades since I first went to the South, I have observed the growing international visibility and new confidence of southern writers, musicians, politics, and tourism and a greater sophistication about the South among Europeans, and indeed U.S. citizens of other regions. European fascination, anxieties, and easy assumptions about an exoticized South have shifted, with more informed TV and journalistic coverage given to the history of slavery, the civil rights movement, and the renaissance of writing and films about a multifarious region. Heated debates about the sexual and familial relationship between founding father Thomas Jefferson and slave Sally Hemings, inspired by James Ivory's film *Jefferson in Paris* (1995), have focused sharper lenses than ever on the birth of a nation and the composition of its children. And in Britain itself, along with London's celebrated Elvis shops and the familiar advertisements for Jack Daniel's and Carte Noire, "Un Café nommé Désir," the end of the century saw a Glasgow University international conference to celebrate the centenary of southern writer Kate Chopin, a Whitbread Prize shortlisting for *No Place Like Home*, black Briton Gary Younge's account of the post–civil rights South, and daily BBC Television repeat screenings, and boxed-video sales promotion, of the acclaimed Ken Burns series *The (American) Civil War* (1990). Transatlantic connections are being made at many levels.

This fluid cultural exchange is not a recent phenomenon. Symbolically important trips across the Atlantic have long been taken by European and American writers and artists, from the earliest transatlantic explorers such as J. Hector St. John de Crèvecoeur and Alexis de Tocqueville, to African American exiles such as W.E.B. Du Bois, Josephine Baker, and Paul Robeson. Thomas Paine's transatlantic conception of America as a brave new world was, in Paul Giles's words, "not so much a political or historical fact but a virtual reality, a realm of difference poised to interrupt the claustrophobic vistas of Old World life."[2] Paine, of course, crossed the Atlantic. But even when no real travel was involved, imaginary journeys were readily taken.

Nineteenth-century writer Henry David Thoreau hated to leave Boston and district, and rarely did so, but engaged in internationalist reading, immersing himself in Greek and Latin texts, German philosophy, English poetry, European newspapers, and Eastern sacred scriptures and poetry.[3] The armchair travel of educated nineteenth-century intellectuals and writers is matched by the Web surfers of the late twentieth, since travel has long been a virtual experience.

Today more than ever, such travel grows between continents, nations, racial and ethnic groups, high and low culture, publisher and chat show, jazz musician and European karaoke bar. In Britain alone, the circum-Atlantic trade in slavery has become the focus of new museums and exhibitions in two cities, Liverpool and Bristol, hitherto silent about their role in that terrible journey. Southern culture, central as it has increasingly become to world music, film, literature, and debates about race, racial pride, and racism, has been well placed to make the most of those transitions.

I have tried to convey the complexity of such cultural journeys. Transatlanticism and circum-Atlanticism sound romantically seamless, but one can all too easily go round in circles. Seas can be fairly choppy, and reluctant travelers can refuse to look out of portholes. There are transatlantic jealousies and hostilities, such as Hollywood's outrage over British casting of *Scarlett*, and southern scholars' fury at Tennessee Williams's trust in Maria St. Just. There are utopian visions, especially of Africa, that do not live up to sustained attention and enquiry (as with Alex Haley and Maya Angelou). Tourists can see only what they wish to and thus—like British New Orleans jazz enthusiasts and drinks advertisers—obfuscate complex histories and experiences. We Europeans can fool ourselves that, by eating British supermarket versions of jambalaya or sobbing over Bessie Smith numbers, we are in touch with the essence of southernness.

The entertainment industries constitute the United States' main global export; this gives cultural production a new economic and ideological importance in world capitalism. It is all too easy to dismiss this cultural imperialism as a reactionary force and a gloomy indicator of the McDonaldization of the world, a U.S.-inspired global dumbing down. But this underestimates the extent to which popular culture is at the center of vigorous readerly and spectatorly debates, and allows spaces for transformation and radical change. The sequels to, and rewritings of, *Gone With the Wind* cast a harsh light on its political subtext in ways that invite critical readings of the whole plantation myth. Alex Haley's *Roots* was a populist spur to multicultural American national pride and has inspired further international Afrocentric links. Anne Rice has given a transatlantic spin to, and provided new international readers and viewers for, European gothic, while the Sister City scheme between Liverpool and New Orleans offers the prospect of future musical collaborations and civic developments. The British theater has discovered a socially engaged, rather than tragi-gothic, Tennessee Williams. And finally, Maya Angelou's unique performances of black southern Christian oratory, spiced with internationalist zeal, have reinvigorated Martin Luther King's moral vision across a black *and* white Atlantic.

I began this book by claiming that I wished to answer a series of questions about the impact of southern culture on my own country, fellow citizens and, indeed, myself. I was intrigued by the opposing images of the South in British popular imagination—the gothic and tragic South of *Mississippi Burning*, the optimistic visions of *Forrest Gump* and Maya Angelou's "And Still I Rise." I have discovered that, given its seismic demographic, political, and cultural changes in the last half of the twentieth century, the South became a symbolically resonant site onto which many of the nation's, and indeed the world's, most pessimistic and hopeful fantasies were projected. The eighties and nineties saw both a new national concern with the increasingly multicultural, multilingual nature of the United States and the "culture wars" between factions that either celebrated or deplored such diversity/divergence. This left little space in which to explore regionalism, so that space was filled by some dangerously reactionary defenders of regional identities that were then seen as bulwarks against an open, multiple society. By contrast, however, the South offered images of a regional solidarity that was communitarian and racially progressive—the happy endings of *The Color Purple* and *Roots*, as well as southern musicians' vibrant contributions to world music. Of all the regions outside Hollywood, the South seems to be having one of the most loquacious "call-and-response" cultural conversations with the rest of the world—not least my own country.

In the 1997 BBC Reith Lectures, African American lawyer and writer Patricia J. Williams posed the following question to British audiences:

How unrestrained—or imperial—is the claim of what we call ours in the world? When I come to London, albeit in the fizzy-cultural wake of the singer Michael Jackson, when you come to the churches of Harlem—how gracefully do we negotiate the accommodation of each other's presence even as the lurking threat of such accommodation is loss—our sacrifice in knowing that inclusion of new faces might change the landscape forever.[4]

This has been an exploration of similar journeys and landscapes. I have documented examples of both "graceful accommodations" and "losses," besides many "new faces," as well as new voices, music, writings, film, television, and theatrical productions, not to mention bitter arguments and old tensions. My conclusion is that these cultural journeys between continents have both transformed transatlantic landscapes and expanded our imaginative journeys in widening circles.

Notes

1. LOOKING TRANSATLANTICALLY

1. John Shelton Reed, *Whistling Dixie: Dispatches from the South* (San Diego: Harcourt Brace Jovanovich, 1990), 3.
2. Jonathan Freedland, "Everyone's Whistling Dixie," *Guardian*, 2 March 1996, 1.
3. Peter Gould and Rodney White, *Mental Maps* (Baltimore: Johns Hopkins University Press, 1974), 93-118, quoted by Richard Gray, "Afterword: Negotiating Differences: Southern Culture(s) Now," in *Dixie Debates: Perspectives on Southern Cultures,* ed. Richard H. King and Helen Taylor (London: Pluto Press, 1996), 225. For a brief summary of definitions of "the South" and "southern" in a cultural context, see King and Taylor, introduction to *Dixie Debates,* 1-11.
4. John Egerton, *The Americanization of Dixie: The Southernization of America* (New York: Harper and Row, 1974), xx; Peter Applebome, *Dixie Rising: How the South Is Shaping American Values, Politics, and Culture* (New York: Random House, 1996), 21.
5. Diane Roberts, *The Myth of Aunt Jemima: Representations of Race and Region* (London: Routledge, 1994), 29.
6. Frances Trollope, *Domestic Manners of the Americans* (1832; New York: Alfred Knopf, 1949), 25, on first arriving at the mouth of the Mississippi; Edward King, *The Great South: A Record of Journeys* (Hartford, Conn.: American Publishing Co., 1879), 17, on Louisiana.
7. Quote from Applebome, *Dixie Rising,* 9.
8. William Faulkner, *Requiem for a Nun* (New York: Random House, 1951), 85.
9. John Berendt, *Midnight in the Garden of Good and Evil: A Savannah Story* (New York: Random House, 1994); John Berendt, "A Sense of Place," the Tennessee Williams/New Orleans Literary Festival, 26 March 1995.
10. For instance, I was struck by the coexistence in British cinema, during August 1998, of a group of southern films alongside Robert Redford's blockbuster *The Horse Whisperer.* In the latter, the female protagonist's husband calls her and asks how things are in "Marlboro Country"; the film abounds with wide open spaces and clichés about freedom associated with the natural. By contrast, in a series of very differently styled films, from Kasi Lemmons's *Eve's Bayou* and Robert Altman's *The Gingerbread Man* to Billy Bob Thornton's *Sling Blade* and Robert Duvall's *The Apostle,* the South is a place where nature is sinister and dangerous and human desire anarchic, violent, and uncontrollable.
11. See Grady McWhiney, *Cracker Culture: Celtic Ways in the Old South* (Tuscaloosa: University of Alabama Press, 1988); E.R.R. Green, ed., *Essays in Scotch-Irish History* (London: Routledge

and Kegan Paul, 1969); and Andrew Hook, *From Goosecreek to Gandercleugh: Studies in Scottish-American Literary and Cultural History* (East Linton, Scotland: Tuckwell Press, 1999).

12. Originally known as the Southern League, it changed its name after complaints from a baseball team with the identical name.

13. Diane Roberts, "Ghosts of the Gallant South," *Guardian*, 22 July 1996, 14.

14. Kirsty Scott, "The Fatal Attraction: The Disturbing Phenomenon of America's Violent Racists and Their Bond with Scotland," *Herald*, 6 August 1997, 12. I am indebted to Colin McArthur for this article and other material on *Braveheart*. See also my discussion of Alexandra Ripley's Celtic-themed sequel to *Gone With the Wind*, *Scarlett* (chapter 2).

15. Robert O. Stephens, *The Family Saga in the South: Generations and Destinies* (Baton Rouge: Louisiana State University Press, 1995), 145.

16. Mark Twain, *Life on the Mississippi* (1883; New York: Harper, 1904), 347.

17. W. J. Cash, *The Mind of the South* (New York: Vintage, 1941), ix, 67, and 68. Also see William R. Taylor, *Cavalier and Yankee: The Old South and American National Character* (New York: Harper and Row, 1961).

18. Alvin R. Sunseri, "Military and Economy," in *Encyclopedia of Southern Culture*, ed. Charles Reagan Wilson and William Ferris (Chapel Hill: University of North Carolina Press, 1989), 731.

19. See James B. McMillan and Michael B. Montgomery, eds., *The Annotated Bibliography of Southern American English*, 2d ed. (Tuscaloosa: University of Alabama Press, 1986).

20. I am indebted for these points to the late Joseph Logsdon.

21. Joseph Roach, *Cities of the Dead: Circum-Atlantic Performance* (New York: Columbia University Press, 1996), 258.

22. Glenn Horowitz, foreword to Thomas M. Verich, *English Magnolias: An Exhibition of Mississippi Fiction Printed in England* (Oxford: University of Mississippi, 1992), n.p.

23. Two excellent examples at random, in the summer of 1998, were a Channel 4 four-part series titled *Naked Nashville* (Oxford Television Company), which produced a CD of the series's music as well as a glossy brochure, *Naked Nashville: Selling and the Soul of Country Music* (London: Broadcasting Support Services, 1998); and BBC Radio 3's four-part documentary on the British jazz revival featuring Humphrey Lyttleton, *Take Me Back to New Orleans*.

24. For an interesting European discussion of Elvis enthusiasts, see Erika Doss, *Elvis in the Public Sphere: Fans, Faith, and Cultural Production in Contemporary America*, Working Paper No. 24 (Odense, Denmark: Odense University, 1996). In 1997 alone, the twentieth anniversary of the singer's death, I noted the following (and this must be the tip of a very large iceberg): BBC and ITV television companies ran more than twenty hours of Elvis programs; the broadsheet and tabloid press ran cartoons and articles on Elvis fans, impersonators, legends, after-life sightings, and the like; an Elvis Festival was held at Pontin's Holiday Village, Hemsby, Norfolk, with ten hours of Presley disco, live rock and roll bands, contests, karaoke, line-dance tuition, and so on; Virgin Holidays offered an Elvis holiday in Memphis; and the King Creole Travel Club organized a six-day Elvis Festival in Exmouth, Devon, with legendary rocker Marty Wilde topping the bill. The same year, Sidney Shaw, owner of Elvisly Yours, went to court to appeal against the sole right of Elvis Presley Enterprises of America to use the singer's name and alleged signature. The Trade Marks Registry had ruled in EPE's favor, but Mr. Shaw won his case.

25. William J. Cooper Jr. and Thomas E. Terrill, *The American South: A History*, 2d ed. (New York: McGraw-Hill, 1996), 718.

26. See a very timely series of articles on the subject in *American Quarterly* 50 (September 1998), especially Nikhil Pal Singh, "Culture/Wars: Recoding Empire in an Age of Democracy," 471-522, and Frederick Buell, "Nationalist Postnationalism: Globalist Discourse in Contemporary American Culture," 548-591.

27. Paul Gilroy, *The Black Atlantic: Modernity and Double Consciousness* (London: Verso, 1993); Edward Said, *Culture and Imperialism* (London: Chatto and Windus, 1993).

28. Said, *Culture and Imperialism*, xxii–xxiii, xxix; Gilroy, *Black Atlantic*, 19.

29. Alan Munton, "Misreading Morrison, Mishearing Jazz: A Response to Toni Morrison's Jazz Critics," *Journal of American Studies* 31 (August 1997): 235-251. See chapter 2, in which this is discussed further.

30. Quoted from ibid., 251.

31. See David Ellwood, Mel van Elteren, Mick Gidley, Rob Kroes, David E. Nye and Robert W. Rydell, *Questions of Cultural Exchange: The NIAS Statement on the European Reception of Ameri-*

can Mass Culture, Working Paper No. 13 (Odense, Denmark: Odense University, 1994). Joseph Roach argues that America is "an ever-shifting ensemble of appropriated traditions" (*Cities of the Dead,* 184). This would also be true of virtually any contemporary nation.

32. Roach, *Cities of the Dead,* 4. For a sustained discussion of creolization in relation to New Orleans, see Arnold R. Hirsch and Joseph Logsdon, eds., *Creole New Orleans: Race and Americanization* (Baton Rouge: Louisiana State University Press, 1992).

33. Charles Joyner, "African and European Roots of Southern Culture: The 'Central Theme' Revisited," in King and Taylor, *Dixie Debates,* 13-14, 28.

34. Berndt Ostendorf, *Creolization and Creoles: The Concepts and Their History with Special Attention to Louisiana,* Working Paper No. 27 (Odense, Denmark: Odense University, 1997), 22.

35. Quoted in ibid., 25. This critique is also made of Joseph Roach's work, in a review of *Cities of the Dead* by Bruce McConachie, in *Theatre Survey* 37 (November 1996): 141-144.

36. Richard Gray, afterword to King and Taylor, *Dixie Debates,* 220.

37. Ursula Branston, *Let the Band Play "Dixie"!: Improvisations on a Southern Signature Tune* (London: George G. Harrap & Co., 1940). I am indebted to Ed Gallafent for finding this book on his junk-shop travels.

38. Gary Younge, *No Place like Home: A Black Briton's Journey through the American South* (London: Picador, 1999), 18-19.

---

2.   "GONE WITH THE WIND" INTO THE MILLENNIUM

1. For a summary of the history of reception and the phenomenon of *Gone With the Wind,* see Richard Harwell, ed., *"Gone With the Wind" as Book and Film* (Columbia: University of South Carolina Press, 1983), and Helen Taylor, *Scarlett's Women: "Gone With the Wind" and Its Female Fans* (New Brunswick, N.J.: Rutgers University Press, 1989; London: Virago, 1989). Books, articles, and vast Web sites detail a plethora of cultural reference, artifacts, and ephemera: memorabilia collection, Scarlett pop-up book, porcelain figurine and music box, Civil War Society costume ball, Scarlett O'Hara impersonator, and so on. See Herb Bridges, *"Frankly, My Dear...": "Gone With the Wind" Memorabilia* (Macon, Ga.: Mercer University Press, 1986). The film, repremiered seven times in Atlanta, shows somewhere daily across the globe and is frequently broadcast on television. The videotape—reissued in a newly colorized print in 1989—is a constant best-seller, and any publication or film relating to the work is guaranteed good sales. And since the book and film anniversaries in 1986 and 1989, there has been a spurt of cultural production of various kinds. In 1989, the sons of David O. Selznick compiled a TV film, *The Making of "Gone With the Wind,"* using unseen footage of screen tests, edited-out scenes, interviews with the cast, and so on. In 1991, the scholar Darden Asbury Pyron published his authoritative, comprehensive biography, *Southern Daughter: The Life of Margaret Mitchell* (New York: Oxford University Press, 1991), a book designed to expand the field of serious scholarship on the writer and her work. In 1995, Mitchell fans were excited by the discovery of a cache of letters, photos, and two unpublished manuscripts of juvenilia. *Lost Laysen* is a 107-page romance novella set in the South Pacific and was swiftly published (ed. Debra Freer [New York: Scribner, 1996]); "Lady Godiva," described enthusiastically on the Margaret Mitchell Web site, will undoubtedly follow into print.

2. See sequels such as Rachel Billington's sequel to Jane Austen's *Emma, Perfect Happiness* (London: Sceptre, 1996); Emma Tennant's sequels to the whole Jane Austen canon (see later in this chapter); Susan Hill, *Mrs de Winter: The Sequel to Daphne du Maurier's "Rebecca"* (London: Sinclair-Stevenson, 1993). Reworkings include Sue Roe's version of *Great Expectations, Estella: Her Expectations* (Brighton: Harvester Press, 1982); "Another Lady," who completed Charlotte Brontë's unfinished fragment, *Emma* (London: J. M. Dent, 1980); and two contemporary versions of *Rebecca,* Mary Wings, *Divine Victim* (London: Women's Press, 1992), and Maureen Freely, *The Other Rebecca* (London: Bloomsbury, 1996). One might also look at a highly successful contemporary film version of Jane Austen's *Emma, Clueless* (1995).

3. "Ghostly Presence" is a term used to refer to William Faulkner's influence on Graham Swift's *Last Orders.*

4. "Classical progression" is a term used about Emma Tennant's sequels to Jane Austen novels.

5. Quoted in Anne Edwards, *The Road to Tara: The Life of Margaret Mitchell* (New Haven: Ticknor and Fields, 1983), 294.

6. Early reports quoted anything from $3 million to $7 million (or pounds sterling—who cared?), while in two author interviews the writer herself quoted very different advances of $160,000 (*New York Times*), then $64,000 (*Hello!*).

7. "Wind Up," *Girl about Town*, 7 October 1991, n.p.

8. Peter Guttridge, "Foreplay, fiddle-dee-dee!" *Independent*, 28 September 1991, 30; Sally Beauman, "Back with the Breeze," *Independent on Sunday*, 29 September 1991, n.p.

9. Philippa Kennedy, "The Woman Entrusted with the Secrets of Scarlett," *Daily Express*, 16 September 1991, 16; Gisèle Galante, "Alexandra Ripley," *Hello!*, 12 October 1991, 92.

10. Ibid., 16.

11. "Scarlett," publicity pack, Pan Macmillan, 1991, n.p.; Galante, "Alexandra Ripley," 93; Kennedy, "Woman Entrusted," 16.

12. Kennedy, "Woman Entrusted," 16.

13. "Scarlett and Rhett Reunited at Last," *Lancashire Evening Telegraph*, 25 September 1991, author and page not cited (Macmillan press cuttings file, 1991).

14. Aileen Jacobson, "An Author Tiptoes through the Times," *Newsday*, 25 September, 1991, p.61.

15. Quoted from Alexandra Ripley, *Scarlett: The Sequel to Margaret Mitchell's "Gone With the Wind"* (London: Macmillan, 1991), 556.

16. Grady McWhiney, *Cracker Culture: Celtic Ways in the Old South* (Tuscaloosa: University of Alabama Press, 1988).

17. This is not the appropriate context for lengthy discussions of McWhiney's thesis. Authoritative countertexts to *Cracker Culture* would, however, include Ted Ownby, *Black and White Cultural Interaction in the Antebellum South* (Oxford: University of Mississippi Press, 1993); William D. Piersen, *Black Legacy: America's Hidden Heritage* (Amherst: University of Massachusetts Press, 1993); Walter Benn Michaels, *Our America: Nativism, Modernism, and Pluralism* (Durham, N.C.: Duke University Press, 1995); and Minrose C. Gwin, *Black and White Women of the Old South: The Peculiar Sisterhood in American Literature* (Knoxville: University of Tennessee Press, 1985).

18. Margaret Mitchell, *Gone With the Wind* (London: Macmillan, 1936), 29.

19. Patricia Storace, "Look Away, Dixie Land!," *New York Times*, 19 December 1991, 37; M. G. Lord, *"GWTW* II," *Newsday*, 25 September 1991; Kate Saunders, *Sunday Times*, 6 October 1991, 6; Justine McCarthy, *Irish Independent*, 26 October 1991, n.p. (Macmillan cuttings file, 10.91).

20. Quoted in Jacobson, "Author Tiptoes through the Times," 61.

21. *Variety*, 4 November 1991, 1.

22. Christopher Goodwin, *Times*, 9 November 1993; Mark Dowdney, 1993, no details; Phil Reeves, *Independent*, 9 November 1993; [no author cited], *Daily Express*, 9 November 1993 (all from SKY TV cuttings file, 1994).

23. "Scarlett Women," *People*, 8 March 1992, 92.

24. "Frankly, She *Gives* a Damn," unattributed article, SKY TV cuttings file, 1994.

25. Baz Bamigboye, "A Chill Wind is Blowing on Scarlett," *Daily Mail*, 14 January 1994, n.p. (SKY TV cuttings file).

26. *Scarlett* publicity pack, SKY TV, December 1994.

27. Pauline Wallin, "No wonder she wishes she was more like Scarlett," reference unknown, cutting from Warner and Macmillan files.

28. Jane Thynne, *Daily Telegraph*, 8 January 1994.

29. Quoted in *Moving Pictures*, 9 December 1993, 8.

30. Ibid.

31. Robert Halmi, *Evening Standard*, 7 January 1994.

32. "Scarlett: Tomorrow Is Another Day," SKY TV publicity pack, 1994, pp. 39, 44, 49, 41.

33. *Scarlett: Tomorrow Is Another Day*, RHI Entertainment Inc., 1994, p. 60.

34. Jane Thynne, *Daily Telegraph*, 8 January 1994, 7; Allison Pearson, "It's Hard to Give a Damn," *Independent on Sunday*, 18 December 1994, 23; "Scarlett Is Simply Off-Colour," *Today*, 17 December 1994.

35. Antonia Fraser, "Rebecca's Story," *Harper's and Queen*, November 1976, 84-88.

36. Sarah Lyall, "It's Hard to Keep a Good Sequel Secret," *New York Times*, 4 May 1995, C12.

37. Emma Tennant, conversation with author, London, 5 November 1995.

38. Emma Tennant, "Gone!," *Telegraph Magazine*, 7 September 1996, 24.

39. Sarah Lyall, "Book Sequel Creates a New Civil War," *New York Times*, 3 June 1996, D7.

40. Ibid.

41. Ibid.

42. Tennant, "Gone!," 26 and 28.

43. Lyall, "Book Sequel," n.p.

44. Régine Deforges, *La bicyclette bleue* (Paris: Ramsay, 1981). See Peter Lennon, "Damned, Frankly," *Guardian*, 28 September 1991, 21.
45. Julian Green, *South: A Play* (New York: Marion Boyars, 1991). The play was first performed on 30 March 1955 at the Arts Theatre Club, in London, produced by Peter Hall.
46. Julian Green, *Les Pays Lointains* (Paris: Fayard, 1987); *The Distant Lands* (London: Marion Boyars, 1990); *The Stars of the South* (1989; London: Marion Boyars, 1996); and *Dixie* (Paris: Fayard, 1995).
47. Julian Green, *The Distant Lands* (1990; London: Mandarin, 1991), 896. Subsequent page numbers in this edition will be given in parenthesis in the text.
48. Laura Jacobs, "Scarlett 'n the Hood," *Vanity Fair*, May 1996, 180-190.
49. "Pass Notes No. 1303: Scarlett O'Hara," *Guardian* G2, 10 November 1998, 3, and John Hiscock, "Gone With the Sequel: Scarlett to Be Killed Off," *Daily Telegraph*, 10 November 1998.
50. Maya Angelou, "Miss Scarlett, Mr. Rhett, and Other Latter-Day Saints," in *Just Give Me a Cool Drink of Water 'Fore I Diiie: The Poetry of Maya Angelou* (London: Virago, 1988), 28.

3.   EVERYBODY'S SEARCH FOR ROOTS

1. Quote from Willie Lee Rose, *Race and Region in American Historical Fiction: Four Episodes in Popular Culture* (Oxford: Clarendon, 1979), 4; Alex Haley, *Roots* (1976; London: Hutchinson, 1977).
2. Joseph R. Millichap, "Television Movies," in *Encyclopedia of Southern Culture*, ed. Charles Reagan Wilson and William Ferris (Chapel Hill: University of North Carolina Press, 1989), 940; Michael Steward Blayney, "*Roots* and the Noble Savage," *North Dakota Quarterly* 54, no. 1 (1986): 1; Bob Knight, "ABC Miniseries Shatters Records," *Variety*, 2 February 1977, page unknown.
3. Leslie Fiedler, *The Inadvertent Epic: From "Uncle Tom's Cabin" to "Roots"* (New York: Simon and Schuster, 1979), 71 and 72.
4. Harold Courlander, "Kunta Kinte's Struggle to Be African," *Phylong: The Atlanta University Review of Race and Culture* 47, no. 4 (1986): 294.
5. Rose, *Race and Region in American Historical Fiction*, 5.
6. John Egerton, *The Americanization of Dixie: The Southernization of America* (New York: Harper and Row, 1974), xx.
7. L. Moody Simms Jr., "Albion W. Tourgée on the Fictional Use of the Post–Civil War South," *Southern Studies* 17 (1978): 405-406, quoted in Robert O. Stephens, *The Family Saga in the South: Generations and Destinies* (Baton Rouge: Louisiana State University Press, 1995), 141.
8. Paul Gilroy, "Living Memory: A Meeting with Toni Morrison," in *Small Acts: Thoughts on the Politics of Black Cultures* (London: Serpent's Tail, 1993), 178-179.
9. Judith Mudd, "Returning a Theft of Identity: This Is Also Me: Two Indian Views of *Roots*," *Indian Journal of American Studies* 10 (July 1980): 50.
10. Quoted in Murray Fisher, "In Memoriam: Alex Haley," *Playboy*, 1 July 1992, 161.
11. Mary Siebert McCauley, "Alex Haley, a Southern Griot: A Literary Biography" (Ph.D. diss., George Peabody College for Teachers of Vanderbilt University, Tennessee, 1983).
12. Chuck Stone, "Roots: An Electronic Orgy in White Guilt," *Black Scholar* 8 (May 1977): 40.
13. *Black Scholar* 8 (May 1977): 36-42.
14. Alice Walker, *The Same River Twice: Honoring the Difficult: A Meditation on Life, Spirit, Art, and the Making of the Film "The Color Purple" Ten Years Later* (New York: Scribner, 1996).
15. A strong exception to this is a good discussion of the text in Stephens, *Family Saga in the South*, especially chap. 5.
16. Henry Louis Gates Jr., *Loose Canons: Notes on the Culture Wars* (New York: Oxford University Press, 1992), 101.
17. Mark Ottaway, "Tangled Roots," *Sunday Times*, 10 April 1977, 17.
18. *Sunday Times*, 17 April 1977, 14.
19. Mark Ottaway to author, 2 February 1995.
20. Philip Nobile, "Uncovering *Roots*," *Village Voice*, 23 February 1993, 32.
21. *Bookmark: The Roots of Alex Haley*, BBC2, 13 September 1997, dir. James Kent.
22. For instance, the authoritative, painstakingly compiled *Encyclopedia of Southern Culture*, edited by Wilson and Ferris (1989) includes approximately a dozen references to Haley and *Roots* without a whisper of the controversies surrounding it. None of the major African American literary critics (Henry Louis Gates Jr., Houston A. Baker Jr., Toni Morrison, bell hooks, or Hazel V. Carby) even cites the man, book, or phenomenon. He is excluded from the authoritative *Norton Anthology of African American Literature* (1997). Maya Angelou and Michele

Wallace make the odd reference to Haley (Angelou made her name by appearing in *Roots*; see chapter 6), but curiously, in an important collection of essays edited by Gina Dent, *Black Popular Culture* (Seattle: Bay Press, 1992), in which one might expect at least a mention, Haley is absent. He is the subject of various essays but never of a major scholarly project by an influential African American critic. David Shirley's study of Haley, in the "Black Americans of Achievement" series, is a largely descriptive account of Haley's life and career, and although it contains a short chapter titled "Backlash," referring to controversies surrounding Haley's use of literary sources and his subsequent wealth, it is primarily (as its series title would suggest) hagiographical. Computer and library searches have yielded a surprisingly small amount of published material on the subject. David Shirley's biography is one of only two; the other is an unpublished Ph.D thesis.

23. Nobile, "Uncovering *Roots*," 36.
24. Fiedler, *Inadvertent Epic*, 17.
25. Rose, *Race and Region in American Historical Fiction*, 2-3.
26. See Paul Gilroy, "A Dialogue with bell hooks," in *Small Acts*, 208-209, on the silence of black nationalists on black popular culture: "To talk about popular culture, one has to confront the whole 'contamination' of supposedly pure African forms. Africa provided the critical substance for that process of mutation and adaptation we call creolization. The serious study of Black popular culture affirms that admixture in some way" (209).
27. Millichap, "Television Movies," 940; Christopher P. Geist, "*Roots*," in Wilson and Ferris, *Encyclopedia of Southern Culture*, 972.
28. Fiedler, *Inadvertent Epic*, 62.
29. As Edward D. C. Campbell has argued, by the 1970s, in films and TV programs featuring blacks (*Mandingo* [1975], *Drum* [1976], the final episode of *Roots* [1977]), "Uncle Tom had become Nat Turner"; see *The Celluloid South: Hollywood and the Southern Myth* (Knoxville: University of Tennessee Press, 1981), 172. The fictional passive slave was replaced by representations of a real, violent revolting slave who owed no allegiance to white society. Other TV movies with a southern plantation theme had appeared in the 1970s. The year 1974 saw the adaptation of Ernest Gaines's *The Autobiography of Miss Jane Pittman*. Cicely Tyson, who played Jane, also appeared four years later in a TV movie about black emancipationist Harriet Tubman, *A Woman Called Moses* (1978; Tyson also had a part in *Roots*). *Freedom Road* (1979) was a thin copy of *Roots* starring Muhammad Ali, and the moonlight-and-magnolias *Beulah Land* appeared in 1980. *Roots* itself was followed in 1979 by *Roots II: The Next Generation*, a twelve-hour miniseries, and *Palmerston, U.S.A.* (1980), a series based on Haley's youth in Henning, Tennessee.
30. Toni Morrison, *Playing in the Dark: Whiteness and the Literary Imagination* (Cambridge: Harvard University Press, 1992), 50-51.
31. Jack Temple Kirby, *Media-Made Dixie: The South in the American Imagination* (Baton Rouge: Louisiana State University Press, 1978), 170.
32. Alex Haley and David Stevens, *Alex Haley's Queen: The Story of an American Family* (New York: William Morrow, 1993).
33. John Fiske, *Reading the Popular* (London: Routledge, 1989), 107.
34. Selwyn R. Cudjoe, "Maya Angelou and the Autobiographical Statement," in *Black Women Writers: Arguments and Interviews*, ed. Mari Evans (London: Pluto, 1985), 6.
35. Toni Morrison in Evans, *Black Women Writers*, 339.
36. Ernest J. Gaines, "Miss Jane and I," *Callaloo* 1 (1978): 23, quoted in Stephens, *Family Saga in the South*, 155.
37. Gates, *Loose Canons*, 62 and 63.
38. Ibid., 63.
39. Toni Morrison in Evans, *Black Women Writers*, 339.
40. Michael Kirkhorn, "A Saga of Slavery That Made the Actors Weep," *New York Times*, 29 June 1976.
41. Houston A. Baker Jr., frontispiece to *Blues, Ideology, and Afro-American Literature* (Chicago: University of Chicago Press, 1984).
42. Henry Louis Gates Jr., *Black Literature and Literary Theory* (New York: Methuen, 1984), 19.
43. Toni Morrison in Evans, *Black Women Writers*, 341.
44. McCauley, *Alex Haley, a Southern Griot*, 114.
45. Ibid., 212.
46. Ibid., 204.
47. Rose, *Race and Region in American Historical Fiction*, 6.

48. American Africanism is defined as "the denotative and connotative Blackness that African peoples have come to signify, as well as the entire range of views, assumptions, readings, and misreadings that accompany Eurocentric learning about these people," in Morrison, *Playing in the Dark*, 6-7; Manning Marable, in Dent, *Black Popular Culture*, 295.
49. McCauley, Interview with Alex Haley, 15 May, 1981, in *Alex Haley*, p.110.
50. McCauley, interview with Alex Haley, 17 July 1982, in "Alex Haley," 212.
51. McCauley, interview with Alex Haley, 15 May 1981, in "Alex Haley," 176.
52. One might suggest that this was a way in which Haley helped southernize the nation. During the conference, "The Configuration of Race in the South," Sidney Sussex College, University of Cambridge, September 1995, Paul Gaston remarked that he had arrived in Virginia thirty-eight years previously and asked what people did there; he was told, "They go climbing about the family tree." Haley's success gave a new fashion to the whole nation for climbing that tree.
53. The BBC2 Bookmark program, *The Roots of Alex Haley*, featured considerable footage of black American tourists taking the Haley family "Roots Tour" of Gambia, wearing Western dress and carrying camcorders, welcomed by villagers to whom they reiterated, "We've come home."
54. Quoted in Blayney, "*Roots* and the Noble Savage," 13.
55. David Harvey, *The Condition of Postmodernity: An Enquiry into the Origins of Cultural Change* (Oxford: Blackwell, 1989), 87.
56. Ibid., 303.
57. McCauley, "Alex Haley," 179.
58. Alex Haley (with the assistance of), *The Autobiography of Malcolm X* (1965; London: Hutchinson, 1966), 501.
59. Haley, *Roots*, 639.
60. McCauley, "Alex Haley," 173.
61. Cornel West, "Nihilism in Black America," in Dent, *Black Popular Culture*, 40 and 43.
62. Paul Gilroy, "It's a Family Affair," in Dent, *Black Popular Culture*, 310, 307.
63. Ed Vulliamy, "Fire in the Blood on the Bayou," *Observer*, 8 February 1998, 11.
64. Walker, *Same River Twice*, 200-201.

4.   NEW ORLEANS, "AMERICA'S EUROPEAN MASTERPIECE"

1. H. Wayne Schuth, "The Image of New Orleans on Film," in *The South and Film*, ed. Warren French (Jackson: University Press of Mississippi, 1981), 241.
2. John Kennedy Toole, *A Confederacy of Dunces* (Baton Rouge: Louisiana State University Press, 1980), 3.
3. Beverly Gianna, director of Public Affairs, New Orleans Convention and Visitors Bureau, interview with author, New Orleans, 31 March 1995.
4. Peirce F. Lewis, *New Orleans: The Making of an Urban Landscape* (Cambridge, Mass.: Ballinger, 1976), 10; Arnold R. Hirsch and Joseph Logsdon, eds., *Creole New Orleans: Race and Americanization* (Baton Rouge: Louisiana State University Press, 1992), x–xi.
5. Walker Percy, "New Orleans, Mon Amour," *Harper's*, September 1968, 81; Gwendolyn Midlo Hall, "The Formation of Afro-Creole Culture," in Hirsch and Logsdon, *Creole New Orleans*, 59.
6. See, for instance, Frances Parkinson Keyes's popular novel *Dinner at Antoine's* (New York: Messner, 1948), dedicated to the owner of Antoine's, Roy Alciatore, who is a character in the novel; Alexandra Ripley's *New Orleans Legacy* (New York: Macmillan, 1987), which ends with a recipe for red beans and rice, the dish of which the heroine reminds the hero; and Alan Parker's film *Angel Heart* (1987), in which one of the victims drowns in the chicken gumbo.
7. Lyle Saxon, Robert Tallant, and Edward Dreyer, *Gumbo Ya-Ya: A Collection of Louisiana Folk Tales* (New York: Bonanza Books, 1945), v, 173.
8. Quote from Bernard M. Hermann and Charles "Pie" Dufour, *New Orleans* (Baton Rouge: Louisiana State University Press, 1980), 8.
9. Ishmael Reed, *Shrovetide in Old New Orleans* (New York: Atheneum, 1989), 25.
10. Saxon et al., *Gumbo Ya-Ya*, 149.
11. Anne Rice, *The Feast of All Saints* (New York: Simon and Schuster, 1979); Noel Rockmore, Larry Borenstein, and Bill Russell, introduction to *Preservation Hall Portraits* (Baton Rouge: Louisiana State University Press, 1968), n.p.

12. Mikhail Bakhtin, *Rabelais and His World* (Cambridge: MIT Press, 1968), 9.

13. Samuel Kinser, *Carnival American Style: Mardi Gras at New Orleans and Mobile* (Chicago: University of Chicago Press, 1990), xv.

14. Lafcadio Hearn, *Creole Sketches* (Boston, 1924), 90-92, in *Literary New Orleans: Essays and Meditations,* ed. Richard S. Kennedy (Baton Rouge: Louisiana State University Press, 1992), 26.

15. Walker Percy described Mardi Gras as a "universal celebration of a public occasion by private, social, and neighborhood groups," but one that is closed to black participation, in "New Orleans Mon Amour," *Harper's,* September 1968, 90; Ishmael Reed described it as "Caucasian Mardi Gras," with a history that is both "scandalous and violent" and "racist," in *Shrovetide in Old New Orleans,* 15. Also see Reid Mitchell's excellent *All on a Mardi Gras Day: Episodes in the History of New Orleans Carnival* (Cambridge: Harvard University Press, 1995).

16. Joseph Roach, *Cities of the Dead: Circum-Atlantic Performance* (New York: Columbia University Press, 1996), 243 and 245. For an excellent autobiographical and journalistic account of the trauma of the ordinance during 1991, see Carol Flake, *New Orleans: Behind the Masks of America's Most Exotic City* (New York: Grove Press, 1994). Also see Mitchell, *All on a Mardi Gras Day,* "Epilogue."

17. "New Orleans" [tourist pamphlet], New Orleans Metropolitan Convention and Visitors Bureau, December 1995.

18. Dean MacCannell, *The Tourist: A New Theory of the Leisure Class* (London: Macmillan, 1976), 76 and 61 (in which he quotes from *Anglo-American Practical Guide to Exhibition Paris: 1900*).

19. Edward W. Soja, *Thirdspace: Journeys to Los Angeles and Other Real-and-Imagined Places* (Cambridge, Mass.: Blackwell, 1996), 112.

20. Diane Roberts, *The Myth of Aunt Jemima: Representations of Race and Region* (London: Routledge, 1994), 27, 29.

21. Roach, *Cities of the Dead,* 231.

22. See, for instance, French director Louis Malle's film *Pretty Baby* (1977), the British musical *Mardi Gras* (1975) by Alan Blaikley, Melvyn Bragg, and Ken Howard, and Australian novelist Lois Battle's *Storyville* (New York: Viking, 1993). A British restaurant chain, Old Orleans, offers its customers "a taste of the Deep South," with sexily named cocktails, "Virgin on the Ridiculous," "Slow Comfortable Screw," and "Wild Thing."

23. See their Web page< http:www.windsorcourthotel.com/story.html>. I am indebted to Joseph Logsdon for the point about the statue.

24. Umberto Eco, *Travels in Hyperreality: Essays* (London: Picador, 1987), 30.

25. Lewis P. Simpson, "New Orleans as a Literary Center," in Kennedy, *Literary New Orleans,* 88.

26. Lewis Lawson, "Pilgrim in the City: Walker Percy," in Kennedy, *Literary New Orleans,* 53.

27. Justin Kaplan, *Walt Whitman: A Life* (1980), 139, quoted by Kenneth W. Holditch, in Kennedy, *Literary New Orleans,* 69.

28. James Campbell, *Talking at the Gates: A Life of James Baldwin* (London: Faber and Faber, 1991), 4.

29. Leaflet produced by Monteleone Hotel, New Orleans, c. 1995.

30. *Time Out,* 9-16 June 1993, 38.

31. Grace King, *New Orleans: The Place and the People* (New York: Macmillan, 1895), xvii, xx–xxi.

32. Carvel Collins, ed., *William Faulkner: New Orleans Sketches* (London: Chatto and Windus, 1958), 13-14.

33. Hamilton Basso, "William Faulkner, Man and Writer," *Saturday Review,* 28 July 1962, 11, quoted in Inez Hollander Lake, "Paris in My Own Backyard: Hamilton Basso," in Richard S. Kennedy, ed., *Literary New Orleans in the Modern World* (Baton Rouge: Louisiana State University Press, 1998), 40.

34. Simone de Beauvoir, *America Day by Day* (London: Gerald Duckworth, 1952), 172.

35. W. Kenneth Holditch, "South toward Freedom: Tennessee Williams," in Kennedy, *Literary New Orleans,* 63.

36. Sallie O'Brien, *Bayou* (New York: Bantam, 1979), cover blurbs. See also fiction by crime writers Julie Smith and James Lee Burke; romances by Lois Battle, Frances Parkinson Keyes, Belva Plain, and Alexandra Ripley; gothic romances by Anne Rice, Poppy Z. Brite, and Blaise Bulot.

37. See Kennedy, *Literary New Orleans in the Modern World*; Helen Taylor, "Walking through New Orleans: Kate Chopin and the Female Flâneur," *Southern Quarterly* 37 (Spring–Summer 1999): 21-29; extended version, *Symbiosis* 1 (April 1997): 69-85.

38. See Dorothy H. Brown and Barbara C. Ewell, eds., *Louisiana Women Writers: New Essays and a Comprehensive Bibliography* (Baton Rouge: Louisiana State University Press, 1992), and Kennedy, *Literary New Orleans in the Modern World*.

39. Britton E. Trice, "Britton E. Trice: An Interview with a Bookseller," in *The Unauthorized Anne Rice Companion*, ed. George Beahm (Kansas City, Mo.: Andrews and McMeel, 1996), 81; W. Kenneth Holditch, "Latter-Day Creoles: A New Age of New Orleans Literature," in Kennedy, *Literary New Orleans in the Modern World*, 141.

40. Anne Rice, *Interview with the Vampire* (New York: Alfred A. Knopf, 1976).

41. See Beahm, *Unauthorized Anne Rice Companion*, various interviews with the author, and Bette B. Roberts, *Anne Rice* (New York: Twayne, 1994).

42. For instance, Anne Rice, Phone Message, 001 504 522 8634, 8 December 1999, recommends that fans see the movie *The Sixth Sense* and the TV programs *Pride and Prejudice* and *Horatio Hornblower*.

43. Quoted in Beahm, *Unauthorized Anne Rice Companion*, 128 and 138.

44. http://www.annerice.com/

45. The novel is due for U.S. publication in summer 2000; see Grace Bradberry, "Interview with the Son of a Vampire Legend," *Times*, Features 3, 28 February 2000, 38. "Commotion Strange" can be found on <earthsystems.org/~shay/commotion.html>, and the Anne Rice fan club is found on <earthsystems.org/~shay/ricereaders.html>. See Jane Plumb, "Dark Angels: A Study of Anne Rice's 'Vampire Chronicles'" (Ph.D. diss., University of Warwick, 1998). With thanks, too, to Steve Jones and Marie Mulvey Roberts, especially for Marie's interview with Rice.

46. Daniel Jeffreys, "Bad Blood," *Sunday Telegraph Magazine*, 6 April 1997, 18-20.

47. Katherine Ramsland is Rice's official biographer, and she has produced not only an authoritative biography, *Prism of the Night: A Biography of Anne Rice* (New York: Dutton, 1991), but also guides to the works, such as *The Vampire Companion: The Official Guide to Anne Rice's "The Vampire Chronicles"* (New York: Ballantine Books, 1993), *The Roquelaure Reader: A Companion to Anne Rice's Erotica* (New York: Plume, 1996), and a collection of writing about Anne Rice, *The Anne Rice Reader* (New York: Alfred A. Knopf, 1997). There are numerous guides to the New Orleans of the novels, as well as an Anne Rice calendar and a trivia book.

48. David Ward, "Dixie Farewell in Blaze of Glory," *Guardian*, 6 July 1995, 7.

49. Adam Sweeting described the CD-ROM with tongue-in-cheek contempt: "You find yourself entering a sprawling mansion in Louisiana, accompanied by the absurd baritone rumblings of Legba, 'Gatekeeper of Voodoo and Master of the Crossroads,' who fancies himself as a philosopher and spouts drivel like 'the wise man knows when to talk and when to listen' and 'don't doubt the meanings of your dreams,'" *Observer*, 31 December 1995, 7.

50. Dave Gelly, *Observer Review*, 14 January 1996, 10.

51. Michael Ondaatje, *Coming through Slaughter* (London: Marion Boyars, 1979).

52. Peter Linebaugh, "All the Atlantic Mountains Shook," *Labour/Le Travailleur* 10 (Autumn 1982): 119, quoted in Paul Gilroy, *The Black Atlantic: Modernity and Double Consciousness* (London: Verso, 1993), 13; Gilroy, *Black Atlantic*, 4.

53. Jeremy Mitchell and John Pearson, "Popular Music," in *The United States in the Twentieth Century: Culture*, ed. Jeremy Mitchell and Richard Maidment (London: Hodder and Stoughton, 1994), 198-209. This also applies to other forms of music. Connie Atkinson notes of contemporary New Orleans, "Musicians often mention 'Europe' as a place of musical discernment where New Orleans music is appreciated," in "'Shakin' Your Butt for the Tourist': Music's Role in the Identification and Selling of New Orleans," in *Dixie Debates: Perspectives on Southern Cultures*, ed. Richard H. King and Helen Taylor (London: Pluto, 1996), 156.

54. See Jerah Johnson, *Congo Square in New Orleans* (New Orleans: Louisiana Landmarks Society, 1995), and Connie Atkinson, "Musicmaking in New Orleans: A Reappraisal" (Ph.D. diss., University of Liverpool, 1997).

55. Alan Munton, "Misreading Morrison, Mishearing Jazz: A Response to Toni Morrison's Jazz Critics," *Journal of American Studies* 31 (August 1997): 251. See the whole article (235-251) for a critique of excessively Afrocentric critical approaches to fiction and jazz; also see Gunther Schuller, *Early Jazz: Its Roots and Musical Development* (New York: Oxford University Press, 1968).

56. Nick Kent, "Miles Davis Interview," *Face* 78 (1986): 22-23; Miles Davis with Quincy Troupe, *Miles: The Autobiography* (New York: Simon and Schuster, 1989), 360-361. Quoted in Gilroy, *Black Atlantic*, 97 and 238-239.

57. Gilroy, *Black Atlantic*, 102.

58. Ibid., 79.
59. Ibid., 199.
60. *Ken Colyer Trust Newsletter and Memorabilia,* June 1995, n.p.
61. John Long, Ken Colyer Trust Band Management, interview with author, Epsom Downs, Surrey, 25 July 1994.
62. Horace Meunier Harris, "A New Orleans Odyssey," unpublished paper, 1.
63. David Cross, quoted in Jeff Nuttall, "Still Trad Mad after All These Years," *Observer Review,* 10 April 1994, 15.
64. John Long, phone conversation with author, 3 April 1999.
65. John Long, "The Band in New Orleans," *Ken Colyer Trust Newsletter and Memorabilia,* June 1995, n.p.
66. This can be seen as part of a general trend in the reception of American cultural forms in Europe. David Ellwood et al. argue, "With the manifest exception of such phenomena as the reception accorded African-American jazz performers in Paris, Europeans did not often recognise the class, ethnic and other origins of forms of popular culture; it was simply American," in David Ellwood et al., *Questions of Cultural Exchange: The NIAS Statement on the European Reception of American Mass Culture,* Working Paper No. 13 (Odense, Denmark: Odense University, 1994), 13.
67. M. Christine Boyer, "Cities for Sale: Merchandising History at South Street Seaport," in *Variations on a Theme Park: The New American City and the End of Public Space,* ed. Michael Sorkin (New York: Hill and Wang, 1992), 201.
68. Allen Toussaint, interview with author, Sea Saint Studios, New Orleans, 28 March 1995.
69. For this information, I am indebted to conversations and interviews with Zane Branson (February 1995 and February 1998) and Connie Atkinson (various occasions), whose unpublished drafts of her Ph.D. thesis and ESRC research have been invaluable in this context. See also Connie Atkinson and Sara Cohen, "Report to the Research Development Office," University of Liverpool, September 1996.
70. Zane Branson, "An American in Liverpool: A Perspective on Tourism," 15 June 1987, 1.
71. Atkinson and Cohen, "Report to the Research Development Office," n.p.
72. Quote from ibid.
73. Andrew Didlick, Peugeot's national advertising manager, told me that twelve city police were only too delighted to close one of the city's main bridges during rush hour, to enable their filming, while several house owners in New Orleans had grown wise to endless requests for permission to photograph their house facades; a few were demanding as much as ten thousand dollars a time. (Interview with author, Coventry, February 1995).
74. Lyons Brown III, president of Brown-Forman Beverages Worldwide, interview with author, London, 13 October 1995.
75. Nicholas Herbert-Jones, assistant vice president, Brown-Forman Beverages Worldwide, interview with author, London, 13 October 1995.
76. Simon Hawtrey-Woore, Court, Berkitt and Company, telephone interview with author, 10 November 1997.
77. http://www.neworleansonline.com/
78. Three examples: an annual, peripatetic Sidney Bechet conference was initiated in Paris in 1997; the first interdisciplinary conference titled "New Orleans in Europe," University of Warwick, England, 4-5 July 1998, was cosponsored by the University of Warwick and the Midlo International Center for New Orleans Studies, University of New Orleans; the Tennessee Williams/New Orleans Literary Festival invites international scholars annually to speak on southern culture topics.
79. Ed Vulliamy, "Degas the Creole," *Observer Magazine,* 1 August 1999, 24-27.

5. TENNESSEE WILLIAMS AND THE CONTEMPORARY BRITISH STAGE

1. Lyle Leverich, *Tom: The Unknown Tennessee Williams* (London: Hodder and Stoughton, 1995), ix.
2. "Beast of the Jungle," *Sun,* 20 April 1992, 2-3. The article referred with relish to the "stinking hell called Desire."
3. Philip C. Kolin, ed., *Confronting Tennessee Williams's "A Streetcar Named Desire": Essays in Cultural Pluralism* (Westport, Conn.: Greenwood Press, 1993), 1, 4.
4. Brian Parker, Book Reviews, *Modern Drama* 39 (Fall 1996): 518. See also Helen Taylor, "'An Archaeological Dig': Tennessee Williams in the 1990s," *Critical Survey* 9, no. 2 (1997): 43-60.
5. Richard Eyre, interview with author, The National Theatre, London, 22 February 1995.

6. Claude Coulon, "Tennessee Williams on the International Scene," panel at the Tennessee Williams/New Orleans Literary Festival, New Orleans, 24 March 1995.
7. Quoted in Kate Bassett, "Tennessee's Time Has Come Again," *Daily Telegraph*, 25 February 1977, 17.
8. Kolin, *Confronting Tennessee Williams's "A Streetcar."*
9. Matthew C. Roudané, ed., *The Cambridge Companion to Tennessee Williams* (Cambridge: Cambridge University Press, 1997), 2 (Roudané) and 45 (Felicia Hardison Londré).
10. Tennessee Williams, quoting Shaw, *The Doctor's Dilemma*, in *Where I Live: Selected Essays* (New York: New Directions, 1978), 69.
11. Nancy M. Tischler, in Roudané, *Cambridge Companion*, 147.
12. See Gilbert Debusscher, "Creative Rewriting: European and American Influences on the Dramas of Tennessee Williams," in Roudané, *Cambridge Companion*, 167-188.
13. Arthur Miller, *Timebends: A Life* (New York: Grove Press, 1987), 182.
14. See Taylor, "'Archaeological Dig,'" 43-60.
15. Nicholas de Jongh, "Tennessee Ascending," *Guardian*, 3 December 1988, n.p.
16. Charles Spencer, "Torrid Triumph with Tennessee," *Daily Telegraph*, 20 June 1994.
17. Coulon, "Tennessee Williams on the International Scene."
18. Matt Wolf, "Britain, Smitten," *Chicago Tribune*, 8 March 1992.
19. Steven Pimlott, quoted in Lynne St. Claire, "Southern Comfort on the Rocks," *Nottingham Evening Post*, 19 May 1995.
20. Robin Thornber, "Glamorous Gloss on Slice of Low-Life," *Guardian*, 24 May 1995.
21. Eyre, interview with author.
22. This may well be a dying tradition, however, since theater schools train fewer students than they did (because of the financial constraints on British students and the absence of grants for such training). Young actors also expect to follow the jobs, thus to be trained in television and film techniques rather than for repertory or classical theater.
23. Benedict Nightingale, "Darkest Flights of the Soul," *Times*, 18 June 1994; Jan Stuart, "Sweet Bird of Youth," *Newsday* (New York), 24 July 1994; Michael Billington, "Leaving Nothing to Chance," *Guardian*, 18 June 1994.
24. Donald Hutera, "Curtain Call: Donald Hutera on Clare Higgins," *What's On*, 15 June 1994.
25. Neil Smith, "A Streetcar Named Desire," *What's On*, 8 January 1997.
26. John Peter, "A Streetcar Named Desire," *Sunday Times*, 5 January 1997; Shaun Usher, *Daily Mail*, 31 December 1996.
27. David Benedict, "Tennessee Williams and His Women," *Independent*, II, 15 June 1994, 23.
28. Quoted in Philip Kolin, *Confronting Tennessee Williams's "A Streetcar,"* 4.
29. Joyce McMillan, "Goforth—and He Did," *Scotland on Sunday*, 6 November 1994.
30. Quoted in Gene D. Phillips, *The Films of Tennessee Williams* (London: Associated University Presses, 1980), 299.
31. Rupert Everett, quoted in Lisa O'Kelly, "Pretenders to the Drag Queen's Throne," *Observer*, 1994, n.d.
32. Michael Coveney, "A Curious Date with Destiny," *Observer Review*, 6 November 1994, 8.
33. John Peter, *Sunday Times*, 2 November 1997, 19; Paul Taylor, *Independent* (Eye on Wednesday), 29 October 1997, 1.
34. Susannah Clapp, "Rupert, Is That You in There?" *Observer Review*, 2 November 1997, 13.
35. Quoted in Richard Eyre, "There Are Times . . . ," Program, *Sweet Bird of Youth*, The National Theatre, 1994, n.p.
36. Christopher Bigsby, "Tennessee Williams: Romantic Radical," Program, *Sweet Bird of Youth*, The National Theatre, 1994, n.p.
37. Eyre, "There Are Times . . . ," n.p.
38. Irving Wardle, "Arms and the Government's Men," *Independent on Sunday*, 19 June 1994; Charles Spencer, "Torrid Triumph with Tennessee," and Clive Hirschhorn, "Deep South Excess Works Wonderfully," *Sunday Express*, 19 June 1994.
39. Carole Woddis, "Awesome Williams," *Glasgow Herald*, 21 June 1994.
40. John Gross, "Heavenly Loses in a Game with Chance," *Sunday Telegraph*, 19 June 1994.
41. Tennessee Williams, *Not about Nightingales* (London: Methuen, 1998).
42. Maria St. Just, *Five o'Clock Angel: Letters of Tennessee Williams to Maria St. Just, 1948–1982* (New York: Alfred A. Knopf, 1990), 388 and 357. His admiration for Redgrave was not shared by his American agents, who in 1982 deeply disapproved of his sharing a public reading with the politically radical actress.
43. Trevor Nunn, talking about the play on BBC Radio 4, *Start the Week*, March 1998.
44. Williams, *Not about Nightingales*, 1.

45. David Nathan, *Jewish Chronicle*, 13 March 1998, n.p., quoted in *Theatre Record*, 26 February–11 March 1998, 254.
46. Nicholas de Jongh, *Evening Standard*, 6 March 1998, quoted in *Theatre Record*, 26 February–11 March 1998, 255.
47. The final British production of the century was an interesting case of creative response to different versions of Williams's work. Director Lucy Bailey opened the newly refurbished Birmingham Repertory Theatre with a highly-acclaimed version of *Baby Doll*, in which she developed a new stage version by drawing on the 1956 Williams–Elia Kazan film script and several versions of Williams's later play script, *Tiger Tail* (1978).
48. This tradition has begun to be honored by scholars, and it is no coincidence that the 1990s saw the publication of two collections of essays about the city's literary heritage: Richard S. Kennedy, ed., *Literary New Orleans: Essays and Meditations* (Baton Rouge: Louisiana State University, 1992) and *Literary New Orleans in the Modern World* (Baton Rouge: Louisiana State University Press, 1998). In 1996, the Historic New Orleans Collection relocated its research departments to a new center on Chartres Street, now called the Williams Research Center.
49. Tennessee Williams, interview by Don Lee Keith, New Orleans, January 25, 1978, quoted in W. Kenneth Holditch, "South toward Freedom: Tennessee Williams," in Kennedy, *Literary New Orleans*, 67.
50. The long weekend comprises a great deal of partying, an element of which the festival's namesake would have heartily approved, as well as high-class gossip about his life and work, only some of which he would have relished. At two festivals I attended (1995 and 1996), events included the Kenneth W. Holditch walking tours of the French Quarter, painstakingly pointing out the writer's every haunt and hangout; the unveiling of the artwork for the 1995 Tennessee postage stamp by the last-surviving conductor who rode on the final 1960s journeys of the streetcar named Desire; a "Stella and Stanley Shouting Contest" at the historic Pontalba Apartments, during which contestants screamed their heads off to the amusement of Jackson Square tourists; and Dakin Williams performing speeches from his brother's plays and regaling rapt audiences with his lurid version of the writer's death, namely, murder by various (named) conspirators. At the tenth anniversary festival, for the first time an academic conference took place alongside the celebrations. In the lobby to Le Petit Théâtre, you could buy a Desire streetcar tie (woven in England), sterling silver pins with images from *Streetcar*, *Cat on a Hot Tin Roof*, and *The Night of the Iguana*, festival mugs and clutch bags.
51. Eliza Kazan, preface to St. Just, *Five o'Clock Angel,* ix.
52. Leverich, *Tom*, 10 n.
53. John Lahr, "The Lady and Tennessee," *New Yorker*, December 1994, 77.
54. As Lyle Leverich and others have argued, the idea of a standard complete edition of Williams's plays is hard to envisage. Williams regarded no play complete until there was a definitive production, and throughout his writing career he worked on different drafts of most of the plays.
55. Lahr, "Lady and Tennessee," 89.
56. Elia Kazan, preface to St. Just, *Five o'Clock Angel*.
57. "Obituaries: Maria Lady St. Just," *Times*, 19 February 1994.
58. Quoted in Lahr, "Lady and Tennessee," 88.
59. Kit Hesketh-Harvey, *Five o'Clock Angel*, dir. Scott Williams, Hampstead Theatre Club, and Théâtre Antibéa, Antibes, October 1999, and The King's Head Theatre, February–March 2000. The play was basically a two-hander, with Nichola McAuliffe playing St. Just and Stefan Bednarczyk Tennessee Williams. Although the play avoided excessive sentimentality about their friendship and the characters themselves (and was especially honest about Maria St. Just's romantic fantasies about the writer), it did represent the relationship in isolation, as if St. Just had very great importance for and influence on the playwright. This was a provocative interpretation that St. Just's detractors would almost certainly refute.
60. Eyre, "There Are Times . . . ," n.p. This is an echo of Elia Kazan's words in the preface to *Five o'Clock Angel*. Kazan spoke of every author needing "someone special" to give a "judgment-in-advance" on his work (ix); this reliable, utterly trustworthy person in Williams's life was, he claimed, Maria St. Just.
61. Peter Hall to author, 7 January 1997.
62. Ibid.; Richard Eyre to author, 23 May 1995.
63. This explanation was offered by Kit Hesketh-Harvey, phone conversation with author, 6 October 1999.

64. John Osborne, quoted in Program, *Sweet Bird of Youth*, June 1994; Eyre, interview with author.

---

6. "A BLACK OCEAN, LEAPING AND WIDE"

1. Maya Angelou, "Still I Rise," in *The Complete Collected Poems* (1994; London: Virago, 1995), 164.
2. Greg Hitt, "Maya Angelou," in *Conversations with Maya Angelou*, ed. Jeffrey M. Elliot (London: Virago, 1989), 208-209.
3. Maya Angelou, "Phenomenal Woman," in *Complete Collected Poems*, 130-131. This phrase is used throughout Angelou's shows and interviews.
4. Maya Angelou, "No No No No," in Angelou, *Complete Collected Poems*, 43.
5. Quotes from Polly Toynbee, *Guardian*, 30 January 1984, 10; Nikki Giovanni, quoted in Deirdre Donahue, "Writer Gives Voice to Injustice," *USA Today*, "Life," 24 May 1990, 2D; Emma Tennant, quoted in "Profile: Maya Angelou, Poet for the New America," *Observer*, 24 January 1993, n.p.; *Cosmopolitan*, June, 1998, n.p. (Virago Press Archive).
6. Donahue, "Writer Gives Voice to Injustice."
7. Maya Angelou, *All God's Children Need Travelling Shoes* (London: Virago, 1987), 173 and 174. In 1960, she was touring in an American production of Jean Genet's *The Blacks*.
8. Mona McKinlay, "Singin' and Swingin'," *Race Today Review*, no details (Virago Press Archive).
9. Brita Lindberg-Seyersted, *Black and Female: Essays on Writings by Black Women in the Diaspora* (Oslo: Scandinavian University Press, 1994), 77.
10. "Very much" quote from ibid.
11. Paul du Feu, *In Good Company: A Story in Black and White* (Edinburgh: Mainstream, 1991), 146.
12. Kadiatu Kanneh, "Marketing Black Women's Texts: The Case of Alice Walker," in *Writing: A Woman's Business: Women, Writing, and the Marketplace*, ed. Judy Simons and Kate Fullbrook (Manchester: Manchester University Press, 1998), 145.
13. Maya Angelou, in Dolly A. McPherson, *Order Out of Chaos: The Autobiographical Works of Maya Angelou* (1990; London: Virago, 1991), 143. She also told Jackie Kay, "I think I am the only serious writer who has chosen the autobiographical form as the main form to carry my work, my expression," "The Maya Character," in Elliot, *Conversations with Maya Angelou*, 195.
14. "In the Psychiatrist's Chair," transcript, 8-9.
15. Elliot, *Conversations with Maya Angelou*, vii, x–xi.
16. Ibid., 219.
17. Ibid., 96.
18. Margaret Busby, "Coming on Strong," *Guardian Weekend*, 14 May 1994, 8. Busby dissents from this view, but see du Feu, *In Good Company*, 219, for the reasons why his marriage to Angelou broke down.
19. "Diary: Maya Angelou," *Private Eye*, 15 May, 1998, 24.
20. Maya Angelou, *Singin' and Swingin' and Gettin' Merry like Christmas* (1976; London: Virago, 1985), 60.
21. Martin Walker, "Angelou's Poetic Source Queried," *Guardian*, 26 November 1993. The writer, Norton Tennille, wrote to Angelou suggesting that her Clinton inauguration poem, "On the Pulse of Morning," contained identical structure and imagery (of rock, rope, river, tree, and human hands) to that of a poem he wrote to celebrate the Outward Bound adventure course. He had written the poem after an adventure course in the North Carolina mountains, at a school supported by Angelou herself. The school's founding trustee told Tennille that the "striking similarities" he noted between the two were "mere coincidences." The story was taken up in the 1993 issue of the American cultural journal *Chronicles*.
22. Bryan D. Bourn, "Maya Angelou and the African American Tradition," http://www.usinternet.com/users/bdbourn/maya.htm, p. 3. For serious critical discussion of the poetry, however, see Priscilla R. Ramsey, "Transcendence: The Poetry of Maya Angelou," and Carol E. Neubauer, "Maya Angelou: Self and a Song of Freedom in the Southern Tradition," in *Maya Angelou*, ed. Harold Bloom (Philadelphia: Chelsea House, 1999), 75-90 and 191-218.
23. For an uncompromising attack on Angelou's success on the reading lists for American high school students, see Francine Prose, "I Know Why the Caged Bird Cannot Read: How American High School Students Learn to Loathe Literature," *Harper's Magazine*, September 1999,

76-84. Prose quotes from *Caged Bird* and asks, "Who seriously believes that murky, turgid, convoluted language of this sort constitutes good writing?" 78.

24. Collections of essays began to emerge in the late 1990s: see Bloom, *Maya Angelou*, and the student textbook *Readings on Maya Angelou*, edited by Mary E. Williams (San Diego: Greenhaven Press, 1997). I see as significant the rather minimal space allotted her work in the single most important collection of African American writing published in the century: Henry Louis Gates Jr. and Nellie Y. McKay, eds., *The Norton Anthology of African American Literature* (New York: W. W. Norton, 1997), gave 13 pages to Angelou (two chapters of *Caged Bird*) by contrast with 29 for Gloria Naylor, 34 for Alice Walker, 86 for Toni Morrison, and even 15 for the much less well known Adrienne Kennedy. At least she is included here; astonishingly, she is completely omitted from the authoritative and comprehensive collection edited by Charles Reagan Wilson and William Ferris, *Encyclopedia of Southern Culture* (Chapel Hill: University of North Carolina Press, 1989).

25. Maya Angelou, interview with author, Llangoed Hall Hotel, Wales, 3 June 1999.

26. Maya Angelou, *Gather Together in My Name* (1974; London: Virago, 1985), 74; *Singin' and Swingin' and Gettin' Merry like Christmas*, 173.

27. Angelou, *Gather Together in My Name*, 73.

28. Quote from ibid.

29. Maya Angelou, *I Know Why the Caged Bird Sings* (New York: Random House, 1969; London: Virago, 1984), 97 and 27.

30. Eudora Welty, *One Writer's Beginnings* (Cambridge: Harvard University Press, 1984), 33-34; McPherson, *Order Out of Chaos*, 10.

31. Maya Angelou, *Wouldn't Take Nothing for My Journey Now* (1993; London: Virago, 1995), 7.

32. Ibid., 11.

33. Maya Angelou, *Even the Stars Look Lonesome* (1997; London: Virago, 1998), 24.

34. Sheila Weller, "Work in Progress: Maya Angelou," *Intellectual Digest*, June 1973, 11-12, 14, in Elliot, *Conversations with Maya Angelou*, 14; Angelou, *Wouldn't Take Nothing*, 75-76.

35. James Baldwin, quoted in Maya Jaggi, "Survival with Style," *Guardian*, 4 April 1998, n.p. (Virago Press Archive); Harold Bloom, introduction to Bloom, *Maya Angelou*, 1, and also see Harold Bloom, ed., *Maya Angelou's "I Know Why the Caged Bird Sings"* (Broomall, Pa.: Chelsea House Publishers, 1998), 6.

36. Nikhil Pal Singh, "Culture/Wars: Recoding Empire in an Age of Democracy," *American Quarterly* 50 (September 1998): 505-506, quoting David Hollinger, *Postethnic America: Beyond Multiculturalism* (New York: Basic Books, 1995), 171.

37. See the useful summary of Martin Buber's writings in Edward Craig, ed., *The Routledge Encyclopedia of Philosophy* (London: Routledge, 1998), 42-48.

38. Angelou, *Wouldn't Take Nothing*, 87.

39. Ibid., 123-124.

40. Angelou, *Even the Stars Look Lonesome*, 139.

41. Walter Blum, "Listening to Maya Angelou," *California Living*, 14 December 1975, 12-23, in Elliott, *Conversations with Maya Angelou*, 39.

42. Ibid.

43. Mary Chamberlain, ed., *Writing Lives: Conversations between Women Writers* (London: Virago, 1988), 1-23, in Elliott, *Conversations with Maya Angelou*, 231.

44. Elliot, *Conversations with Maya Angelou*, 70.

45. Angelou, *Even the Stars Look Lonesome*, 102.

46. Ibid., 112.

47. Angelou, *Wouldn't Take Nothing*, 103.

48. "A goo" from Bill Moyers, "A Conversation with Maya Angelou," in Elliot, *Conversations with Maya Angelou*, 28.

49. Angelou, *Wouldn't Take Nothing*, 12.

50. McPherson, *Order Out of Chaos*, 145, 140.

51. Angelou, *I Know Why the Caged Bird Sings*, 154; Maya Angelou, quoted in Mari Evans, ed., *Black Women Writers: Arguments and Interviews* (1984; London: Pluto Press, 1985), 3.

52. Du Feu, *In Good Company*, 108.

53. Sal Manna, "The West Interview: Maya Angelou," 22 June 1986, in Elliot, *Conversations with Maya Angelou*, 158.

54. Angelou, *The Heart of a Woman* (1981; New York: Bantam, 1982), 135.

55. Ibid., 135-139.

56. Maya Angelou to author, 3 June 1999, and *All God's Children Need Travelling Shoes*, 204; in these views Angelou is reiterating the line taken by many southern scholars that southern culture was largely shaped and defined by African slave culture.

57. Angelou, *All God's Children Need Travelling Shoes*, 137-138, 113-114. The term *motherfucker* is never actually printed, but it is very clear exactly what is meant.
58. Angelou, *All God's Children Need Travelling Shoes*, 158-159.
59. Ibid., 76.
60. Ibid., 201-207.
61. Ibid., 206.
62. James Baldwin, *Notes of a Native Son* (London: Michael Joseph, 1964), 14.
63. Lindberg-Seyersted, *Black and Female*, 122.
64. Lawrence Toppman, "Maya Angelou: The Serene Spirit of a Survivor," 11 December 1983, in Elliot, *Conversations with Maya Angelou*, 143.
65. Natasha Walter, "Decca Mitford Likes a Good Sing-Song," *Observer Review*, 16 February 1997, 9.
66. Lennie Goodings, publisher, Virago Press, interview with author, London, 17 August 1999.
67. *King*, with music by Richard Blackford and lyrics by Angelou, opened at London's Piccadilly Theatre on 4 April 1990, starring Simon Estes as King and Cynthia Haymon as Coretta Scott King. On 17 March, Angelou stormed out of the production and London, claiming the play was "terrible," and complaining about the amount of attention paid to the white, rather than black, characters. Her lyrics remained, because of the nature of her contract, but she withdrew her name from the play program. The production came off the London stage almost immediately. Angelou's production of *Moon on a Rainbow Shawl*, which made its world premiere in London in 1958 and New York in 1962, ran in London from 4 May to 4 June 1998. Angelou, invited to come to London by the Greater London Arts Investment Scheme, chose John's play because it dealt with a variety of types of love, the subject she considers most important.
68. Lennie Goodings, interview with author.
69. Ann Donald, *Herald* (Glasgow), 14 May 1998, n.p.
70. *Angelou on Burns*, dir. Elly M. Taylor (BBC TV and the Scottish Arts Council, 1997).
71. McPherson, *Order Out of Chaos*, 8 and 11.
72. Sondra O'Neale, "Reconstruction of the Composite Self: New Images of Black Women in Maya Angelou's Continuing Autobiography," in Evans, *Black Women Writers*, 26.
73. McPherson, *Order Out of Chaos*, 81; Françoise Lionnet, "Con Artists and Storytellers: Maya Angelou's Problematic Sense of Audience," in Bloom, *Maya Angelou*, 146-154.
74. See McPherson, *Order Out of Chaos*, 120-121.
75. Lindberg-Seyersted, *Black and Female*, 70.
76. Angelou, *Singin' and Swingin' and Gettin' Merry like Christmas*, 189.
77. Angelou, *All God's Children Need Travelling Shoes*, 182-184.
78. The first screenplay Angelou wrote, *Georgia, Georgia*, produced and set in Sweden, focused on a story of miscegenation, a black expatriate singer in love with a white photographer. This suggests that Angelou was concerned and troubled by issues of mixed-race relationships in ways she rarely explores in her autobiographies.
79. Maya Angelou, phone conversation with author, 30 November 1999.
80. Julie Herd, "Uncaged Bird Sings for the Gift of Life," *Australian Woman*, 3 September 1987, n.p. (Virago Press Archive)
81. Angelou, phone conversation with author.
82. O'Neale, "Reconstruction of the Composite Self," 26.
83. Joanne M. Braxton, *Black Women Writing Autobiographiy: A Tradition within a Tradition* (Philadelphia: Temple University Press, 1989), 186.

EPILOGUE

1. On using the term *American*, see Janice Radway's Presidential Address to the American Studies Association, 20 November 1998, reprinted in *American Quarterly* 51 (March 1999): 1-32.
2. Paul Giles, "Virtual Americas: The Internationalization of American Studies and the Ideology of Exchange," *American Quarterly* 50 (September 1998): 524.
3. Robert A. Gross, Opening Address to the British Association of American Studies Conference, Glasgow, 27 March 1999, 3-4.
4. Patricia J. Williams, *Seeing a Colour-Blind Future: The Paradox of Race* (London: Virago, 1997), 67.

Selected Bibliography

Note: The following titles are selected for their relevance to the arguments in this book. Many other primary and secondary works, journal and newspaper articles, personal interviews, and reviews, are quoted in the text and given full citation in the notes.

Applebome, Peter. *Dixie Rising: How the South Is Shaping American Values, Politics, and Culture.* New York: Random House, 1996.

Atkinson, Connie. "Musicmaking in New Orleans: A Reappraisal." Ph.D. diss., University of Liverpool, England, 1997.

Baker, Houston A., Jr. *Blues, Ideology, and Afro-American Literature.* Chicago: University of Chicago Press, 1984.

Beahm, George, ed. *The Unauthorized Anne Rice Companion.* Kansas City, Mo.: Andrews and McMeel, 1996.

Beauvoir, Simone de. *America Day by Day.* London: Gerald Duckworth, 1952.

Berendt, John. *Midnight in the Garden of Good and Evil: A Savannah Story.* New York: Random House, 1994.

Berry, Jason, Jonathan Foose, and Tad Jones. *Up from the Cradle of Jazz: New Orleans Music since World War II.* New York: Da Capo Press, 1992.

Bloom, Harold, ed. *Maya Angelou's "I Know Why the Caged Bird Sings."* Broomall, Pa.: Chelsea House, 1998.

———. *Maya Angelou.* Philadelphia: Chelsea House, 1999.

Branston, Ursula. *Let the Band Play "Dixie"!: Improvisations on a Southern Signature Tune.* London: George G. Harrap, 1940.

Braxton, Joanne M. *Black Women Writing Autobiography: A Tradition within a Tradition.* Philadelphia: Temple University Press, 1989.

Brown, Dorothy H., and Barbara C. Ewell, eds. *Louisiana Women Writers: New Essays and a Comprehensive Bibliography.* Baton Rouge: Louisiana State University Press, 1992.

Cash, W. J. *The Mind of the South.* New York: Vintage, 1941.

Collins, Carvel, ed. *William Faulkner: New Orleans Sketches.* London: Chatto and Windus, 1958.

Cooper, William J., Jr., and Thomas E. Terrill. *The American South: A History.* 2d ed. New York: McGraw-Hill, 1996.

Dent, Gina, ed. *Black Popular Culture: A Project by Michele Wallace.* Seattle: Bay Press, 1992.

Doss, Erica. *Elvis in the Public Sphere: Fans, Faith, and Cultural Production in Contemporary America,* Working Paper No. 24. Odense, Denmark: Odense University, 1996.

du Feu, Paul. *In Good Company: A Story in Black and White.* Edinburgh: Mainstream, 1991.

Dyer, Richard. *White.* London: Routledge, 1997.

Eco, Umberto. *Travels in Hyperreality: Essays.* London: Picador, 1987.

Edwards, Anne. *The Road to Tara: The Life of Margaret Mitchell.* New Haven: Ticknor and Fields, 1983.

Egerton, John. *The Americanization of Dixie: The Southernization of America.* New York: Harper and Row, 1974.

Elliot, Jeffrey M., ed. *Conversations with Maya Angelou.* London: Virago, 1989.

Ellwood, David, Mel van Elteren, Mick Gidley, Rob Kroes, David E. Nye, and Robert W. Rydell. *Questions of Cultural Exchange: The NIAS Statement on the European Reception of American Mass Culture,* Working Paper No. 13. Odense, Denmark: Odense University, 1994.

Evans, Mari, ed. *Black Women Writers: Arguments and Interviews.* London: Pluto Press, 1985.

Fiedler, Leslie. *The Inadvertent Epic: From "Uncle Tom's Cabin" to "Roots."* New York: Simon and Schuster, 1979.

Fiske, John. *Reading the Popular.* London: Routledge, 1989.

Flake, Carol. *New Orleans: Behind the Masks of America's Most Exotic City.* New York: Grove Press, 1994.

French, Warren. *The South and Film.* Jackson: University Press of Mississippi, 1981.

Gates, Henry Louis, Jr. *Black Literature and Literary Theory.* New York: Methuen, 1984.

———. *Loose Canons: Notes on the Culture Wars.* New York: Oxford University Press, 1992.

Gates, Henry Louis, Jr., and Nellie Y. McKay. *The Norton Anthology of African American Literature.* New York: W. W. Norton, 1997.

Gilroy, Paul. *The Black Atlantic: Modernity and Double Consciousness.* London: Verso, 1993.

———. *Small Acts: Thoughts on the Politics of Black Cultures.* London: Serpent's Tail, 1993.

Gould, Peter, and Rodney White. *Mental Maps.* Baltimore: Johns Hopkins University Press, 1974.

Harvey, David. *The Condition of Postmodernity: An Enquiry into the Origins of Cultural Change.* Oxford: Blackwell, 1989.

Harwell, Richard, ed. *"Gone With the Wind" as Book and Film.* Columbia: University of South Carolina Press, 1983.

Hirsch, Arnold R., and Joseph Logsdon, eds. *Creole New Orleans: Race and Americanization.* Baton Rouge: Louisiana State University Press, 1992.

Hook, Andrew. *From Goosecreek to Gandercleugh: Studies in Scottish-American Literary and Cultural History.* East Linton, Scotland: Tuckwell Press, 1999.

Kanneh, Kadiatu. "Marketing Black Women's Texts: The Case of Alice Walker." In *Writing: A Woman's Business: Women, Writing, and the Marketplace,* edited by Judy Simons and Kate Fullbrook, 145-160. Manchester: Manchester University Press, 1998.

Kennedy, Richard S., ed. *Literary New Orleans: Essays and Meditations.* Baton Rouge: Louisiana State University Press, 1992.

———. *Literary New Orleans in the Modern World.* Baton Rouge: Louisiana State University Press, 1998.

King, Grace. *New Orleans: The Place and the People.* New York: Macmillan, 1895.

King, Richard H., and Helen Taylor. *Dixie Debates: Perspectives on Southern Cultures.* London: Pluto Press, 1996; New York: New York University Press, 1996.

Kinser, Samuel. *Carnival American Style: Mardi Gras at New Orleans and Mobile.* Chicago: University of Chicago Press, 1990.

Kirby, Jack Temple. *Media-Made Dixie: The South in the American Imagination.* Baton Rouge: Louisiana State University Press, 1978.

Kolin, Philip C., ed. *Confronting Tennessee Williams's "A Streetcar Named Desire": Essays in Cultural Pluralism.* Westport, Conn.: Greenwood Press, 1993.

Kroes, Rob, Robert W. Rydell, and Doeko F. J. Bosscher, eds. *Cultural Transmissions and Receptions: American Mass Culture in Europe.* Amsterdam: VU University Press, 1993.

Leverich, Lyle. *Tom: The Unknown Tennessee Williams.* New York: Crown, 1995; London: Hodder and Stoughton, 1995.

Lewis, Peirce F. *New Orleans: The Making of an Urban Landscape.* Cambridge, Mass.: Ballinger, 1976.

Lindberg-Seyersted, Brita. *Black and Female: Essays on Writings by Black Women in the Diaspora.* Oslo: Scandinavian University Press, 1994.

MacCannell, Dean. *The Tourist: A New Theory of the Leisure Class.* London: Macmillan, 1976.

McCauley, Mary Siebert. "Alex Haley, a Southern Griot: A Literary Biography." Ph.D. diss., George Peabody College for Teachers of Vanderbilt University, Tennessee, 1983.

McMillan, James B., and Michael B. Montgomery, eds. *The Annotated Bibliography of Southern American English*. 2d ed. Tuscaloosa: University of Alabama Press, 1986.

McPherson, Dolly A. *Order out of Chaos: The Autobiographical Works of Maya Angelou*. London: Virago, 1991.

McWhiney, Grady. *Cracker Culture: Celtic Ways in the Old South*. Tuscaloosa: University of Alabama Press, 1988.

Michaels, Walter Benn. *Our America: Nativism, Modernism, and Pluralism*. Durham, N.C.: Duke University Press, 1995.

Mitchell, Margaret. *Gone With the Wind*. New York: Macmillan, 1936.

Mitchell, Reid. *All on a Mardi Gras Day: Episodes in the History of New Orleans Carnival*. Cambridge: Harvard University Press, 1995.

Morrison, Toni. *Playing in the Dark: Whiteness and the Literary Imagination*. Cambridge: Harvard University Press, 1992.

Nobile, Philip. "Uncovering Roots." *Village Voice*, 23 February 1993, 31–38.

Ondaatje, Michael. *Coming through Slaughter*. London: Marion Boyars, 1979.

Ostendorf, Berndt. *Creolization and Creoles: The Concepts and Their History with Special Attention to Louisiana*, Working Paper No. 27. Odense, Denmark: Odense University, 1997.

Phillips, Gene D. *The Films of Tennessee Williams*. London: Associated University Presses, 1980.

Piersen, William D. *Black Legacy: America's Hidden Heritage*. Amherst: University of Massachusetts Press, 1993.

Pyron, Darden Asbury. *Southern Daughter: The Life of Margaret Mitchell*. New York: Oxford University Press, 1991.

Reed, Ishmael. *Shrovetide in Old New Orleans*. New York: Atheneum, 1989.

Reed, John Shelton. *Whistling Dixie: Dispatches from the South*. San Diego: Harcourt Brace Jovanovich, 1990.

Rice, Anne. *Interview with the Vampire*. New York: Alfred A. Knopf, 1976.

Ripley, Alexandra. *Scarlett: The Sequel to Margaret Mitchell's "Gone With the Wind."* New York: Warner, 1991; London: Macmillan, 1991.

Roach, Joseph. *Cities of the Dead: Circum-Atlantic Performance*. New York: Columbia University Press, 1996.

Roberts, Bette B. *Anne Rice*. New York: Twayne, 1994.

Roberts, Diane. *The Myth of Aunt Jemima: Representations of Race and Region*. London: Routledge, 1994.

Rose, Willie Lee. *Race and Region in American Historical Fiction: Four Episodes in Popular Culture*. Oxford: Clarendon, 1979.

Roudané, Matthew C., ed. *The Cambridge Companion to Tennessee Williams*. Cambridge: Cambridge University Press, 1997.

Said, Edward. *Culture and Imperialism*. London: Chatto and Windus, 1993.

St. Just, Maria. *Five o'Clock Angel: Letters of Tennessee Williams to Maria St. Just, 1948-1982*. New York: Alfred A. Knopf, 1990.

Saxon, Lyle, Robert Tallant, and Edward Dreyer. *Gumbo Ya-Ya: A Collection of Louisiana Folk Tales*. New York: Bonanza Books, 1945.

Soja, Edward W. *Thirdspace: Journeys to Los Angeles and Other Real-and-Imagined Places*. Cambridge, Mass.: Blackwell, 1996.

Sorkin, Michael, ed. *Variations on a Theme Park: The New American City and the End of Public Space*. New York: Hill and Wang, 1992.

Stephens, Robert O. *The Family Saga in the South: Generations and Destinies*. Baton Rouge: Louisiana State University Press, 1995.

Symbiosis: A Journal of Anglo-American Literary Relations. Plymouth: University College of St. Mark and St. John, 1997–.

Taylor, Helen. *Scarlett's Women: "Gone With the Wind" and Its Female Fans*. New Brunswick, N.J.: Rutgers University Press, 1989; London: Virago Press, 1989.

———. "'An Archaeological Dig': Tennessee Williams in the 1990s." *Critical Survey* 9, no. 2 (1997): 43-60.

———. "Walking through New Orleans: Kate Chopin and the Female Flâneur." *Southern Quarterly* 37 (Spring–Summer 1999): 21-29.

Taylor, William R. *Cavalier and Yankee: The Old South and American National Character*. New York: Harper and Row, 1961.

Toole, John Kennedy. *A Confederacy of Dunces*. Baton Rouge: Louisiana State University Press, 1980.

Twain, Mark. *Life on the Mississippi*. New York: Harper, 1904.

Verich, Thomas M. *English Magnolias: An Exhibition of Mississippi Fiction Printed in England*. Oxford: University of Mississippi, 1992.

Walker, Alice. *The Same River Twice: Honoring the Difficult: A Meditation on Life, Spirit, Art, and the Making of the Film "The Color Purple" Ten Years Later*. New York: Scribner, 1996.

Williams, Mary E., ed. *Readings on Maya Angelou*. San Diego: Greenhaven Press, 1997.

Williams, Patricia J. *Seeing a Colour-Blind Future: The Paradox of Race*. London: Virago, 1997.

Wilson, Charles Reagan, and William Ferris, eds. *Encyclopedia of Southern Culture*. Chapel Hill: University of North Carolina Press, 1989.

Younge, Gary. *No Place like Home: A Black Briton's Journey through the American South*. London: Picador, 1999.

Index

Gray, Richard, 25, 203n3
Green, Julian, 33; *The Distant Lands*, 56–60; *South* (play), 56, 207n45
griots, 70–71, 82–83
Gross, John, 149
Gross, Robert A., 197, 217n3
Guardian, 144, 158
gumbo, 94
Gumbo Ya-Ya, 209n7
Guttridge, Peter (*Independent*), 36
Gwin, Minrose C., 206n17

Haley, Alex, 33, 71, 175, 207–208n22; reputation, 164–167
    Roots, 63–90, 184
    – British impact of, 70
    – criticism of, 72–77
    – sequel to, 78
    – sources of, 72
    – spin-offs of, 65
Hall, Gwendolyn Midlo, 93
Hall, Peter, 135, 136, 145, 158, 159
Halmi, Robert Sr., 44–48
Hammond, James Henry, 20
Handlin, Oscar, 75
Harris, Horace Meunier, 212n62
Harvey, David, 86
Harvey, Laurence, 134
Hawkins, Coleman, 110
Hawtrey-Woore, Simon, 212n76
Hearn, Lafcadio, 95
Hellman, Lillian, *Pentimento*, 175
Herbert-Jones, Nicholas, 212n75
Hermann, Bernard M., 209n8
Hesketh-Harvey, Kit, 158, 159, 214n59
Higgins, Clare, 138, 141
Hill, Susan, 205n2
hip-hop culture, 111
Historic New Orleans Collection, 214n48
history, sense of, 13–16, 99
Hitt, Greg, 215n2
Holditch, W. Kenneth, 210nn35, 39, 214n49
Hook, Andrew, 203–204n11
hooks, bell, 207–208n22
Horowitz, Glenn, 204n22
Horsfield, Peter, 108
"Hot South," 10, 161
Hunter-Gault, Charlayne, 84

Hurston, Zora Neale, 68, 174
hybridity, 23, 66–67, 197, 204n26. *See also* cultural exchange and flow; fusion

identity: hybrid, 23, 66–67; regional, 200; sexual, 144. *See also* gender identity
imperialism, 23
Independent, 36, 141
Innus, Dagnija, 74
international music, 109, 117
Interview with the Vampire (film), 120. *See also* Rice, Anne
Irish heritage, in U.S., 42
Irish Independent, 43
Irishness: in Ripley, 41–43; romance of, 39
Iyer, V. R. Krishna, 68

Jack Daniel's bourbon, 15, 18
Jackson, Jesse, 68
Jacobs, Harriet, 20, 173, 185
Jakes, John, 33
jambalaya, 94
jazz, 24, 107–116
Jeffreys, Daniel, 211n46
Jezebel (film), 120
John, Errol, *Moon on a Rainbow Shawl*, 188, 217n67
Johnson, Jerah, 211n54
Jones, Quincey, 111
journeys: in American history, 191, 198–199; in Angelou, 164, 189, 194
Joyner, Charles, 25

Kanneh, Kadiatu, 169
Kaplan, Julius, 99
Kauffman, Stanley, 141
Kay, Jackie, 188, 215n13
Kay, Tony, 124
Kazan, Elia, 130, 156, 214n60
Keith, Don Lee, 214n49
Kemble, Fanny, 101
Ken Colyer Trust, 111–116
Kennedy, Richard S., 210n37, 211nn38, 39, 214nn48, 49
Keyes, Frances Parkinson, 209n6, 210n36
King, Edward, 10, 203n6
King, Grace, 100

About the Author

Helen Taylor is a professor and head of the School of English at the University of Exeter, England. She has taught English and American literature at the universities of Louisiana State, West of England, and Warwick and has published widely on the writing and culture of the American South. Her publications include *Gender, Race, and Region in the Writings of Grace King, Ruth McEnery Stuart, and Kate Chopin* (Louisiana State University Press, 1989), *Scarlett's Women: "Gone With the Wind" and Its Female Fans* (Rutgers University Press and Virago, 1989), and (with Richard H. King, eds.) *Dixie Debates: Perspectives on Southern Cultures* (Pluto, 1996), as well as many scholarly articles on British and American women's writing and popular culture.